BROWN ENOUGH

A TALE OF A MIXED-RACE BASEBALL TEAM
SUMMER OF '56

KEN OHM

Disclaimer
This story is based on actual events. In certain cases, incidents, characters and timelines have been changed for dramatic purposes. Certain characters may be composites or entirely fictitious. When quoting characters, any accents of their true speech are not distinguished from standard spelling.

Copyright © 2018 Kenneth R. Ohm

All rights reserved. No part of this publication may be reproduced, distributed, or transmitted in any form or by any means, including photocopying, recording, or other electronic or mechanical methods, without the prior written permission of the copyright holder.

Cover design, book design and layout by Jim L. Friesen

Library of Congress Control Number: 2018937767

Table of Contents

Prologue v
1 Summer Prospects 1
2 Possum 5
3 Philip and The Brown Bombers 13
4 Sundown 23
5 The Lebo Wolves 29
6 The Bat 37
7 Two Arrowheads 43
8 July 4th, 1956 49
9 Olpe and the Browns 57
10 An Ace? 63
11 A Long, Hot Day 71
12 Good News All Around 83
13 Madison 87
14 A Little Time Off 97
15 Tension in the Ranks 111
16: A Big Leaguer 121
17 Harold and Clyde 127
18 Gridley 137
19 First Chance, Last Chance 147
20 Home Field Advantage 157
21 Steve 163
22 Reading 171
23 Melvern 181
24 A Long 40 Hours 193
25 Turnpike Tussle 201
26 Lawrence Stadium 209
27 Game One 217

28 Monday, the Day Before 229
29 Hazel's Boarding House...235
30 Game Two 245
31 Possum's Story...257
32 Commercial Street Parade 269
33 Jeers from the Crowd 281
34 The First Pitch 289
Epilogue 297
Acknowledgements 303
About the Author 305

Prologue

During the first several years of my youth I lived on an isolated farm about twenty miles southwest of Emporia, Kansas. However, I had early contact with baseball when my dad and granddad (Pop) listened each year to the World Series via the battery-powered radio in our farmhouse. The Series was played during the daytime in those years. I remembered this because the two-mile walk from my one-room school stood in the way of these exciting broadcasts. I generally arrived home during week days to hear the last few innings of each game but heard nearly the whole game on the weekend.

These championship games almost always involved the New York Yankees with Lefty Gomez, Joe DiMaggio and Phil Rizzuto as key-player icons. To hear their exploits over the airways was a feast for my imagination. The careful set-up by broadcaster Mel Allen, with his description of the sights and sounds of Yankee Stadium, excited each of us as we huddled near the Silverton radio in our tiny living room.

While carefully listening to the games, Dad would occasionally give me a quick minute to describe a rule or explain a play that we heard. Gradually, I became familiar with the basics of the game and soon found it almost as exciting as did Dad and Pop.

We also watched live Sunday afternoon games of the local team playing in nearby cow pastures which further added to my knowledge of the game. These were exciting times with cars surrounding the outfield and picnic lunches spread out on blankets on the soft prairie grass.

We moved to Emporia in early 1946 when I was nine years old and the game of baseball became even more a part of my life with my own radio near my bedside and live broadcasts of the St. Louis Cardinals from Sportsmans Park. I loved announcer Harry Caray with his unique voice and exciting descriptions. My imagination provided a mental picture of greats, Stan Musial, Red Schoendinst and Enos Slaughter—along with many others.

The organization of major league baseball was much simpler than it is today. St. Louis had the only two teams west of the Mississippi, and this made it easy for a Kansas kid to choose either of them as a favorite team. One boy my age, Jerry Trowbridge, attended Cardinal games with his parents, and his departure and return from a trip to St. Louis fascinated the rest of us. A classmate, Jerry Brown, attended St. Louis Browns games on occasion. They both had a special way of detailing their trips and their big-league experiences.

The local YMCA began a baseball instruction program for kids up to grade six that first summer in town. A single coach was hired, and he inspired many of the nearly forty boys who showed up for the first practice. Marc Rose was an exceptional young man. He not only taught us the fundamentals of the game, but also shared his personal experiences as a minor league player and as an ex-Marine. We started each day's meeting under a shade tree near the ball diamond and were encouraged to join the conversation as it touched not only on baseball but many other aspects of our young lives.

After several minutes under the tree, Mr. Rose dragged out a gunny sack with a few old baseballs, a catcher's glove, mask, and chest protector, and a couple of bats. We had great fun learning the fundamentals using simulations of various game situations. Finally, after some two or three weeks, he posted a listing of players on four teams to start actual game play. He issued long-sleeved shirts provided by different civic organizations. A few of us had baseball gloves and often shared them with the opposing team. Positions were determined for the most part by player preference. Since Dad and I often played catch in our driveway where he taught me how to throw a roundhouse curve ball, I chose to become a pitcher.

In those years of the mid 1940s, no one thought about protecting a kid's pitching arm, so I experienced great success as my frequent slow curve and faster "fast" ball struck out many players. As a result, I enjoyed some notoriety among my teammates and members of the opposing teams. Our Eagles team won the competition during the following several weeks and baseball became my obsession.

The next four summers offered no organized baseball after a move back to the farm. We finally returned to Emporia for my junior year in high school. I found several boys in my new neighborhood enjoying baseball as much as I did. We started regular practices at Peter Pan Park in the early summer of 1953 and somehow caught the eye of the Junior Legion coach, Frank Griffith. He invited a few of us to join the team and we performed well.

I played third base for most of the Legion games. We had a talented group of experienced pitchers, so my pitching days at that level were limited. With my eighteenth birthday falling that winter, I was not eligible to play Legion ball in the summer of 1954. But, in the fall of 1955, after a one year lay-off from baseball, I walked on to become a pitcher for the Emporia State University varsity. Following a successful season, I scrambled to play the game during that summer—and therein lies my story of the fabled Brown Bombers.

Ken Ohm
Summer, 2018
Ken.Ohm@hotmail.com
www.flinthillsstories.com
Topeka, Kansas

Chapter One

Summary Prospects

A tiny article in tonight's newspaper catches my attention. It is not in the sports pages but in an obscure "About Town" section.

Baseball has steadily filled my mind for the few weeks since the end of my first year playing college baseball. Might this ad offer me an alternative to a dreaded baseball-free summer? I do have a deep, dark tan after weeks in the haying fields and working in construction. I wonder if I can pass an all-black test.

> Tryouts for an all-black baseball team will be held at Soden's Grove in Emporia on Wednesday evening, June 13, from 6-8pm. The coach and general manager of this new team is William "Possum" Williams. Please bring your own glove, bat and shoes. Coach Possum may be reached at Browns Barber shop at Sixth and Commercial for further details.

I hesitate to contact coach Possum in fear of rejection for any number of reasons, not the least the color of my skin.

The thought of playing with highly-talented, mature men also gives me second thoughts. Wednesday arrives and I decide not to attend the tryout.

On this Thursday morning, though, I face another day pushing wheelbarrow loads of concrete from a cement truck, over an inclined ramp, to dump into forms for basement walls in a new house. Thinking about baseball gives me a daily diversion from this hard and very hot work. We need to finish pouring concrete today, so quitting time extends past eight o'clock. I finally decide that I must contact coach Possum.

It rains heavily the next day and my foreman assigns me to another work site in a farmhouse several miles from town. I am late arriving home and, with the forecast for continued rain throughout the night, my prospects vanish for finding Possum this evening. In addition, earlier today, my sister gave birth to her first child and my parent's first grandchild. After supper, I visit the hospital to see my new niece.

I finally collect the newspaper from the front porch. As usual, I turn first to the sports page. This article catches my attention:

Brown Bombers to Play Here Saturday

The Emporia Brown Bombers will open their home season Sunday night at Soden's Grove, meeting the Emporia Aces, a team composed of former Emporia State players at eight o'clock. Bob Smith will do the pitching for the Brown Bombers, according to manager William "Possum" Williams. Adults will be admitted to the game for 50 cents.

The Bombers will begin the season after only one or two practices. Perhaps this game might give me an idea as to whether I can play at this talent level. As an active Emporia State player, I figure that I might not be welcomed to play for a team composed of "former Emporia State players." So, I rule out that possibility. My only hope seems to rest with the Brown Bombers. First, though, I need to see the make-up of that team before I contact coach Possum. As I re-read the article, the headline lists a Saturday game, but the article, itself, reads a Sunday game time.

I decide to drive to Soden's Grove on this Saturday, in case it is game day, but neither team shows up. Several fans drive in and out of the park showing some discontent with no game being played. I wonder if this scheduling uncertainty might be a precursor for the Bombers' season. I assume the game will be played on Sunday instead, so I arrive at the park for the eight o'clock start. Both teams are warming up and a very small crowd begins to occupy the stands.

Sitting alone near the top of the bleacher seats, I'm surprised to see the Aces dressed in new white uniforms, trimmed in red, while only a few Bombers wear mismatched uniforms with the others wearing regular street clothes, some with tennis shoes and some with street shoes. Nevertheless, the Bombers have some incredible athletes who hold their own against the seasoned Aces. It seems that a few Mexicans as well as blacks are on the team, but I do not recognize any of them. The Bombers' Bob Smith pitches very well for the first five innings before tiring. He is then relieved by a few players who show very little pitching experience and are hit hard by the Aces.

During the game, I see a routine I have not seen since my early Legion baseball days. After each half-inning, all the fielders toss their baseball gloves onto the outfield grass. We did that so that each player would be assured a glove while playing in the field. It seems that some of the players for the Bombers do not own a glove. We certainly do not have that problem while playing in college. Apparently, summer baseball at this level must be played on a shoe-string budget!

The Bombers lose the game, 14 to 9, but from my point of view the prospects of playing with them are more realistic. I promise myself that I will visit Possum at his place of business next week—if I can get off work. What do I have to lose?

Chapter Two

Possum

Fritz's barbershop, downstairs at the corner of Commercial Street and Sixth Avenue, is most popular for the average guy in my age group. However, his fifty-cent haircut charge is, for me, too expensive. Instead, I pay twenty-five cents at a shop on the other side of Commercial Street, several blocks to the south.

On several occasions, though, I accompany friends of mine who are regular customers at Fritz's. During these times, I visit with Possum, a very friendly black man probably in his late 50s or early 60s. His hair and chin whiskers show signs of graying, while his piercing dark eyes center his being. His shoe-shine service, with his step-up bench and shoe-shine kit positioned along the left wall, has been in Fritz's shop for years. He freely, and with quiet dignity, engages those waiting for their turn in the barber chair. He is by nature an easy conversationalist with no topic out of bounds, or without some personal knowledge, and is always eager to share.

"I'll never forget that day. March 31, 1931," Possum says with a frown. "I was living here in Emporia and getting ready to go to the *Gazette* to get my newspapers to deliver. It was almost one o'clock and people started shouting that an airplane has crashed near Cottonwood Falls. Then, the sad news comes out that the Notre Dame coach, Knute Rockne, was on that plane and had died in the crash."

And another story. "I remember Babe Ruth calling his shot to right field back in '32. I wasn't there, of course, but I heard it on the radio. Man, that was something. The crowd roared and roared after he hit that thing."

The one incident, of which he seemed most passionate, occurred in 1935. "Some of us guys heard that Satchel Paige was going to bring a team down from North Dakota to play in the NBC World Series in Wichita. There are over sixty teams from all over the United States playing there each year. So, we hop in a car and drive there just in time to see Satchel strike out about seventeen batters and win the championship. He wins four games and strikes out over sixty batters during that series. I hear that record still stands." He seems to have a tear in his eye whenever he tells that story.

Possum has us right there. Over my high school years, and during my recent first year in college, I look forward to seeing him anytime I can to pick up on one of his colorful stories.

On this day, Thursday, however, I feel my stomach tumbling and a little sweat on the back of my neck. With rain coming down, I finally get off work early and decide that now is the time to drop in to see Possum. I step down the stairway leading to the barber shop. This time, I am to see Possum for a different reason than for merely a visit. My summer baseball future is at stake and, I feel, perhaps my whole baseball life hinges on the outcome of this scary plan.

I enter the shop and am immediately relieved to find that Possum is alone with no customers and with Fritz and his assistant apparently on break. I approach Possum with a nod, no handshake, as he seems to recognize me from my many previous visits.

"Possum, I have a proposition for you that you may not like, but I have to give it a try."

"Shoot," he says.

"I attended your ball game last weekend and was really impressed by what a fine team you have. I noticed, though, that after your starting pitcher tired, you did not seem to have many good back-ups. I pitched for the E-State Hornets this spring and sure wish I could find a team to play for this summer."

Possum just looks at me over his glasses, without a word, waiting for me to continue.

"The problem is, of course, that I am not black, but you might notice that I have a pretty good tan! I was wondering if you think we could work something out so that I could play for you and the Brown Bombers."

"Man, we could sure use some help," he says. "I saw a few Hornet games several weeks ago and I remember seeing you pitch. Seems like you have a pretty good curve ball."

After several more seconds, he says, "Heck, you're brown enough. We're having practice east of the Peter Pan diamond tomorrow evening at about six if it's not raining, so why don't you drop by and we'll see how it goes? Otherwise, just show up for the game Saturday with whatever you want to wear. Bring your glove and a bat for sure."

As I turn to walk out, Possum calls to me, "Hey, Kenny, since you're here, I'd like to get a little information."

Possum reaches for a notebook and a pencil from a nearby shelf. "I've several of the Bombers listed in here with their jobs and families and such. You may take a look at them if you want and then add a few things of your own on one of the back pages. I'm hoping to get the rest of the team in this book before long."

As Possum walks back to the shoe-shine stand, I take a seat in a barber chair and open the notebook cover.

At the top of the first page, I see Steve Jones listed and several hand-written notes: *He is right-handed, bats right and plays second base. He played only one year of Legion ball but loves the game. He supports his mother, several brothers and sisters and works at the greenhouse. Seems to be a really tough guy.*

I flip to the second page and see a similar listing for Harold Turner. *He is right-handed and bats right and plays the outfield. The tallest and fastest Bomber. He lives and works on a farm north of town. Came in from Georgia about a year ago with no family.*

Clyde Matson's name is at the top of the third page. *Throws left and bats right and is a natural first-baseman. Lives on a farm and drives his own car. Likes to read and listen to the radio. Arrived from back east a few years ago after some difficulty with the law and has no family. Large frame with muscle.*

Page number four headlines Don Graham. *A great Bomber. He is a natural right fielder with a terrific arm. Bats right and throws right. He is by far the oldest Bomber—around 35. Has a wife and several kids. Works at a lumberyard and can hit the ball a mile!*

The fifth player is Bob Smith. *He pitches and can play third* base or the outfield. He works at the Booster station south of town. He played some Legion ball and seems dedicated to the game and will make a great utility player.

Mike Garcia's name tops the sixth page. I am finding these entries very interesting. Possum must certainly be a detail man. The page reads: *A slick shortstop with no flaws on defense. Bats right and throws right and will center the team with quiet and determined play. He is a teller at a local bank. He will hit well at the top of the order. Lived in Emporia for several years but did not play baseball locally. He seems older than the other team members, except for Don Graham.*

David Carter is the player listed on the last page. I remember a David Carter in junior high, but it probably isn't him. *David is a player who can play several positions. He could be our catcher or pitcher if necessary. Throws right and bats right. He works in the printing department of the* Gazette *and has his own apartment. He seems to really like playing baseball and being a member of the Bombers.*

The next several pages are blank, but I note that near the back of the notebook are a great number of baseball playing situations and diagrams, all written in Possum's longhand. I will have a fun time with this team if I can make it.

I turn to another page and find the starting lineup for the game played last Sunday. It reads:

This explains the need for other players. They only have nine guys on the team. I page back to the players' listings and enter my name on the top of the first

Starting Lineup for Bombers, June 17, '56
Steve Jones, 2b
Mike Garcia ss
Don Graham rf
Bob Smith p
Jesse Solis lf
Harold Turner cf
David Carter 3b
Philip Solis c
Clyde Matson 1b
Note: Clyde and David may also pitch

blank page. I follow it with a few comments about me and my interest in baseball. I guess Possum won't mind these entries in my own handwriting. *I played Legion ball in Emporia and am now an E-State player. I work for my dad in house building and live with my parents.*

On second thought, should I put down my living with my parents with all these other guys living so differently? I decide I might as well. That is what I do.

I continue a few more lines: *I am a pitcher and third baseman, throw right and hit right. I really look forward to playing with the Bombers this summer!*

We are still alone in the barber shop as I hand Possum the notebook with my page open to him. He reads it and smiles. "Live with your parents, huh?"

I do my best to show confidence with a positive nod. "Yup, see you tomorrow."

Possum smiles once again as he gives me a short wave with his left hand.

I drive home with a good feeling that I have found a fine team to play for this summer.

Even though it is raining hard the next day, I hurry to the park after work and wait, hopefully, as the six o'clock hour arrives. But no others show up, so practice is obviously cancelled.

Arriving home, I pick up the *Gazette* and find the announcement for the next game tomorrow and am delighted to read of the addition of two new pitchers.

Possum must already be counting on me, I think. I will not sleep well tonight but will do my best to impress the team tomorrow evening. I remember that he said to "bring a bat for sure." At Emporia State, I did not need a bat of my own, and the only one I have is pretty beat up. I go to the closet and find it leaning against the side wall. I bought it for a quarter or so at a second-hand store a few years ago. I pick it up to see the numerous dents and scrapes resulting from, I think, some kid hitting rocks with it. It is a standard bat, though, with the numeral "34" on the knob end and the familiar "Louisville Slugger" brand barely visible on the barrel. Oh well, it will have to do. I do not want to get cross-ways with Possum for my first game!

Brown Bombers Play Allen Here Saturday

Emporia's Brown Bombers will make their second start of the season Saturday night at Soden's Grove, meeting the Allen town team at eight o'clock. Manager William "Possum" Williams says that the club has added several new players, including two pitchers, and that it will be stronger than the one that lost the opening game last Sunday to the Emporia Aces, 14-9. Admission to the game will be 50 cents.

Chapter Three

Philip and the Brown Bombers

I arrive early at Soden's Grove and find one other player waiting in his car. After a few moments, I think I recognize him from our very early baseball-playing days at Peter Pan Park on the south side of Emporia. I open the car door and swing my legs out. It is the Philip Solis I remember!

Philip greets me with a quick nod and steps out of his car. He starts pulling out catching equipment from the trunk. He had been a real friend so many years ago when we were kids. I have not seen him since our early junior high school days. But, from up close, he has hardly changed in appearance, except for more muscle and a little mustache. He wears old jeans and a dark short-sleeved shirt and carries a chest protector, mask, and glove with a ball resting in the pocket.

My mind flashes back quickly to a memory of Philip and his

brothers living with their grandparents who had immigrated from Mexico some years earlier.

I thought about wearing my old woolen uniform hanging in my closet, but, after some deliberation, and remembering that Possum said to wear anything, I decided on a cotton warm-up bottom, with draw string around my waist and a single button-down back pocket. My top consists of a simple white T-shirt.

I quickly grab my baseball spikes from the back seat and lace them up. I pull my baseball hat tight over my forehead hoping that my white skin will not expose my deception. This is my uniform for the day. I grab my glove and old bat from the back seat and close the door.

"Hi, Philip," I say, with a quick wave. "It's been a long time. How are you doing?"

He hesitates for a few seconds before recognizing me and smiles. "Fine, Kenny, and how about you?"

I am eager to get the formality behind me so simply blurt, "I'm doing good, but hey, I talked to Possum a few days ago and he suggested I might drop by for the game this evening. He seemed to think it would be OK for me to maybe join you guys."

His look carries me back some ten years when he was my catcher when I pitched for the Eagles in our little league games at Peter Pan Park. "What was that you said?"

"Man, I've been looking for a chance to play ball this summer and this seems to be my chance." I am getting a little shaky at this point. I so want Philip's response and am hoping it to be a positive one.

As a catcher, Philip had always been a no-nonsense kind of guy. When he put a finger down for a fast ball or a curve or a change-up, I do not remember ever shaking him off. His catcher's glove was positioned where he wanted to receive the pitch.

His glove showed no movement as it provided a clear target. Of the dozens of catchers I have pitched to over the years, Philip was the smoothest of all. His arm was excellent, and few runners attempted to steal on him. However, as with most of us, hitting was the big problem. To truly succeed at this level, our batting average needed to be well above .300 and we had to show some power with homeruns and extra-base hits. Only a few reached that level and Philip and I were destined to hit in the .280s, so our strengths had to be in other aspects of the game. Mine was pitching and his was catching.

After a few more minutes, Philip finally says, "I don't know how you're going to get away with playing on the Brown Bombers, Kenny, but I have no problem with it. I'm guessing that others on the team might want to give it some thought, though."

That startles me a bit. I have been feeling rather comfortable after visiting with Possum, but deep down I also know that some players might feel a bit betrayed by a white boy joining an advertised brown or black team.

"I surely don't want to cause trouble with this. Do you think you would be able to help out a little bit—when the other players show up?"

"Oh, man, I don't know," Philip says with a frown. "Let's just see how it goes. Possum should be here pretty soon and we'll just let him handle it with the rest of the players." It is obvious Philip does not want to get in the middle of what might become a controversy. As is typical for Philip, he is most likely thinking about the game and not wanting any distractions to get in the way.

I take a deep breath and suggest we start warming up since Philip was already carrying a baseball. We walk through a nearby gate to the third base side of the diamond. Philip drops his catching gear on the dugout bench and we begin to toss a few short balls, gradually increasing the distance to about twenty feet. A few minutes pass with no words spoken.

Suddenly, several cars enter the parking lot and players in all manner of dress stroll across the lot to the third base dugout. I notice especially that only a couple of the guys have baseball spikes while the others either have high-top tennis shoes or simply street shoes to play in.

One player wears dark blue-bib overalls with no shirt. The buttons on the sides are open and his white shorts show clearly. Further, he is wearing no socks with his street shoes. He must be six feet 5, or so. What a sight!

I recognize Possum with his short stature and deliberate gait. He has a small notebook in one hand and a bag with a couple of bats and an old glove. He quickly recognizes Philip and me as we play catch a few yards away.

"Hi, Kenny," he says. Then, only raising his voice a little, he asks the players close by to say "Hi" to me. It is as if in passing; no ceremony or formality, whatsoever. It seems he automatically makes me a member of the team, and there will be no further discussion.

One of the players comes over and shakes my hand, "Hi, I am Philip's brother, Jesse. You may not remember me. Just call me Peanuts."

"Nice to meet you", I say with a nervous smile.

"Hey, why do folks call you Peanuts?" I ask a little too quickly.

He smiles back. "When I was in junior high, I'd walk across the street to the YMCA when school was out. Grandmother always gave me a dime to spend each day and I would buy a coke for a nickel and a handful of peanuts and some red-hots for a penny from the machines there. Then I'd dump them all in the coke and watch the bubbles. Joe Stine was a great basketball player for E-State and he was a volunteer at the "Y" and saw me and started calling me Peanuts. That's the story."

I provide an open laugh, "That's a good one."

A couple of the other players look at us with sideway glances but show no concern one way or the other. That suits me fine.

We continue with our warm-ups including a little pepper and then infield practice for some players. Others, including Peanuts, fan out across the outfield grass. Possum does not direct any positioning as the players seem already accustomed to where they play. I continue to throw with Philip as we increase the distance to sixty feet or so.

Suddenly, I hear "Hold That Tiger," coming from a record player near a loud speaker. This is my first introduction to that song as it is played over and over during infield practice. Neither team has "Tigers" as their mascot tonight, so I wonder why that record is chosen.

Several minutes later, members of the Allen town team arrive in three or four cars and begin their preparation near the first base dugout. It has always seemed to me that the opposing team, whether baseball or basketball, are older than the teammates on my teams. This is the situation again this evening as the Allen team is made up of several players seemingly over thirty years old and most wear regular baseball uniforms with no stirrup stockings. This hairy, bare-legged image seems to make them even more formidable.

Of course, I do not know yet the names of the players for the Bombers, except for Philip and Peanuts. I saw them in the game last week but did not recognize anyone—not even Philip. While Philip is inviting a few other players to join us playing catch, I look around the field. It turns out that the Bombers are as tall and muscular as any of the Allen team and, once again, as in the game last Sunday night, show considerable skill and enthusiasm in their warm-ups. At this point, the teams look even to me. The excitement is starting to build within me as I can feel the normal pre-game jitters.

After the warm-ups are over for both teams, Possum calls the eleven of us to the dugout to relay the lineup for today's game. "Jones will lead off at second base, and then Garcia, Graham, Smith, Jesse, and Turner."

It turns out that Turner is the guy in the over-alls. Seeing him up-close, I bet he is not eighteen years old and likely doesn't even weigh 170 pounds.

Possum continues, "Kenny Young, you'll be pitching, Philip, catching, and Matson will be batting ninth."

I am greatly relieved not to have my name called to start. It would likely have been a surprise to the rest of the team, anyway, since I have just joined them. Sitting next to me, I overhear Mike Garcia whisper to Clyde Matson, "Kenny Young is from Georgia and just moved here to be with his dad." Young is 6 feet tall or more, I think. He sure looks like he will be a good pitcher, and he must be the second pitcher Possum was writing about in the newspaper article.

Now it is game time and the Bombers run from the dugout to the field, leaving me alone with one other player. It is quite light at eight o'clock these first days of summer, so the field lights are still turned off. It looks like a crowd of a few hundred and they are giving our team a nice greeting with applause and shouts. Wow, the Bombers surely look like a powerful team from my dugout position! The butterflies are quieting a little as I scoot over on the bench closer to the other player.

"Hi, I'm Ken Ohm."

"I'm David Carter," he answers, as he holds out his hand for a shake.

I look at him with sudden recognition. "Did you go to junior high here in Emporia?"

"Sure did, but left Emporia a few years after that. I only got back here last fall, and I'm working in the printing department at the *Gazette*."

"I met with Possum last week and he suggested I join the team tonight as a pitcher," I say. "Did you join the Bombers right away when they had the tryouts?"

"Yeah, Possum was anxious that we all sign up as he had a schedule already planned. In fact, he also said that he could almost assure us that we would get paid… maybe as much as five to ten dollars a game. Did he talk to you about that, Kenny?"

"No, he didn't. I was not even thinking about that when I talked to him."

"Well, I know some of the guys will be working on him a little bit. He probably got several dollars for tickets from the last game."

The first pitch from Kenny Young is a strike and the game is underway.

"Hey, I just thought of something," David says. "We got two Kenny's on our team and they're both pitchers. Isn't that something?"

David and I sit quietly as the first inning ends for the Allen batters with three up and three down. I watch as each Bomber turns and flips his glove to the outfield grass, with Kenny Young carefully dropping his glove behind the mound.

"David, what's the deal with the tossed gloves?" I ask.

"Possum told us to talk with the opposing team during warm-ups so that we can share gloves with anyone who doesn't have one. Bob Smith and Harold Turner don't have a glove for our team, and Clyde's is a really old one," David answers. "Besides, this way we don't have to carry our gloves in and out each time."

"Well, at least everybody has a glove that way," I add.

The nine guys in the field come running into the dugout and offer each other encouragement as Steve Jones goes to the plate as the first batter for the Bombers. The Allen pitcher stoops to pick up and wear Kenny's glove before his warm-up pitches. Steve promptly hits a first-pitch single to right field but is stranded as the next three Bombers fly out to end the inning.

The game continues a scoreless tie until the bottom of the fifth inning. The field lights are turned on and the ball park turns into a beautiful gem in the night. Don Graham is at bat. On the second pitch, he hits a line drive well over the left field fence. His homerun is followed by several other hits until the score reads 3 to 0, Bombers.

Now in the top of the seventh inning, Possum walks by and directs David to center field in place of Harold Turner. Possum does not look at me during the substitution and I do not care at all. In fact, I am hoping that I will not have to enter the game this evening. I am just beginning to get to know the names of the players. They are all playing very well, and I am still a bit nervous.

Kenny Young has been sailing along allowing only two hits going into the top of the eighth inning. Suddenly, the first two Allen batters are walked. The next hitter pulls an inside pitch to the wall in left field, scoring both runners, and ends up at second base. Possum strolls by and says, "Kenny, go out and warm up. We might need you."

Harold Turner grabs a glove and a ball, and I follow him out the dugout to the bullpen along the foul line. As Turner and I start throwing, I see looseness and a fluid motion in him that suggests that he is an incredible athlete. I wonder why Possum substituted for him.

The next batter walks and Possum jogs to the mound to talk to Young. I start throwing harder and I am feeling quite relaxed—which surprises me. Allen's clean-up batter hits a ground ball to shortstop Mike Garcia who tags second base and throws to first for a double play. The final batter in the inning flies out to right field and the Bombers go into the bottom of the eighth inning leading 3 to 2. Whew!

Turner and I continue to throw lightly and pause to watch the Bombers at bat. "That's a moth-eaten glove you have there, Harold," I say.

"Yeah, it's the one Possum always brings as an extra, but it's like not having a glove at all," Harold grins.

"I'm sorry. Did I throw too hard on our warm-ups?"

"Didn't hurt a bit," Harold shrugs.

The Bombers score no runs in the eighth. As I am warmed up, I decide to return to the dugout for the top of the ninth inning. Instead, Possum meets me and says, "It's all yours, Kenny. Go get em."

"OK, I'll give it a try," I mumble. I nod to Philip who walks to the mound with me. I notice Kenny's glove resting behind the mound and leave it there. I have my own glove.

"I've not pitched under the lights in college, but since both game balls are pretty worn and dark, I think if I keep my pitches low, the hitters will have a tough time seeing them against the background of the dirt around home plate," I say a little too fast for Philip's liking.

He puts a hand on my shoulder and says, "Take it easy, Kenny. Just throw your stuff. No big deal."

He is right. The first batter hits a slow ground ball to first base for out-number one. I reach a 3-2 count on the second batter before he strikes out on my roundhouse curve! Philip throws the ball back to me with a smile under his face mask. I feel very confident right now. On the first pitch, the next batter hits a high fastball deep into left field and all I can see is the back of Jesse Solis as he runs full speed before catching the ball over his right shoulder. Game over!

The players all rush in with happy chatter. Some grab my hand on the way by. Philip walks over and pats me on the back. Well, the first trial is over.

Perhaps this will be a fun summer after all. I deliberately wait near my car in the parking lot hoping to hear of any reaction to me pitching for the Brown Bombers. It is late—almost eleven thirty, so many fans left earlier, even with a close game. Maybe they don't know that I'm not black or maybe they don't care.

I notice Possum some distance away walking toward his car. He sees me and shouts, "He sure got a hold of your last pitch, didn't he?"

"Yeah, I missed with a high one, I guess." That ended the conversation. I get in my car and head home.

Chapter Four

Sundown

Two days later I look in the *Gazette* for a box score or at least a game summary. However, none appears. I see Philip at the next practice and he says, "Forget it, Kenny. Possum doesn't keep a box score. His main interest is the final score of the game and whether we win or lose. I also think he doesn't want to rely on anyone else to keep score, especially since we have just eleven guys on our team. The only time the Bombers are in the paper is when Possum manages to get to the *Gazette* office with a final score and a preview of the next game. I am guessing that only about half our games will ever be covered by the press.

"By the way, some of the guys are meeting with Possum after practice today. They are wondering if he is getting some money together to pay us as he promised when we signed up. We got some out of town games coming up so at least we need to get some gas money. Do you want to join us to meet him?"

"I think I'll pass on that, Philip. I feel that I am barely on the team as it is. Good luck, though. It does cost money to get to games. I know that."

It is our final practice before the next game with the Lebo Wolves in Lebo. It will be a Wednesday night game and we spend several minutes determining car assignments when Possum surprises us by handing out a five-dollar bill to each of the two drivers. That brings smiles all around. I will be riding in Philip's car with Clyde, Don, Steve, and Mike. These assignments are critical as each of us will work all day on Wednesday and coordinating meeting times and places are necessary to get to the game on time after the short drive to Lebo. Possum likes to drive alone to games and we do not argue with him about that.

The payment to the drivers is not the only surprise today, however. With some fanfare, Possum asks us to take a seat on the ground in a circle around him. He stands, smiling. "We just signed a deal to play an exhibition game with the Americus All-Stars at their park on July 26."

This is nice news, but why is Possum making such a big deal out of it?

"Turns out that Ross Grimsley will be on his way from Omaha to pitch in Louisville and will be stopping off in Americus to see his friends and family. He has agreed to pitch a few innings for Americus, and that will give each of you a chance to try your hand against a major leaguer."

Silence, with a few soft whistles. We have all heard of Mr. Grimsley and know that he pitched for the Chicago White Sox a few years ago and is now having a terrific career in the Class AAA League. Although this game is about a month away, we are excited.

"Oh, one more thing," Possum says while pointing his index finger into the air. "You all know Cliff Hodges. He dropped by the barber shop yesterday and said he would like to donate a couple of bats to our team and they should be here by the Lebo game. When you see him around, be sure to thank him.

"By the way, I noticed some of you are working on finding some regular uniforms for our games and I think that is a good idea. Harold, you might try to find a shirt to wear under your overalls," Possum says, smiling. I wonder if that is why he took Harold out of the game the other night.

It will be our first out of town game and we know very little about the other team. Someone rumored that a few players for Lebo do not live in or around Lebo. In fact, Don tells us that three of their guys are from Ottawa University and includes one of their best pitchers. Possum overhears us and shouts, "Forget all that. Let's work on a run-down play between second and third and be sure we understand what we are supposed to do. Ohm, you be the runner. Kenny Young, hit some fungoes to the outfield. Philip, catch the balls coming in for Young."

The four infielders line up, two behind second and two behind third base. Possum watches from the side with a baseball in his hand. I stand between the two bases. "You all know how to do this, so let's get it right and tag Kenny out." He rifles a throw to second baseman Steve Jones. I take off running to third as Jones throws over my head to Bob Smith at third. I stop quickly and head back to second as Bob bluffs several throws back to Steve. Just as I am about to arrive at second safely, Bob throws to Steve and Steve catches me as I turn back to third with a tag hard on my back just above the tailbone. "Ow!" I shout, as I bend over in some pain.

"Perfect," shouts Possum. "Sometimes the umpires miss the tag, but if the runner gets tagged hard enough, there will be no doubt he's out. Let's try that again. Kenny, get back in there."

After several more trials, the shortstop Mike Garcia and first baseman Clyde Matson begin to rotate into the play as I become a little more elusive. Now, with four infielders chasing me, it is impossible to escape without a hard tag most often in the same spot on my back. In my first year at E-State as a pitcher, I do not remember seeing this kind of drill. I will be sore tonight.

After what seems to be the longest practice session of the summer, we are called together for what we believe will be some final reminders relating to our trip to Lebo.

Possum asks us to sit on the grass around him. I hear grumbles here and there as we are exhausted and ready to go home. Possum stands for a minute with a serious expression. "Men, I've been waiting until now to talk to you about a very serious issue that affects us all and will determine how well we play and win games. It relates to our being an all-black team and how we must handle ourselves, especially on out of town trips. I'll get right to the point. As we travel on the highways and roads getting to the towns, we'll likely see signs warning us about the so-called Sundown Law. Almost all small towns enforce it and it says that no black man or Mexican may find himself in that town after sundown. Bluntly, some of the signs might simply read: 'Colored people, don't let the sun set on you in this town.'"

Possum slowly turns, momentarily looking each of us in the eye. I lower my head and lift my shoulders while shifting my eyes to the near grass below. I will not glance either to the right or to the left. I do not want to be seen staring at any of my teammates and I do not want to see them looking at me. I feel a strange guilt.

Possum continues loudly, "When I was traveling the country in my early days I came across several signs reading, A-N-N-A. What they mean is 'Ain't No Negros Allowed.' It may also mean other nasty words." I hear a few angry whispers around me.

A few more seconds pass before Possum adds, "We probably won't have to worry much about that since we're invited by their baseball teams to play night games in their ball parks. However, you might hear all sorts of things during the game. I'm telling you right now that you'll act like you have not heard a thing. Just catch the ball, hit the ball and win the game. After the game, we all need to head right down the road and not visit more than to say 'Hi.' Do not buy anything from the concession stands. Just wait until you get home. No use looking for trouble."

He pauses as if looking for a reaction. No one says a word. Possum waves to us, indicating the end of practice for this evening.

I drop my shoulders a little while getting up from my sitting position and walk straight to my car. The other players do the same. I think our minds are all focused on Possum's message.

Clyde walks near me and softly shares, "I remember last summer that two guys in my church finished a haying job in western Kansas and were trying to hitch a ride home when they decided to rest in the park of a small town. Even though it was in the early afternoon, within minutes a sheriff found them and escorted them outside the town limits, with the demand that 'Your kind cannot stay here overnight. Don't come back.' It really scared them, so they are trying to find work close by this summer."

I shake my head in sympathy. It seems that Clyde, at least, is not blaming me for the worries Possum shared. I wonder what I am getting into as the lone white boy on this team. Might I have to deal with a potential conflict and help defend my black or brown teammates? The short drive home is an uneasy one!

Chapter Five

The Lebo Wolves

My work day has been a tiring one as I finish hanging sheet rock in a new house on Sunnyslope Street. My dad, Frank, contracted this house from the ground up and I have been working here for the past week. At $1.25 an hour, I cannot complain. My haying job ran out and the outside concrete construction job has been delayed for a time. I am lucky to live at home and Mom is a good cook. Now though, I have just enough time to get to the street in front of the *Gazette* building to meet Philip and the rest of the guys for our twenty-five-mile trip to Lebo. I make much longer trips with the E-State Hornet baseball team, but I find this to be exciting as the Bombers first out-of-town game.

All six of us cram into Philip's light blue, 1946 Plymouth four-door. Mike is the only one who works inside during the day as a bank teller, while the rest of us work in hot and sweaty labor jobs. We had no time for a bath or clean up, so for most of us, our regular work clothes are our travel clothes for the evening. In a small bag, I carry my flannel pants with drawstring to wear as replacement for my dirty jeans, along with my spiked shoes and a white T-shirt, as my playing uniform. I wear my steel-toed work boots until we get to the Lebo diamond and then will change clothes in the car. We also bring along our gloves, bats, a single baseball and, of course, all of Philip's catching gear. With the windows wide open, we head out of Emporia, and we figure it will take about thirty-five minutes to get to Lebo.

I find the ride quite interesting as most of the guys are talkers and the conversation is becoming quite animated. It seems that no one is interested in looking for or talking about Sundown signs—and that is fine with me.

"Did you see Gib last night? He was pretty tipsy…"

"Yeah, but he wasn't the only one. Even Sarah…"

"Hey, Mike. Who was that lovely lady who dropped you off for practice the other day?" Steve asks.

Mike hesitates. "Oh, that's Rosa. She works at a bank across the street from mine and says she likes baseball a lot. She just bought a '48 Chevy so I caught a ride with her to get to practice on time."

With two or three conversations going on, it is hard to follow all of them.

I keep quiet and listen and am rather happy to relax for this short time and try to think a bit about the game this evening. I notice that Don only nods now and then to some conversations. He is by far the oldest member of the team. I imagine somewhere in the mid-thirties. I heard he has a wife and a couple of kids. Probably he is wondering why he keeps playing baseball while working full time and raising a family. I feel some kinship with him. I cannot imagine life without baseball, even when I get to be his age. Philip is eighteen, Jesse and Harold about a year younger, Clyde and I are nineteen, and Steve mentioned a twenty-first birthday a few days ago. The other members of the team seem a little older. This may be the only summer this bunch of guys will get to play together.

Philip enjoys shouting back at the talkers in the back seat while hanging his left arm out the window. "OK, guys, there's Lebo up ahead. As I recall, the diamond is about half way through town…should be there in a few minutes."

Sure enough, we turn into the parking lot near the diamond and find a large crowd milling around, mostly near the concession stand. I could sure use a hot dog right now but as Possum told us, "…especially in out-of-town games, just don't buy anything. No use looking for trouble."

Although it is 1956, I am reminded over and over that the country is still not at peace among the races. Nevertheless, my association so far with the Mexicans and the blacks on this team has been rather easy. These are nice guys, and, besides that, they want to play baseball at every opportunity. That may be what holds us together. Enough of that. I need to get my mind on the game and a good way to start is to get my pants changed and my spikes on.

"Move over, Steve. I need a place to sit."

"It's all yours, Kenny," he shouts. It is such a relief to get these boots off and air my feet for a few seconds. My spikes are fitted with a pitching toe protector. This curved metal piece keeps the shoe leather on my right shoe from wearing out as fast when I drag it in the dirt after each pitch. The piece is screwed to the bottom of my shoe and up to the top where it joins a leather patch secured by my laces. I then check the inside of my right shoe for any sign of screw points protruding through the sole. They seem smooth tonight. Good, no worries there. I tighten the laces and jog to the field. It's time to warm up for a few minutes before heading for the dugout. As a possible relief pitcher, I need to be careful how much warming up I do before I throw seriously later in the bull pen.

As I walk back to the dugout, I hear Possum calling. "Kenny, come here a minute. I am starting you at third base tonight, batting sixth. You did play third at E-State, didn't you?" It takes me a few seconds to catch my breath.

"Yeah, sure. No problem. Who's pitching tonight?" I ask.

"Bob Smith. I'm saving Young until Saturday night at Bushong. They're going to be a tough bunch. By the way, David is not feeling well so we'll be a little shorthanded."

Boy, I must give Possum credit. He takes his job very seriously and is already looking ahead to the next game. I see David Carter standing by the dugout on my way back to the field.

"Hey, David, you feeling alright?"

"No, some kind of stomach problem I guess. Good luck out there on third base."

Infield practice goes well, and third base feels good again.

There is no public-address system and no music is playing before the game. I like that much better than "Hold That Tiger," played over and over again.

The game begins, and we go down in order in the top of the first inning. In the bottom of the inning, I take my position at third base and find myself in a routine dating back to my Junior Legion days. Between each pitch, I glance around on the infield dirt looking for rocks or pebbles or spike marks that might cause a bad hop on a ground ball. I see two or three small stones and toss them into the grass in foul territory to my right.

Lebo goes down in order and I fling my glove to the outfield grass before running into the dugout. The other Bombers do the same with their gloves.

The game for the fans is turning out to be a good one. The teams are tied at one each at the end of the sixth inning. I have two hits so far and no errors at third base. We go into the bottom of the seventh inning still tied at two. The Wolves score one run and lead 3 to 2 as we bat in the eighth inning. We go down one-two-three, and Lebo also goes down in order in the bottom of the eighth.

This is it; the top of the ninth, one run down with the top of our order coming to bat. Possum walks by and says, "Kenny, if we tie or go ahead, you will have to pitch. Looks like Bob is out of gas."

"That's fine with me. I'll be ready," I reply.

The inning starts out well with Jones and Garcia both hitting singles. We have men on first and second. Our power hitter, Don Graham, lines out to third base with the runners holding. Peanuts pops up foul to first base. There are two outs and two on with Harold Turner batting. After a 3-2 count, Turner walks, loading the bases. I feel confident as I stride to the plate. I take the first pitch strike and the next two, both balls. I swing late on the next pitch and hit the ball high off the light pole behind first base. The next pitch is a fast ball way outside for a ball three. Now the count is 3-2 and the pitcher steps off the rubber and rubs the ball in his glove. I step out of the box and take a couple of practice swings. As the pitcher goes into his windup, I concentrate on the ball as it leaves his hand. I start my swing as the ball streaks before my eyes, but I miss it by a foot, and strike out. Game over, we lose 3 to 2.

I am furious and, as the umpire and the catcher walk away, I slam my old bat hard on home plate. With a loud crack, splinters fly and the bat barrel rolls to one side, leaving me holding the handle. My eyes are tightly closed in agony when I hear Possum shouting as he storms from the dugout. I turn around to see him approach me yelling, "Why did you do that, Kenny? You are going to have to buy us a new bat. You are going to have to buy us a new bat!"

We are now toe to toe and looking at each other from just inches away. "This's my bat, Possum!" I shout. "It's not yours."

He pauses for a brief second and pivots away back toward the dugout, shouting words not clear to me. I guess that my days as a Brown Bomber are over. I continue to stand near the plate for a minute or two before I pick up the larger pieces of the bat and then drift toward the dugout.

As I am about to toss them into a nearby trash barrel, I feel a tug on my shirt. "Sir, are you going to throw that bat away?"

I look down at the saddest, yet brightest blue eyes I have ever seen. His little body is covered with patches of dirt and grime from his hair to his bare feet. I doubt he is no more than six years old.

"Yes, it's no good anymore."

"I just want the big part. I bet I could hit a ball with it," he explained.

The barrel of the bat broke off rather cleanly, so I hand it to him. "Thanks," he says. He swings the bat-piece as he runs off onto a narrow path along the wheat field beyond left field and disappears into the darkness. I see no adult in sight. He must live close by. He is the first person who has ever called me, "Sir." I bet I will always remember him.

I walk to Philip's car. I pull off my spikes, tie the shoes laces together, and toss them, along with my glove and hat, into the open trunk.

Some of the other players nod in sympathy. Clyde leans close to me and whispers, "I think Possum was so mad because he thought you broke one of our new bats that Mr. Hodges just gave us. Don't worry about it."

A car goes by with horns honking along with the passengers' shouts of victory. The trip home is a long one. Not much is said on the drive back to Emporia. Everyone is exhausted, both from the long day at work and then with the late night of a losing game.

I picture over and over again the ball sailing past my eyes and my desperate attempt to hit it. I have been playing baseball long enough to know that it is hard to hit a ball that high. Further, the umpire would certainly have called it a ball and we would have tied the game. Then, if it remained tied or we went ahead, I would get to pitch in the bottom of the ninth inning and perhaps even more. This is a tough one to shake off!

We part ways back on the deserted street where we left our cars. "See you tomorrow at practice," was the extent of conversation. Mike jumps on his bicycle and heads down the dark street for home.

Chapter Six

The Bat

After arriving home and in my bedroom, I cannot sleep. I see the little Lebo boy with his sad, blue eyes. Then, my memory reflects to a time shortly after World War Two ended. My family moved to Emporia and Dad achieved his lifelong dream of becoming a carpenter. Among some used tools he purchased, he found an old wood lathe and began to experiment with it. He decided after turning several lamp bases and table legs that he would build a baseball bat for my future use. Although I was only eleven years old, he was certain that I would grow up to handle any legal man-size baseball bat.

After a little research, he found the major league limit on the length of a bat was forty-two inches, so used it as his starting point. For some reason, he picked a walnut log as the raw material for the bat and, over the next several evenings, spun out a beautiful and well-shaped prize. He swung it a few times and handed it to me. It was surprisingly heavy to me and I nearly dropped it. I could see the disappointment on Dad's face but assured him that I would grow into it and make him proud one day with a home run. He smiled at that and the bat became a fixture around the house until I was strong enough to take it outside and try to hit a pitch or two from my neighbor friend, John Whittington.

My thoughts continue, but I am finally becoming drowsy.

I recall a long-ago evening, with darkness approaching, when I ran into the kitchen for supper and forgot the bat outside. It rained that night and when I recovered the bat the next day, it had a very distinct curve to it. From the handle to the far end, the curve extended at least three inches. I did not mention my oversight to Dad and he never did react even when later seeing the disfigurement for the first time. He shrugged and focused on other problems that he may have had at the time.

The bat has been in our basement for several years; all through my high school and now in my college baseball days. Since I have used other bats furnished by the baseball teams and, up until tonight, my own "bat-worth-a-quarter," I have thought little of the "hunker," downstairs.

Rather than to part with the two- or three-dollar asking price for a new bat, I think I might just try that old one in the basement. Heck, what have I got to lose? Possum will probably kick me off the team tomorrow anyway. I am suddenly wide awake as I move silently down the dark stairway, past the rooms of our two boarders, Willis and Russell.

I pull the string to the basement light bulb and there is the bat, lying on an upper shelf along the wall—probably untouched for all these years. I lift it from the shelf, blow off a little dust and give it a few swings. It seems quite light and, as I

The Bat

look down the curved barrel, I see myself giving it a try on the practice field. I study the curve. I know the bat will have to be held with the end of the bat curved either to the right or to the left of the handle. The curve held up or down will, of course, guarantee missing the pitch. After some deliberation, I decide that I will hold the bat so that the curve will be to the right. I know that if my swing is a normal one, the contact point will likely direct any hit to right field. But, that is my decision and I am anxious to try it out.

The next day, Philip drops by my work site during the lunch break. "I heard you were working here on Union Street," he said. "I just saw Possum and he said to tell everyone that we will not have practice today or tomorrow. He said for everyone to rest up a bit and meet as usual on Saturday for the drive to Bushong."

"Did he say anything about me striking out or breaking my bat?" I ask.

"Not a word. I think he was way more concerned with losing the game and then getting ready for Bushong. I think you have nothing to worry about. Possum knows this game pretty well and realizes that is all part of the game."

"I found a different bat, Philip. I am going to bring it along to Bushong and give it a try. You might get a kick out of it. I don't think I'll mention it to Possum."

Game day finds us all on time at the *Gazette* building for the ride to Bushong. I quickly transfer my shoes, glove, and new bat into Philip's car trunk.

As we head north for the short 20-mile trip, I mention I am going to try out a new bat tonight that my dad made for me several years ago. Although I am excited about the possibility, the players in the car show little response.

Don changes the subject. "Did you guys know that Bushong is named after a major-league catcher?" That gets our attention. He continues.

"Back in the 1880s, the St. Louis Browns won what was then the world series and their players became very popular in Missouri and Kansas. The Missouri-Pacific railroad ran a line down through this part of Kansas and their officials decided on naming some of the whistle-stops they used to fill up their engines with water. They renamed the little town of Weeks to become Bushong. They also gave original names in honor of several other St. Louis players, including Allen, Comiski, Raff, Admire, Wilmet, Burns and several others I can't remember." Don pauses.

"Are you making this up, or what?" Philip shouts.

"No, I read it just a few days ago. It turns out that Bushong was a dentist along with being a major-league player. If you look him up, he goes by Doc Bushong. By the way, he also invented the catcher's glove."

Just then we arrive in Bushong and file out of our car a few minutes ahead of Bob Smith's and Possum's cars. We smile at Don on our walk to the playing field.

The Bushong baseball diamond is dirt with a patchy grass outfield. The outfield has no fence, but is surrounded by a cornfield, averaging about 350 feet from home plate. The corn is nearly six feet tall and quite dense; a beautiful sight with the setting sun and soon in the dim lighting provided by a few light bulbs resting on three forty-foot poles. After dark, any fly ball hit that high disappears into the night and infielders as well as outfielders must guess where the ball might land. I recall some rather serious acrobatics on the part of fielders as they reposition and try to catch the ball after suddenly seeing it drop below light level.

Two Arrowheads

We do not have batting practice tonight, since we arrive just several minutes before game time and we have a limited number of bats and balls. So, my first hitting attempt with the walnut bat will be in a game situation. I am playing third base again tonight. Possum had no other comment for me except to say that I will bat sixth. Other than the guys who rode in Philip's car, the others have not heard the bat story and of my intention to use it this evening. After a short warm-up, the game begins.

I take my position at third base and, as usual, check for rocks and pebbles on the infield. I find a small rock but, before throwing it to the side, I notice a distinct arrowhead shape. My mind quickly recalls one of Dad's stories about finding an arrowhead on the dirt infield of a ball diamond deep in the Flint Hills. I place the stone in my rear picket and concentrate on Kenney's first pitch to the Bushong lead-off hitter. Neither team scores in the first inning.

I stroll into the batter's box in the top of the second inning. With two teammates on base, I prepare to face my first pitch with the walnut lumber and with my adrenaline pumping strongly. The pitch is a fast ball nearly eye high and I give it a great swing and catch it squarely. The ball flies high and deep into center field. I watch the beautiful sight for a second or two while still in the batter's box and then take off running full speed to first base. I see the ball land far into the corn field and shift to my highest running gear around second base and catch sight of Possum swinging his arms to round third and to head for home. The next batter up, my friend Philip, signals me to slow down as there is no play at the plate. I am ecstatic with the first home run of my playing career. Glancing toward center field, an opposing player has just found the ball and is throwing it into the infield. I could have run the bases twice with that hit.

As I arrive to our dugout, I am greeted by my team mates and a smiling Possum. He has no comment about my "new" bat but shakes my hand briefly and returns to the third base coaching box with hopes of adding to our three-run lead. I sit in the dugout and analyze the home run and realize that I must have been out in front of that pitch a good way to hit it up the center that far. Also, I wonder what possessed me to swing at such a high pitch after my strike out disaster in Lebo.

I get two more hits and a ground out to first base as we end up winning 7 to 2. The ride home is much easier than the other night from Lebo. Kenny Young pitched a three-hitter and gets the win. The guys are talking up the team and its prospects with about as much energy as I have seen at any time so far, this season. Maybe we are now on a winning path. The next game will be at home on July 4 against Allen.

On my drive home, I feel the arrowhead in my back pocket. Did it give me luck tonight?

Chapter Seven

Two Arrowheads

I did not sleep any better last night than I did after my strike out in the Lebo game. But I am much happier now. I smell bacon and pancakes. I grab my "hero" bat, and my arrowhead and walk down the stairs to the kitchen. Mom and Dad are already there as usual, with Dad drinking coffee and Mom cooking breakfast for the three of us and for Willis and Russell. They are both graduate students at Emporia State and boarding with us for the summer. As I walk into the kitchen, I hold my bat up high for Dad to see, and exclaim, "I hit a home run with this last night, Dad!"

Dad smiles broadly and replies, "Well, that is what I made it for, son."

"By the way, Dad, I meant to show you this arrowhead."

I hand it to him.

"I found it yesterday on the Bushong diamond. When I was a

little kid, you showed me one you found on a baseball diamond in the Flint Hills."

Dad lights up. "I forgot all about that."

Dad carefully turns the arrowhead over and over and notes a slight chip on one edge. "Kenny, this is the real thing. I cannot believe we both found arrowheads on baseball diamonds. Let me go see if I can find mine in the dresser drawer."

Dad returns a few minutes later with his arrowhead. We compare the two. Our shared happiness is electric.

After breakfast, we drive to the Lutheran Church at Eleventh Avenue and Neosho Street. As I walk in, I hear Uncle Chet call to me, "I just heard that you got a home run and beat Bushong last night, Kenny. Congratulations." He shakes my hand and pats me on the back.

"How did you know that?" I ask.

"I worked last night at the Santa Fe with Kenny Young's father. Kenny came by after you guys got home and told us all about it. How is it that you play for an all-black team?"

"Well, it is actually black and Mexican, but I wanted a place to play and they don't seem to mind. Besides, look at my dark tan. So far, nobody has said anything about it. I hope it stays that way."

Chet is with Aunt Gladys and Cousins Carolyn and Larry and the three are smiling at me during the conversation.

"We are going to play a game in the afternoon on July 4 at Soden's Grove. Come by if you get a chance," I say.

"With Pop's eighty-first birthday, we'll all be at the Peter Pan Park grape arbor for a noon picnic," Gladys says. "Don't forget, it is also Aunt Dorothy's, and cousins Karen's and Don's birthdays," she adds.

"Of course, I know that. Mom and Dad have been talking about it for several weeks, right Mom?"

She nods and says, "We'll be there for sure before going to the game. "I think the game starts at three. Is that right, Kenny?"

I nod my head, yes.

Mom turns to Gladys, "What are we supposed to bring? I always bring potato salad and fried chicken." Gladys and Mom visit for a few minutes before we all file in for the service.

Well, the word is out, I think to myself. If baseball fans in the area know that a white boy is playing for the Brown Bombers, they are not making a fuss over it. In a way, that is a relief, but it is kind of disappointing that my charade has been uncovered.

Monday morning is here and time to go to work. I spend the day hauling concrete to fill basement forms for a new house on Prairie Avenue. Although hard work, I do have time to rehash the past game and the success using my "new" bat. I wonder what tonight's paper will say about the game.

As usual, I drive from work directly to practice at Peter Pan Park. When I get there, the guys recognize me with various compliments and, in some cases, over-acted gestures of adoration. With a broad grin, David Carter hands me a copy of the sports page of tonight's *Gazette*. There it is:

As practice is about to start, we see a '48 Chevy drive up and out jumps Mike with glove in hand. Rather than drive off as on other practice days, the car parks along Congress Street and Mike's friend, Rosa, steps out and sits on the car's right-front

Ohm Powers Brown Bombers Past Bushong

With two men on base in the top of the second inning, Kenny Ohm hit a towering home run to center field, making the score 3-0. Coach Possum said the ball traveled over 400 feet and was the spark the Bombers needed to coast to a 7-2 victory. Kenny Young went all the way for the victory. The next game for the Bombers against the Allen town team will be on July 4th at 3pm at Soden's Grove. Bob Smith will start on the mound for the Bombers.

fender. What a sight! She is wearing a bright red dress and her dark black hair and bright eyes capture the attention of each Bomber. Mike joins a group of players warming up with, "OK, guys. Keep your eyes on the ball. Rosa is going to watch practice today before driving me home, so let's get to work."

We all immediately continue our warm-up routine, but with a noticeable change in intensity and with an obvious effort to capture Rosa's attention. Possum notices our distraction with a smile of understanding. However, he begins serious practice with a spirited series of wind sprints followed by a heavy concentration on situational plays.

"Hit the cut-off man!" is a command coach Possum makes over and over. The third baseman and shortstop are an integral part of each of these plays, but Possum insists that the pitcher back up home or go down halfway to third in case the ball is overthrown. We did a little of this in college, but Possum pays special attention to certain types of defenses. More and more, I see him as some kind of baseball genius. Perhaps he would have been a great ball player or coach if only he had been given the chance.

Practice ends today with the Bombers in high spirits while stealing glances in the direction of the '48 Chevy and lovely Rosa still sitting attentively on the front fender. "Hey, Mike," Clyde shouts. "Will you introduce us to your new girlfriend?"

Mike waves him off and quickly trots to the car, driving this time with Rosa at his side in the front passenger seat. He is smiling broadly as they drive away. I look forward to practice tomorrow evening as I suspect does each other Bomber. We are quietly hoping Rosa will once again drive Mike to practice.

Indeed, the next day Rosa takes her position sitting on the Chevy fender, this time in a white dress, but with the same air of confidence and apparent interest in the practice going on before her. We all find extra spring in our step, and I am sure are looking more like a respectable baseball team than during any previous practice session.

Possum reviews several strategies we learned yesterday and then follows with some new ideas. He suggests several ways for infielders to signal who will be covering second base on a steal, and for who will back up the pitcher on every throw back from the catcher. He also emphasizes that the center fielder and left fielder be constantly alert for overthrows on steal attempts. Otherwise, we throw long tosses from the outfield to home plate—even as pitchers, since Possum says it will help to strengthen our arms. I will have to agree.

Before practice ends today, Possum calls us in for a final suggestion to improve our alertness while in the field.

Without expecting an answer, he asks, "What are you guys thinking between pitches? Here is what you should be thinking. What do I do when the ball is hit to me? You must know the instant the ball leaves the bat of an opponent what your reaction will be, whether you make the play directly or a team member makes the play. That includes throwing to the right base and backing up other players as we have been practicing all evening."

Possum pauses as most of us try to concentrate on these suggestions. He seems satisfied as he then dismisses us with a wave of his hand and a "Get some rest tonight. See you tomorrow."

As we begin to leave the practice field, Mike quickly runs over to Rosa and takes her hand. He leads her toward us and says, "Guys, this is Rosa Muniz. She says she wants to meet you all."

We stop as a group and some of us tip our hats. Mike points a finger at each of us as he calls off our names. Rosa smiles and nods with each name. We nervously mumble assorted greetings and then move on. Rosa and Mike, hand in hand, walk to their car and drive off. Each Bomber is smiling.

Chapter Eight

July 4th, 1956

I make a special effort today to get to Peter Pan Park, and to wish my grandfather, "Pop," a happy birthday. We sometimes see relatives only once a year, but today they turn out in full number. At least four generations are represented with old folks in the shade under the grape vines and young kids eyeing the wading pool.

I move from one group of relatives to the other talking little about baseball, but with considerable discussion of the hot weather and the prospects for rain. This makes for easy conversation for a young guy like me having other thoughts to occupy my mind.

On a park bench nearby, photos are being taken of Pop, Aunt Dorothy, Cousin Karen and Cousin Don, all with birthdays today. We are so proud of Fourth of July birthdays extending over four generations within our family.

After lunch, I say goodbye to the folks at the picnic and drive the few blocks to Soden's Grove. It is very warm, approaching 100 degrees, but I look forward to the battle with Allen in hopes of avenging our earlier loss.

I will be playing third base and Possum earlier suggested I be ready for some time on the mound. It is nearly 1:30 and already a crowd is gathering. Two different concession stands are open, and it looks like they are doing a good business selling hotdogs and soft drinks. Several picnic tables under the trees near the Cottonwood River are already occupied by fans enjoying their July 4 celebration. I was careful not to overdo eating at our family picnic and will also resist a hotdog here. As other Bombers arrive, I notice that none of them are visiting the concession stands. "No use looking for trouble," as Possum says. I think we all understand that means even in our home town.

Oh, my goodness! The guy turned on "Hold That Tiger," again. "Hey, Peanuts, do you know what is going on with that song?" I shout.

"That's Charley Songer, an old guy, almost 80. He is said to have been quite a jazz musician in his day."

"I guess it kind of grows on you, but man, do you think he is going to play just that one song over and over before every game?"

Peanuts shrugs.

As our players arrive, we begin our warm-up as usual. We only have two baseballs, so we start a game of catch designed to include any number of players. Up to six or eight players stand in parallel lines of three or four, short-tossing diagonally across from one player to the next across the approximate fifteen-foot space. A player might catch and throw a dozen or more times during this warm up.

July 4th, 1956

Since we are playing at home and not spending time on the road, we next start regular infield practice. We often begin this regimented exercise a half hour or so before a home game—and it is a luxury!

Possum hits ground balls to each player around the diamond who then throws the ball to first base, with Clyde Matson catching it and then throwing to second base. Steve Jones then throws it to me at third. I receive the ball in the glove on my left hand and start a full spin to my left letting it fly to home. The ball hits Philip's glove with a loud pop. We repeat this "around the horn" process two or three times before ending infield practice. It is a nice warm-up, great fun, and gets the blood pumping.

With game time near, I glance to the crowd in the stands and find members of my extended family waving and smiling at me. What a great surprise! They all drove over from Peter Pan Park. There is Pop standing in the front row near our dugout with his suspenders and long-sleeved shirt. He is a good student of the game as he spent many years watching his five boys play baseball in the pastures near his farm.

I am not certain if I feel pressure or pride with such an audience. Quickly, in my mind, I see each of my family shelling out 50 cents for admission to this game. As tight fisted as they are, this is, indeed, an honor.

The game begins precisely at three o'clock. Bob Smith is our pitcher and has a difficult start, giving up three runs on three hits and two errors by our defense, one by me at third base, all in the top of the first inning.

In the bottom of the first, Steve Jones and Mike Garcia both get on base with singles before Don Graham hits a home-run over the left field fence to tie the score. I follow by smashing the first pitch for a double to right-center field. I suddenly remember the arrowhead in my back pocket. I had forgotten about it, even as I washed my pants after the last game. I will leave it there. It certainly is bringing me good luck! Peanuts and David both get base hits and I score a run before our side is retired. Our lead after one inning is 4 to 3.

Going into the sixth inning, we have built a comfortable lead of 12 to 6. The Allen team has nine hits so far and Possum decides to change pitchers, shifting me from third base to the mound with Smith going to third base. The Allen team gets three more hits and one run off my pitching during the rest of the game. In the meantime, the Bombers add five more runs, with Don Graham hitting his second home run of the game, for a final score of 17 to 7.

It has been a great day as my family meets me on my walk from the dugout to the parking lot. They express their enthusiasm for the Brown Bombers and seem to enjoy their time at the ball park. A few of them still question my playing for a black team, but say they'll be back for more games if I'm still playing.

In an unusual departure from our regular post-game routine, Possum calls us back to the dugout before anyone can leave the park. Once we have all gathered, he becomes quite serious as he announces, "I want you all to take the day off from practice tomorrow and try to get a little rest after work. Then let's meet on Friday and Saturday at about six for a short practice." His expression suddenly changes. He is smiling broadly!

"I have just agreed with some folks in Olpe to have our team play them an exhibition game this coming Sunday evening in Olpe. It seems that several of the people there have been following us so far this season and want a chance to see us in their home park."

July 4th, 1956

Each of us, without exception, knows what is coming next. For nearly twenty years, Possum has been working for one of the most famous Olpe baseball players of all time. Fritz Brown owns the barber shop where Possum runs his shoe shine stand. We have all followed the playing careers of Fritz and his brother Justin and know about their successes in the semi-pro and lower minor league levels. Smiles all around.

Possum continues, "The Brown brothers will be on the team and it will give each of you a chance to see great ballplayers in action. They'll be joined by several older and former players from teams in the area, so expect some good competition. Since we have three very tough games the following week with the Kansas City Stars, the Emporia Aces, again, and Madison, I want to pitch Young, Smith and Ohm three innings each. We do not want to overwork our pitching staff against Olpe."

We can still hear the competitive spirit rising in Possum's voice. "This is a game we want to win. We need to get a good winning streak going if we want to get people to go to our games."

We easily see that this will be more than an exhibition for Possum, even though he is trying to hide it. He temporarily pauses, likely finishing a thought. Then, "Great game today. Let's keep it going. See you all on Friday evening."

Thursday's workday is an easy one since rain interrupted us installing rafters in a new house. During rainy times, we sit in our cars and wait out the storm but must stick around to go back to work when the rain stops. It is an aggravating time for me since the new construction boss told us that he would not be paying us for any lost time due to rain. Jobs are not that easy to find, so I guess we must just accept it. Sure seems unfair though.

I arrive home and pick up the newspaper from the front porch and quickly open it to the sports section. There it is. It is a great story on our win over Allen. Perhaps publicity will start to improve, and we can get bigger crowds and even get paid someday.

Brown Bombers Beat Allen by 17-7 Score

After jumping off to a lead in the first inning, the Emporia Brown Bombers went on to coast to a 17-7 triumph over Allen in the featured game of the Fourth of July celebration at Soden's Grove Wednesday afternoon.

Allen managed to get 12 hits off two Brown Bombers hurlers but the Emporians came up with an 18-hit attack to pave the way for Allen to get the loss.

After Allen jumped off to a three-run lead in the top of the first, the Emporians came back with four runs to take a lead they never relinquished.

Practice on Friday starts out with the Bombers taking notice of Rosa assuming her now familiar sitting position on the front fender of her Chevy. I see several players attempting to make eye contact from their practice positions and, in some cases, tipping their hats to her. She smiles regularly.

As the evening progresses, we find practice to be much more than "short." Possum seems to have a new fire in his expression. He drills us for the first time on his using hand signs to signal steals, takes, bunts for hitters and for base runners, and for positioning fielders on defense. This is a new tact since we have always used our own judgment on each of these plays. Our team has exhibited excellent athletic ability with good success. Stealing a base, bunting a base runner to the next base, or to get a hit, have not been problems.

Nevertheless, Possum is on a mission. He starts out, "First of all, we will use these signs from my coaching box at third base. I will touch my nose and then my ear if I want you to bunt. So be looking at me before each at bat. Just step out of the box and I will give you some kind of signal. For a steal when you are on base, I will clap my hands three times, and then touch my ear. Steve, what will you do when you see this sign?" Possum touches his ear and then his nose.

Steve mumbles, "I guess I will bunt."

"No!" Possum shouts. "I said I will touch my nose first and then my ear to bunt. Do you get it now?"

"Yeah."

The team is getting restless, and I don't blame them. This is something quite different than what we have been doing all season, but Possum is insisting.

"If I want you to take a pitch, I will take off my hat with my left hand and rub my hair with my right hand. Now, as far as you infielders and outfielders are concerned, each of you just check with me before each pitch and I will motion where I want you to play on the field. I want you to talk to each other about these signs and make sure you understand them before our game on Sunday. That's all for today."

The Bombers walk quietly from the practice field to their cars.

We review the new signs thoroughly again during Saturday's practice. I notice a little more grumbling among the players than I have heard all season. We regularly use signs at E-State, but for most of these guys, they have been pretty much on their own. It will be interesting to see how all this works out in our next few games.

Final travel arrangements are made for the short trip to Olpe tomorrow afternoon. With a wave of Possum's hand, practice ends in darkness.

Clyde asks Mike if Rosa will be attending the game tomorrow.

"No, she will stay home for that. She says she would not feel comfortable with all the out-of-town fans." That is a good answer for us. We wave at Mike and Rosa as they drive off on the deserted street. We are a tired bunch of Bombers on our way home for the night.

Chapter Nine

Olpe and the Browns

Olpe has the closest high school to my original little one-room school, Stony Ridge, some fifteen miles to the southwest. When students graduate from Stony Ridge, they either enroll in Olpe High School or in Emporia High School. The twenty to twenty-five-mile distance to Emporia often requires finding a place to stay during the school year and that can be a problem. The natural choice, then, is Olpe. Emporia, though, is the market capital of the area and is frequented by Olpe residents on a regular basis. The relationship between Olpe and Emporia is cordial and not normally tested with athletic competition.

So, when Possum made the surprising announcement that Olpe was scheduled for our next game, it created some excitement for our team. But, we found out, on our drive to the game in Olpe in the early evening, that the Olpe residents were also promoting the game in a big way. On nearly every tele-

Baseball Sunday

The Olpe Town Team will play the All-Black Emporia Brown Bombers on Sunday, July 8 at 8 o'clock on the Olpe diamond. Everyone welcome Adults: 50 cents

phone pole along Highway-99, was tacked a poster declaring:

"Hey, Philip, stop the car," I shout.

Philip pulls to the side of the road and I get out and pull one of the posters off the pole. "This will be a great souvenir," I say, as I fold the poster and toss it on the shelf behind the back seat.

We arrive at the Olpe diamond and a large crowd is already gathering. In a similar layout, as with the Bushong diamond, there are no outfield fences and corn grows high in the fields beyond. Our regular warm-ups go well. We watch Fritz and Justin Brown on the infield with their pre-game routine. Fritz is normally a pitcher or catcher but is playing third base tonight and Justin is catching. They are in their 40s but move with a special grace that we have seldom seen this summer. The lights are turned on as the game begins.

Steve Jones pounds a single to center field on the first pitch of the game. Mike Garcia follows with another single to the same spot in center field. Our dugout guys are already cheering as emotions seem higher than usual for this exhibition game. Harold Turner, the third hitter, hits a line drive to the shortstop with the two runners holding. Possum decided right before game time to bat a red-hot Don Graham at clean-up for the first time this season. He is leading the team in home runs with a total of six in the last six games.

Don does not disappoint. On a 2-2 count, he connects for a towering home run deep into the corn field in left-center. He scores before the fielder reaches the ball and the Bombers lead 3 to 0. I glance down the bench to see Bob as the only player not up and shouting. I walk over to him.

"Hey, Bob, are you OK?"

"No, some kind of sinus problem, I guess."

"Shall I get Possum over here?"

"Yeah, maybe so."

Clyde Matson and Peanuts Solis both fly out to end the inning.

I interrupt Possum as he runs into the dugout to congratulate Don before Don takes his position in right field. "Possum, Bob is not feeling well. I think you should talk to him."

Possum pats Don on the back and walks swiftly to Bob's side for a short visit.

He returns with a casual look of concern. "Kenny, I think we should drop Smith from pitching tonight. I will try to get five innings out of Young and you can come in then in the sixth to finish up. Plan on that and I will check with you again as we get closer."

"Sounds good to me, Possum. Let's hope we can get a few more runs."

Maybe he heard me and maybe he did not. He is already at the far end of the bench scribbling in his little note book.

Kenny Young starts out well in the bottom of the first inning. The first two Olpe batters strike out and Fritz Brown flies out to deep left field to end the inning.

The next three innings fly by with no more runs scored by either side.

It is the top of the fifth inning and David Carter leads off with a double down the left field line. Philip Solis hits a single to score David, increasing our lead to 4 to 0. Kenny Young is batting now in an unusual number nine position. Possum says he wants to start resting his pitchers by allowing fewer times at bat. Kenny hits a long ball on the first pitch into the corn field in dead center. By the time the Olpe fielder retrieves the ball, Philip has scored, and Kenny has a triple.

With the score 5 to 0, Jones, Garcia, and Turner all ground out leaving Young stranded on third.

Young runs into the dugout from third before returning to the mound for the bottom of the fifth inning. He still seems a little winded after the triple but is smiling broadly. The number 8, 9 and 1 hitters for Olpe are due up next. Young strikes out the first batter, but the next two reach base on walks before the Olpe number two batter hits into an inning-ending double play. Wow, Garcia to Jones to Matson. It could not be done any better!

Young is greeted by Possum as he enters the dugout. Possum looks to me and says, "It's all yours now, Kenny. Let's work hard out there."

I feel well warmed-up but grab my glove and toss a few to Bob Smith outside the dugout. I pause for a few minutes while watching as our guys go down one-two-three. I realize suddenly that Fritz Brown will be batting leadoff this next inning, followed by Justin Brown in the clean-up spot. Well, I am looking for a challenge and this will be one, for sure. I pat the arrowhead in my rear pocket.

Fritz hits my first pitch for a hard single to left field, his third hit of the night. Now, Justin comes to the plate and I feel a few butterflies in my stomach. He has already hit a double and a single off Young. Philip walks in front of the plate and motions with both hands to calm down and concentrate. I reach a 2-2 count when Philip calls for my round house curve. I deliver it toward the batter and it breaks to the outside corner of the plate for called strike three.

Justin looks at the umpire for a second before walking to the dugout. I feel relief. The next batter flies out to shallow left field with Fritz holding at first. On my next pitch, the number six hitter hits a long drive in the gap between center and right field, easily scoring Fritz from first. The score is 5 to 1. I need to get out of this inning and finally strike out Olpe's number seven hitter on a 3-2 count.

Back in the dugout, Possum quickly reminds me that we have only three more innings to go. I feel quite confident.

Don Graham hits his second home run of the night to lead off the top of the seventh and to make our lead 6 to 1. We then go down in order and hold Olpe to no runs in the bottom of the seventh inning.

Once more we go down one-two-three in the top of the eighth inning, with me striking out on three pitches.

Olpe's number two hitter opens the bottom of the eighth inning with a line drive single on my first pitch. Fritz Brown promptly follows with his fourth hit of the night, a single to left field. Justin Brown is up next and taps the plate with his bat a few times before looking out to me. I try not to notice a batter's face but, in this case, it strikes me as one of certain confidence.

I throw a few fast balls just off the plate, but then on the next pitch, he takes a called strike one. Philip calls for another fast ball and it is fouled off to the fence directly behind home plate. With the count 2-2, Philip calls once more for my round house curve. It has been working well all night, so I try it again. It seems that the ball travels in slow motion to the plate. Justin's eyes widen as the ball curves over the center of the plate, belt high. With a mighty swing and a loud crack, the ball disappears above the dim lights directed to left-center field. Jesse and Harold run for it, but it is over their heads before they can take even a few steps. They both vanish into the cornfield.

The crowd erupts as the two runners score before Justin, making the score 6 to 4. As Justin circles the bases, I briefly think of my home run in Bushong a few weeks ago, which was nearly lost in the corn field. However, this ball must have traveled five hundred feet or more and Jesse and Harold still have not found it. After another minute, the umpire calls them back onto the playing field and throws out the second game ball.

The next three batters ground out to the infield to end the bottom of the eighth inning.

Possum walks up and down the bench encouraging us to get another run or two in this last at-bat. However, we go down in order.

Olpe's last chance to tie or go ahead is uneventful as they also go down in order with two fly-outs to center field and a soft ground-ball out to second base. I feel relief. I guess the arrowhead gave me luck after all. The final score of 6 to 4 is satisfying to all of us, especially having had the honor of playing against two of the finest players in the history of Lyon County. On the way to our cars, Possum calls us to surround his car for a few minutes.

"I thought I might mention that I have been giving signals most of the evening from my coaching box and not even one of you looked at me. Was that on purpose or did you just forget all about it?" Collectively, we look at each other with surprise. Sure enough, we had completely forgotten this new plan of Possum's. But Possum is smiling broadly.

The short trip back to Emporia is filled with personal observations, but mostly centered about the incredible home run by Justin Brown. It will be a long-time memory for all of us.

Chapter Ten

An Ace?

This week has been an easy one for the Brown Bombers. Possum acts relieved that we pulled out the victory over Olpe last Sunday night. He does not mention our missing his signs, so we have decided not to remind him of it. Perhaps the team will not have to worry about signs this weekend or even for the rest of the season. Possum has not pushed us on special plays or on any other variation from our normal routine. We can only imagine that his reception at the barber shop on Monday morning was an interesting one—but none of us have the courage to bring it up!

Practice for the week winds up this Friday evening with Possum reminding us of the three games to be played in the next four days. He says that both the Kansas City team and the Aces will give us a good challenge in back to back games tomorrow and Sunday, at Soden's Grove.

Possum shows some fatigue as he continues, "The tougher game might be at Madison on Tuesday night. They've been playing good ball so far this season and they have some powerful and experienced players. A bigger problem might be that the heat wave we now have will likely continue throughout the weekend. Try to pace yourself at work on Monday and on Tuesday before Madison. I don't think we need to leave before seven o'clock on Tuesday. Let's plan on the same drivers if that is OK with you, Philip and Bob."

Both nod in agreement as practice ends with Possum reminding us that game time tomorrow is eight o'clock and that we will have no heavy pregame warm-ups considering the heat.

I open the *Gazette* this evening and find just a small article about our games this weekend:

Brown Bombers to Play Twice at Soden's Grove

Two games will be played by the Emporia Brown Bombers this weekend opening Saturday night against the Kansas City All-Stars at Soden's Grove.

Starting time for the game is 8 o'clock. Sunday afternoon the Brown Bombers play a return contest with the Emporia Aces at Soden's Grove starting at 3 o'clock.

As usual, no mention appeared in the newspaper this past week about our victory over Olpe. It seems that with three active teams in Emporia this summer, there must not be enough reporters available to cover them all. Possum is most interested in the next scheduled game and makes certain the fans of the Bombers know when and where that game will be played. The crowds are getting bigger and bigger, so he must know what he is doing.

When I wake up the next morning, I feel the humidity and heat already at highs for the summer. My guess is that the late

An Ace?

afternoon temperatures will be well over one hundred degrees, perhaps extending through game time tonight.

A home game once again allows us to show up to the playing field an hour early, but I am the first one to arrive.

The heat is almost unbearable with no breeze at all. I step out of my car and walk to the dugout. I decide to leave my glove, bat and shoes in the car until more players arrive. I run the water hydrant located near the dugout for a few minutes until the water feels cold. I allow the water to flow over my right wrist and can feel the coolness sweep through my body. Most of our team will use this water spout for drinking and for cooling this evening.

Sometimes the heat on the diamond will travel through my metal spikes and burn my feet. I find that walking through the water standing near the hydrant cools the spikes, at least temporarily. I will likely do this several times today.

After several minutes, Philip drives into the parking lot. He waves and shouts, "Is it hot enough for you?"

"Sure is. We will need to pace ourselves tonight for sure," I reply.

I notice Clyde driving in with Harold, as usual. I wonder how they know each other. I will have to ask some day.

I walk to my car and change my shoes and carry my glove and bat to the dugout as Philip walks beside me. I can sense both of us are thinking about the long, hot night ahead.

A half-hour later, Possum collects us to the dugout and offers a rare speech about the importance of this game and the one tomorrow. "We have no idea who the Kansas City All-Stars are, but if they are going to drive all this distance in all this heat, we can be sure they will be here to play a tough game. So, let's take this game seriously tonight. Kenny Young will start on the mound. I plan to hold Bob out until tomorrow's game against the Aces. The batting order will be about the same as it was against Olpe with Don batting clean-up again, but Ohm, you will play third base instead of David."

Possum had decided not to take infield practice nor does the Kansas City team. Even "Hold That Tiger" sounds a little scratchy in this heat. Clyde calls out to us as he holds up a small thermometer and takes it to the field near first base. He places it on the dirt and walks back to the dugout. After a few minutes, he goes back out, retrieves the thermometer and shouts, "Over 120 degrees!"

As tonight's third baseman, I wish he had not done that experiment. Nevertheless, our team gets a big kick out of it and even the Kansas City players give a shout as they hear the number.

The crowd numbers are very low tonight as the eight o'clock game time approaches. I overhear Clyde asking Mike if Rosa will be attending the game tonight.

"No, too hot," Mike replies.

I notice some of the other players listening to this short conversation. We are getting used to Rosa attending our practices and would welcome her to watch our team in action.

Kenny has no trouble in mowing down the All-Stars in order in the first three innings. From my view at third base, it seems that some members of the KC team may be only sixteen or seventeen years old, and they are all white kids. When compared with Kenny's gigantic frame, these players are simply overpowered.

An Ace?

We quickly score three runs in the first inning, including a home run by Don Graham, and then add one more in the second and fourth. With our 5 to 0 lead, both teams seem to go through the motions of at-bats and fielding. The All-Stars score two runs in both the fifth and sixth innings. I lead off the bottom of the sixth with a single giving me two hits for the day, followed by the first home run of the season for Philip. His grin is a classic. Three more runs follow for a score of 10 to 4 after six innings. The heat must still be above one hundred degrees.

What small crowd we have is already starting to leave. Although Kenny Young has not been pushed by the Kansas City team, he comes into the dugout sweating heavily.

A couple of our players, including Kenny, arrived this evening with newly-acquired tops and bottoms of woolen baseball uniforms. They are complaining the most about the heat, suggesting a loss of some eight or ten pounds. Who can believe that? Those of us in t-shirts and sweatpants are drenched as well.

The game ends with no more scoring by either team. The stands are nearly empty as a slight breeze comes up. I gather my glove and bat and walk out of the dugout.

As I near my car, I see a bunch of my teammates laughing and showing all kinds of animation as they are gathered around Bob's car. I cannot resist. I walk over and ask David what is going on. He turns and yells, "Hey, Peanuts, tell Kenny what happened."

Peanuts walks a few steps toward me, parting from the crowd around him. "Did you notice this old guy with no teeth standing at the fence?"

"Yeah, I saw some guy with a brown shirt. He was hollering something to me for a few innings, but I didn't pay much attention, although I saw him take a swig or two from a bottle in a paper sack."

"Well, he kept moving down the fence until he was directly across from me in left field," Peanuts says. "Then he really started on me, calling me all kinds of names sometimes thinking I was Mexican and sometimes thinking I was black. I think he was more than a little drunk, and the dark field didn't help.

Finally, in the ninth inning, I took a few steps toward him and smiled the broadest grin I could find. Boy, you should have seen him head off toward the river!" And the guys started again laughing and shoving each other with great delight.

"We always knew you have the whitest teeth on the team, Peanuts," I say. "It sounds like it paid off this time."

Someone asks the group if we should tell Possum about this. "No," Don says, "Possum might be a little upset. He wants us all to play like Jackie Robinson and not answer back on these things."

As usual, Don has a way of diffusing troublesome things.

We all go our separate ways and I walk to my car. Just when I am about to open the driver's door, Possum shouts from behind me, "Hey, Kenny. I need to talk to you for a few minutes."

"Sure, Possum, what's on your mind?"

"First of all, what was that all about with Jesse?"

"Nothing much. Just a lot of happiness with our win, I guess."

Possum changes the subject. "As you may have noticed, I have been visiting with the manager of the Aces who we play

An Ace?

tomorrow. They had an afternoon game in Gridley today, and won. But they are not looking forward to playing us tomorrow because of the heat and the fact that they have no starting pitchers ready to go."

Interesting, I think, but why are you talking to me about it?

Possum continues, "As you know Bob Smith did not play tonight and will be fresh and ready for us tomorrow against the Aces. I realize that playing third was hot and dusty for you, but we are wondering if you would be willing to pitch for the Aces tomorrow?"

I am shocked. After six or so games this season as a Brown Bomber, has there been some complaint about me not being black on an all-black team, or what? Before I can ask that question to Possum, he continues:

"They are willing to help us out a little if you will pitch for them. He offered me three brand new baseballs and ten-dollars. If the gate is good, he said he might even be able to pay you five-dollars or so if you will pitch for them. I really need you to help us all out, Kenny. The crowd tomorrow should be very good, especially if it cools off a bit. The Aces manager is waiting in his car over there for your answer. What do you say?"

All I can think of is how tired and hot I am, in need of a bath and a night's sleep. Playing with a bunch of E-State former players against the team I have been practicing and playing with all season seems totally unthinkable. However, I look into the eyes of Possum behind those dark-rimmed glasses and I finally manage to say, "Ok, I'll give it a try."

"Thanks, Kenny. If you will hang around for a few minutes, the Aces manager wants to give you one of their uniforms, size

40. I think it'll fit and it's a nice red and white with stirrups and a matching hat."

The surprises keep coming! I walk over as Manager John McFarland shakes my hand, thanks me and gives me a full uniform nicely folded. It has the numeral 10 on the back—my number at E-State! "I guess I will see you tomorrow," I barely mumble. Possum and the Aces manager both look relieved and give me a quick wave as I walk back to my car.

On my short drive home, I think back on the summer so far and recall the days in the middle of June when I had no prospects of playing baseball. Now I am playing for two teams at one time. I shall remember these days forever!

Chapter Eleven

A Long, Hot Day

Sunday morning brings no relief. Temperatures are as high as yesterday and, this time, we are playing baseball in the heat of mid-afternoon. We have no air-conditioning at home, so getting out of bed and away from the sweaty sheets is welcomed.

I arrive a bit later than usual at Soden's Grove and see the Bombers taking over the visitors' dugout. Apparently, the Aces are the home team today. Most of the Bombers wave at me, in my new red and white uniform, but do not show any emotion one way or the other.

They have apparently been told by Possum what to expect and they seem OK with it. The matter at hand, as usual, is to get ready to play my best game possible. I suddenly realize that I forgot to put my arrowhead into the pocket of my new Aces uniform. Oh, well.

At about fifteen minutes before game time, I begin my warm-up with the Ace catcher, Jim Glaze, a former teammate and third string catcher at E-State. The crowd, indeed, is a large one. For the first time this season, I do not feel the need to hide my non-blackness.

I interrupt my warm ups, take off my hat, and look over the crowd. They are nearly all white with a few Mexicans, but I see no blacks. I noticed Mike driving Rosa's Chevy today, but Rosa was not with him. I feel some strange disappointment once again with Rosa not in the stands. With such terrific athletes as we have on the Bombers, and with their devotion to the game, it would seem that their families and loved ones would like to come out to the ball park and share their experiences. I guess they are heeding Possum's advice and "not looking for trouble." I imagine, too, that the 50-cent admission is a little steep for some of them. Possum said recently that he might start passing a hat around for donations since it is so hard to control the entrance to the park when selling admission tickets.

In the far back row, I see Joe and Jerry Brown, my friends from high school, and their father, Joe, and a family friend, Wilbur O'Mara. They rarely miss a baseball or softball game played in Emporia. Another regular fan, "Pop" Griffitts, has taken his seat directly behind home plate and begins his loud chirping with, "Come on, let's get the game going. It is already five till." As usual, he brings a laugh from those gathered around.

The temperature might be a few degrees cooler than last evening and it is easy to get my pitching arm loose and ready. Oh my, there it goes! "Hold That Tiger." I guess even at Bomber away games, that tune will be played.

The Bombers have nearly the same line-up as in previous games but have shifted David Carter to third base with Kenny Young on the bench. The Aces take the field and the umpire hands catcher Glaze the game ball. He tosses it to me for a few warm-up throws. The ball feels slippery but hard and a spark of energy comes from it to my hand and shoulder. It is truly new and probably just removed from the box.

Still, I am a little jittery as I face the Bomber's lead-off batter, Steve Jones. It may be my imagination, but did he just tip his hat toward me and show a slight smile? I cannot help but nod to him as I take the sign for my first pitch. It is a ball, low and inside. He swings at the next pitch and rolls it to the second baseman for the first out. I feel relieved and quite comfortable on the mound, even with these unusual circumstances.

This is short-lived as the next two batters both strike singles. The clean-up hitter, my friend Don Graham, next strolls to the plate with his usual serious look. Since this is the first time I have seen him from this perspective, I am startled by his confident stance and obvious focus.

I know I must pitch him carefully but, still, with two men on base, I surely do not want to walk him. My first two pitches are close-called balls. Down, 2 to 0, I fire my best high fast ball hoping he will either swing and miss or take for a strike. He swings with a full stride, catching the ball squarely. It goes over the left field fence before I can straighten my follow-through.

I barely glimpse the ball landing between the fence and Commercial Avenue. As Don circles the bases, I notice that he is looking to the ground the entire way. He neither recognizes me or anyone else as he crosses home plate. The crowd continues to cheer loudly, and all I can do is wait for the ball to be returned. Instead the umpire throws me the second game ball. I grab it into my glove and walk back to the pitching rubber.

I pick the ball out of my glove and see it as the darkest, most scarred, and misshapen ball I have ever seen. Apparently, as the home team must provide the game balls, and since they gave three new balls to Possum for my appearance on the mound today, this is the only ball they have left. Fine, I think. Maybe I will have an advantage for a while, at least until the new ball is retrieved from over the left field fence.

As I take my pitch sign from Jim Glaze, I feel the seams of the ball significantly raised. I briefly remember during the flood of '51 when I found a couple of baseballs at the edge of the rising waters. I took them home and, when dried, they were rock hard with heavy, raised seams. That must be the history of this ball.

I throw high fast balls with my grip across all four seams and strike out the next two batters. I return to the dugout and manager McFarland nods to me but has no comment. So, we are already behind 3 to 0, but now we come to bat.

I only recognize two players on this E-State old-timer roster, catcher Glaze and second baseman, Ron Bates. They were both seniors last year during my freshman year and played sparingly. They are apparently like the rest of us, needing a place to play this summer in hopes of improving our games or, at least, to have a final fling with the game we love.

I resist looking over to the Bomber dugout. I really do not want to see any reaction that might be directed my way. I am batting sixth tonight and after the Aces go down in order, I briefly consider that I will be batting for the first time in the second inning.

After I retire the Bombers in order in the top of the second inning, I come to bat in the bottom of the inning and hit a line drive to David at third for out number three. The score still stands at 3 to 0.

The heat does not recede as we enter the seventh inning with no further scoring by either team. I feel a bit tired as I walk to the mound. Sweat is pouring from my body with a familiar but unwelcome stream running down my left arm and into my glove. My right hand and wrist are wet also. I must keep rubbing them on my new uniform blouse and pants. Still it is hard to maintain a firm grip on the ball. Droplets of sweat fall off the bill of my cap in regular rhythm.

Bob continues to pitch very well for the Bombers and I notice he is having the same problem with the heat as I am. I guess we both must try to ignore the rising temperatures as best we can.

The Bombers put together two hits along with a walk from me in the top of the seventh, scoring one more run. We are down 4 to 0 going into the bottom of the inning. I lead off with my first hit of the day. It is a right field shot down the foul line and I scramble to stretch it to a double. As I slide into second base, I remind myself that the arrowhead is not in my rear pocket. Otherwise, it could cause some serious damage. I need to remember that!

My former E-State teammate, Jim Glaze, knocks me in with his first hit of the night. At least we scored. Now, down 4 to 1, we play into the top of the eighth inning.

Before I go to the mound, I quickly stop by the water hydrant and carefully step on the stones now flooded with water from the afternoon's use. I find the cold water cooling my spikes and relieving the burn on my feet. Water also on my wrists provides some cooling which I can feel in my temples.

As usual, I take only a brief sip of water to moisten my lips and mouth. My coaches from junior high through college have all warned us not to drink while participating in sports since "it will bog you down and you will likely get sick." I walk slowly to the mound and face the first batter, taking no warm-up pitches.

The sweat falling from the bill of my cap suddenly turns into a steady stream. In my experiences with pitching, this has never occurred before. My arm still feels loose but tiring. After a ground out to third, a pop up to the shortstop and a lazy fly out to right field we surprisingly get through the inning with no runs scored.

It is the bottom of the eighth inning, and we manage to score one run off Bob Smith, making the score 4 to 2. Perhaps, if I can hold the Bombers down a bit in the top of the ninth, we might still have a chance of winning this game. Manager McFarland seems to think so as he pats me on the back, and says, "Just one more inning, Kenny. We might win this thing yet."

After another cooling off at the hydrant, I walk to the mound and feel my legs rather shaky and a hollow feeling inside. I take no warm-ups with Jim Glaze and face the first batter, my buddy Philip Solis. I promptly walk him on four pitches.

The sweat stream from my cap continues steadily. The second batter up, Bob Smith, hits my next pitch deep to the gap in left-center field for a double with Philip scoring. The top of the Bombers batting order comes up next with Steve Jones getting another base hit to center field, scoring Smith.

The score stands at 6-2 and I am exhausted. I glance to the dugout and see McFarland continuing to clap his hands with encouragement. I see no signs of a relief pitcher.

I get both Mike Garcia and Clyde Matson to pop up to the

infield. I walk Peanuts Solis. Don Graham strolls to the plate and I can barely see him through my glasses as they are fogged with the sweat and heat. I suddenly realize that I am the only Bomber or Ace who is wearing glasses. Lucky them.

For some reason catcher Glaze calls for me to throw a knuckleball pitch for the first time in this game. Normally, it is a surprise pitch for most batters, but Don catches it squarely and lifts a high fly ball well over the center field fence. The score is now 8-2 and the game is out of reach.

Harold Turner next hits a gapper between right and center field and scores an inside-the-park home run. I have never seen such speed on the bases.

The Aces look exhausted. I retire the next batter on a pop up to the catcher for the final out. I am barely able to walk from the mound to the dugout.

Our center fielder approaches me and has a smile on his face. I cannot see any humor in all this and wait for him to explain. He says, "Kenny, you will never believe this, but when the ball went over my head, and over the fence, it was not spinning at all. It was dead quiet." I even grin a little at that one.

"Well, I threw him a knuckleball, and I guess he hit it so squarely that it still had no spin. I've never heard of that before." I sit, trying to regain focus while sweating heavily.

The center fielder, still smiling, walks away, happily sharing the story with anyone who will listen.

The Aces are retired in order in the bottom of the ninth inning making the final score 9 to 2.

Manager McFarland approaches me with a slight smile and congratulates me on a "Great effort out there. Except for the last inning, it was a very good game. I am hoping to hear about the gate receipts this afternoon and when I do, I will get you the five dollars. You really earned it today." And then he is off to the parking lot.

I catch up with Philip. "Sorry, Kenny, but we hit you pretty hard today," he says. He seems to be as saturated with sweat as I am. "Possum asked me to let you know that we will have a short practice at Peter Pan tomorrow about six. He said he might have a surprise announcement for us."

"I'm glad it's all over and I hope I'll never have to pitch against you guys again. I hope the crowd enjoyed it a little, though," I struggle to find words.

Philip heads for his car and I to mine. I have an old towel across the driver's seat in my car so that I won't get the seat wet from my saturated uniform, but today I am not sure how well it will work. I take off my spikes and start my drive home with only wet socks on my feet. I briefly think of my absent arrowhead but doubt it would have given me the luck necessary to win this game anyway.

When I get home, I walk around to the back porch where I normally change from my work clothes and take off my uniform. This takes some effort as my muscles are very weak and I am still sweating. I grab underwear from the floor, accumulated during the work week, and then lift the top and bottom of my uniform from the floor for the trip to the basement and the washing machine.

I can barely lift the uniform. It surely weighs over fifteen pounds. When people say they can lose ten to fifteen pounds from a hard effort in the sun, I now believe them.

I toss my uniform and several pairs of white shorts and undershirts into the washing machine and struggle upstairs to the bathroom. Mom and Dad are visiting Uncle Fritz and Aunt Verna this afternoon and Willis and Russell are likely studying at the library. The house is quiet. I smell meatloaf in the oven for supper tonight.

I struggle to get the bath water running and then find myself, finally, cooling down. After several glasses of water and a half-hour in the tub, I begin to feel better with a chance to reflect on the very long afternoon.

All in all, I am not that disappointed with the loss. I just hope that I don't have to play against the Bombers again this summer. I really like the guys on the Bombers and they seem to be fine with me playing with them. We only have another month or so to play and I am looking forward to a good end to the season.

The wash-cycle is finished. I lift the lid of the washing machine and see a startling sight. The entire load is a bright pink! The red from the lettering on my new uniform has obviously bled out to the white of the uniform as well as to the underwear. I put the whole wash into the dryer with considerable sadness. I know for sure that I will have to use the underwear until they wear out and that I will have to deal with the uniform, and the Aces, sometime soon.

Mom and Dad get home about six thirty and, with Russell and Willis, we sit down for supper. I tell them about the game and then about the ill-fated wash. The men give me some sympathy, but Mom just smiles and says she hopes I learned something.

The next morning, I get up at my usual time of seven or so and find Mom left early for her job at Newman Hospital and Dad likely a little later to his construction site. I will be working for Frank Love today on sheeting the roof on a new house on Morningside Drive. I can barely walk at first but loosen up as the morning goes along. I am sure I will be OK for the game tomorrow night in Madison.

At about two o'clock in the afternoon, I find some difficulty in sizing a plywood sheet for the upper corner of the roof. I climb down the ladder carrying the three foot by six foot piece with my pencil markings to cut for a snug fit.

As I reach the bottom of the ladder, I notice Frank sitting on a saw horse with his right hand over his chest. I ask him if he is OK. "Yes," he replies. "Just a little indigestion, I guess."

"I'm having trouble making this board fit and need to trim it a little," I say.

"Here, let me have it. I can use the table saw to get it done right here," he says.

He can do it faster than I can, I think, so I hand it to him as he struggles to stand up. I watch as he carefully cuts the piece along the pencil lines. I look at him and he suddenly shows pain in his face. "Frank, we need to get you to the hospital," I shout. He doesn't argue.

I drive as fast as I can with Frank in the passenger seat. After the six-or seven-block drive, I help Frank into the emergency entrance of the hospital. They take him into an examination room and I use the hospital phone to call Frank's wife. She says she will be right there. I wait with her another hour or so when, finally, the doctor says it looks like Frank will be alright but will have to stay in the hospital a few days. What a relief.

I travel to Dad's work site and share the information with him. We speak for a time, with tears in our eyes, about our friendship with Frank. Dad has known Frank for over twenty years as they have both built numerous houses in the Emporia area. We travel to Frank's new house site and load up the tools and secure the house the best we can for the night.

A Long Hot Day

As I start my drive to practice at Peter Pan Park, the skies open up with a hard shower and I turn around for home. We will not practice today and that is a blessing from my view. As I am driving home, I wonder if I will get paid for the few hours I did not work driving to the hospital and taking care of Frank. Not a very nice thought, I conclude.

Chapter Twelve

Good News All Around

Dad called Mrs. Love and volunteered that he and I would work today at Frank Love's building site to make certain it was closed in and safe. She indicated that Frank had a good night and was expecting to come home in a few days. Dad told her that he would visit Frank at the hospital after work. We decide to take a short lunch break today with so many things going on. We sit down on sawhorses and open our lunch pails.

"You know, Kenny, what I would like to see?"

Before I have a chance to answer, Dad continues. "As you know, on my panel truck it says *Frank Ohm, General Construction*. What would you think of me having it repainted to read, *Frank Ohm and Son, General Construction*?

I know what I should say, but cannot do better than, "I don't know, Dad. I have three more years of college and then I would really like to try playing professional baseball or working in the science field somewhere."

Dad kind of sighs and drops his shoulders. He was likely expecting this answer but was hoping for a different one. We both change the subject quickly. We work hard to finish the sheeting and manage to get tar paper spread over the roof before a light rain starts in the middle of the afternoon.

This time I hold my enthusiasm for the game at Madison and wonder if the weather will be dry enough to play tonight. At about four o'clock, I ride with Dad to visit Frank in his hospital room. When we get there, he is sitting up, smiling and happy to see us. We know he is feeling better when he starts to tell us some of his famous stories.

Frank had visited Colorado a few years earlier and loved to tell his fellow Kansans about the incredible mountains and valleys he discovered. "In fact, we were driving along a narrow road, and when I looked down, it took me a half hour to see the bottom it was so deep." That always gets a laugh.

As we are about to leave the room, Frank suddenly turns serious. "Frank," he says to Dad. "The doctor tells me that my working days are over. I'm going on sixty-five, so I guess it's time to hang up my hammer."

Dad pauses for a minute. "I'll drop by tomorrow and maybe we can work something out to finish your house. My current job is about done, and I know Kenny will help out, too."

This catches me by surprise, but since the hayfields are pretty much dried up and the concrete work is ending, this plan will work out well. Besides, maybe I can keep my dark tan going and still play with the Bombers.

Dad and I walk slowly to his truck for the ride home. "I hope I was not speaking out of turn when offering your help

Good News All Around

with Franks house," Dad says.

"No, not at all. I like the idea and I need to start thinking about paying for tuition and books for next semester." I answer with a smile.

It is raining lightly when we get home. It has been so hectic around here that Monday's paper is still on the table unopened. I have another hour before starting the trip to Madison. I quickly turn to the sports page and find a summary of the Bombers games last weekend.

Well, there it is, "Ohm Hurled!" If anybody has been paying attention to some of the Bombers and Aces game results this season and notice or care that I played for both teams, then I should hear about it soon. Are they wondering why a black guy is pitching for the Aces? The way I feel now, I want to end the season with the Bombers and wish no further detractions. We shall see.

Brown Bombers in A Double Victory

Emporia's Brown Bombers swept two games over the weekend downing the Kansas City All-Stars 10 to 4 Saturday night and defeating The Emporia Aces 9-2 Sunday afternoon in games played at Sodens's Grove.

Kenny Young went all the way for the win Saturday night while Bob Smith picked up the victory in Sunday's contest.

The winners scored three times in the first inning against the Kansas City team to grab the lead they never relinquished. They added single tallies in the second and fourth before icing the decision in the sixth with a five run outburst.

A five-run rally in the top of ninth sewed up the Sunday game against the Aces after the winners had gained a three-run lead in the first inning. Ohm hurled all the way to take the loss for the Aces.

Chapter Thirteen

Madison

As seven o'clock nears, I drive to the *Gazette* building and see Possum and all the guys for the first time since I was shellacked by them last Sunday afternoon. Most of them nod or wave as they obviously gathered here several minutes before my arrival. I step out of my car and then, before I can react, they grab me and lift me to the shoulders of Kenny and Peanuts, all the while shouting "We love Kenny pitching. We love Kenny pitching!"

As I bounce around above the crowd, I find myself smiling and cannot hide my surprise. Heck, they knocked the daylights out of the ball and I hung in there for even more of a beating. They are all smiles after what had been a well-rehearsed demonstration. Possum was in on this for sure as he stands by smiling. As they lower me to the ground, I have no words to say but understand and appreciate this fine gesture.

A few minutes pass and then Possum raises his hands and asks us to gather around.

"First of all," he says. "Nice game Sunday, guys. And, Kenny, we appreciate your effort out there on such a hot day." He continues, "We still have several minutes before we have to leave, and it looks like the rain is stopping. I'm guessing that the game might be delayed a little, anyway. I want to use this time to up-date you on the rest of the Bombers' schedule for the season.

"I'm going to drop it off at the *Gazette* for this coming Friday evening. We have nine games left after tonight with the first one not until next week, Tuesday, July 24 at Lyndon. I know little about them but will find out what I can before our practice tomorrow or by the next day. That means, then, that we will be off from playing for about a week, but I still want to have regular practices."

With that, we pile into our cars and head south down Highway-99 for the twenty-five-mile trip to Madison.

"So, how did you like your ride, Kenny?" Philip asks.

"Peanuts' shoulders were a little bumpy, but otherwise it was fine," I smile.

Everyone in the car laughs.

After a moment of silence, I hear a gentle whistling coming from Mike in the back seat. That triggers a question I have wanted to ask him all season. "When did you learn to whistle like that? Whether I am at third base or pitching, I hear it loud and clear."

Mike looks a little startled. "I didn't realize I was whistling just now. I do that a lot, I guess. When I was in Korea, we had lots of time on our hands and I decided to learn the trick of loud whistles that I had heard from so many of my coaches over the years. Then, when I played baseball in the military, I used the whistle to help me keep focus and it seemed to help the other players as well."

"You were in Korea? I was there, too," Don exclaims.

"All this time and just now we find this out." Mike says.

"So, where were you stationed?" Don asks.

"I was in Korea for most of '52 and got out in '53." Mike answers. "I was an artilleryman in the Twenty-Fifth Infantry Division. My division and others were pushed by the North Korean Army almost down to Pusan in the early days of the war. We had a very difficult time advancing in mountainous regions and were always on the move."

Don looks a little surprised. "I have the same story, but during '51 and '52, I was a battalion cook in the First Marine Division. The cold was brutal, our losses heavy and try as I might, hot food was almost unheard of."

Without thinking, I blurt, "So, did you guys ever run across each other over there?"

Mike and Don look at each other and Don answers, "Kenny, there were thousands of soldiers along the line and it was almost one hundred and fifty miles long, so not much of a chance…"

I can't catch what else he is saying under his breath. It is hard to hear with all the windows open and going down the highway at fifty miles an hour.

"Well, I guess it is time for me to learn a little history," is my feeble reply.

The other three in the car have been listening quietly while discovering this association of two of our very favorite teammates.

The last few miles to Madison are traveled in silence.

We arrive near Madison and find a cloud of dark smoke rising from the playing field. Philip cautiously drives into the parking lot. He parks near other cars some distance away from the field. "Let's get out and see what is going on and leave our stuff here," he suggests.

As the playing field comes into view, we see a sight unlike any we have ever seen. Two guys are walking back and forth across the field pulling chains wrapped around burning car tires.

"They are trying to dry out the infield!" Clyde shouts.

That must be the plan. The men are now concentrating their efforts around home plate and the pitcher's mound. Possum arrives and directs us to the field. We gather our equipment, walk to the visitor's dugout and settle in. It seems that the rain has stopped for good and that we can surely start the game. The crowd so far is very small.

From our view in the dugout the Madison stadium is a cozy one with short outfield fences. As usual, Harold shares his view of the distances.

"Man, look at center field. It's only three hundred and fifty feet away and look at right field, it's only three hundred and ten feet."

We have all heard this before.

"Why don't you hit one over it then?" Steve shouts back.

Harold grins.

Since there will be no infield warm-ups this evening, we sit together in the dugout. I notice that Mike and Don have taken seats near the far end of the dugout. I am still interested in what they have to say so I stroll casually to sit near them.

They are in a regular conversation and not interested in including me. I sit quietly.

"I was about twenty-eight years old when my unit was called

up. I was already married and had two kids by then. I was a mess sergeant, but when the First Marines became encircled just south of the Yalu River, several of us cooks had to join the rifle units. We had to 'advance' to the south!" Don attempts to smile.

He continues, "It got pretty hot when the Chinese stormed the south, but my squad made it through despite heavy losses. It was sure nice to finally get out and start my job. I needed a way to support my family and working for the lumberyard has worked out well for me so far."

Mike pauses for a few seconds. "Ever since I was a kid, I wanted to work in a bank. I am not sure if it was because of all the money around or because the people working there looked so nice. When I got out of the service, I applied to the State Bank and hired on as a teller. I've been doing that for almost three years now and really like it. I got some news the other day that I might be up for a promotion as a loan officer. I would really like that. Heck, maybe Rosa and I could get serious then."

Don smiles and taps Mike on the shoulder. "She is surely a pretty gal, Mike. I hope things will work out for you two." Both are smiling.

A short pause, then Mike and Don look out over the field as the two guys with the burning rubber tires start to douse the tires with gasoline again as they are flickering out. It is still a sight to behold, but with apparent good progress.

I glance to the opposing dugout to see some of the Madison players starting to play catch nearby. Surprisingly, I recognize two of them. They are my cousins Dale and Gale Schroeder. I do not see them often. I know they live in Madison, but I didn't realize they would be playing for their own town team.

They were at the July 4 get-together at Peter Pan Park a few weeks ago. I did not visit with them more than to say, "Hi." Possum would likely not approve of me running over to see them, so I will wait until after the game.

Finally, at eight thirty, the umpire calls to Possum and the Madison coach that the game will start in five minutes. Tire smoke continues to rise slowly into the lights. The smell of burning rubber will likely be with us the whole evening.

Possum waves to the umpire that we are ready and then stands to announce the starting line-ups. "The batting order will be pretty much as it has been the last few weeks. One change is that I want to start Ohm at third base for just a few innings and then substitute David for him. Kenny will get at least one at bat and then can continue to rest up from his effort last Sunday."

Once again, Possum surprises. If he had asked me how I wanted to play tonight, it would be just as he announced. I am still a little weak from Sunday, but it will be nice to get into the game for a few innings. My love for baseball is the only way to explain my feeling.

"Kenny Young will start pitching tonight and bat ninth, as usual. Jones leads off at second, Garcia at shortstop, Matson batting third at first-base, Don in right field, cleanup, Harold in center field, Ohm at third, batting sixth, Philip, catching, followed by Peanuts…I mean Jesse. I am not going to call you Peanuts. You bat eighth, and Kenny Young, ninth." Possum is smiling broadly—once again showing an obvious love for the game.

Steve Jones strolls to the plate to lead off the game. He hits the first pitch up the middle for a single. Mike Garcia follows with a line-drive out to the Madison third baseman. Clyde Matson follows with a double along the left field line scoring Steve. Don Graham works the count to two balls and two strikes before launching a home run ball well over the three hundred fifty-foot sign in center field. The score now stands at 3 to 0. Harold Turner strikes out, followed by my ground-out to shortstop to retire the side.

We feel good with a nice lead after the first half inning. Kenny Young steps to the mound with his usual look of confidence. I check the third base area for rocks and find several—likely because of the flaming tires being pulled over the dirt infield.

The first two Madison batters smash hard singles to the outfield. Kenny fidgets a bit on the mound as he adjusts his cap and looks around to the infield. I hear the shrill whistle of Mike Garcia to my left and a pickup of chatter from the rest of the infield.

Batter number three, my cousin Dale, connects for a long drive to center field where Harold makes an excellent grab on the run. Both runners advance. The Madison clean-up hitter scores both runners with a double down the left-field line. Kenny again stalks around the pitcher's mound, toeing the dirt where his landing foot hits after every pitch.

I trot to the mound for a quick conference with Kenny.

"What seems to be the problem?" I ask.

"The dirt is still wet here and my foot lands about a foot farther than the Madison pitcher. I'm slipping on every pitch."

Together we quickly smooth the dirt in front of the mound.

"Throw hard," I say on the way back to my third base position.

The next pitch is a line-drive out to Steve at second base. Madison batter number six hits a 3-2 count well over the left field fence. We are suddenly behind 4 to 3. The next batter strikes out and the inning is over.

We hustle in to our dugout with confidence that we can come back as we often do. Kenny Young finds a seat near Possum. "No problem, Possum. I think I got the mound figured out and feel pretty good out there right now."

Possum pats him on the back. "You are in it for the game, Kenny. Just pitch your stuff and you'll be fine."

Philip leads off the second inning with a ground-ball single to left field. Peanuts follows with a single to right field. Kenny Young, batting number nine, slugs a two-ball and two-strike count well over the center field fence. Philip and Peanuts score before him and we lead 6 to 4. We greet Kenny at the dugout with handshakes. He smiles broadly. Even though it is early, I think we have this game under control.

With no outs, Steve hits a line drive to third base for out-number one. Mike and Clyde both fly out to left field and we go into the bottom of the second inning.

The first hitter strikes out for Madison. I recognize the next batter as Cousin Gale. He promptly lines a drive off the left field wall, barely in fair territory, and slides into second base for a double. Madison's ninth hitter drills the first pitch hard on the ground to Steve at second base and is thrown out at first base. Gale takes third on the play. I nod at him and he does a double take, before recognizing me.

"Kenny, what are you doing playing for the Brown Bombers?"

"Long story. Let's talk after the game," I say.

Gale and I both know the trouble we would have with our coaches if we said anything more.

Gale nods.

The next batter hits a single to center field, scoring Gale. Kenny strikes out Madison hitter number two to retire the side. We still lead 6-5, at the end of the second inning.

Don leads off the third inning with a towering drive over the center field fence, his second home run of the night. Harold singles to center field and I follow with a double to right center, scoring Harold. We now lead 8 to 5. As I stand at second, the Madison shortstop, Cousin Dale, trots over and kicks the second base bag.

"Hi Cousin," he says quietly. Gale told me you were playing. What a surprise." He trots back to his position.

I nod.

Neither team scores going into the top of the sixth inning. As I return to the dugout, Possum motions for David to take my place to bat in this inning. I end up with one hit in three times at bat and I am happy to call it a day.

We do not score in the sixth inning, but Madison scores three runs on a homerun by Cousin Dale to tie the score in the bottom of the inning at 8 to 8.

Both teams score runs during the next two innings making the score 11 to 10 in our favor going into the top of the ninth inning.

A couple of singles and three walks adds two more runs for the Bombers to make the score 13 to 10. With two outs and the bases loaded, David Carter walks to the plate. After working a three ball, two strike count, David hits a high drive to left field. The left-fielder runs hard and leaps high with his glove hand over the fence. We are all frozen.

The fielder drops to the ground with an empty glove. A grand slam! David is smiling as he rounds third base. We storm out of the dugout to greet him. We lead 17 to 10. Back in the dugout, the noise from the Bombers continues with lots of back slapping and handshakes in honor of David.

Madison scores one run in the bottom of the ninth inning making the final score 17 to 11.

I quickly trot to the Madison dugout and find Dale and Gale. They are both smiling as we shake hands. "Have you been playing with the Brown Bombers all season?" Dale asks.

"Almost the entire season and I hope to continue the rest of the summer," I reply.

"Once the season ends and we get into winter, I want to hear the whole story," Gale says.

"Good idea. We will need quite a bit of time to get it all explained," I say.

"Good luck, Kenny. You guys have a really good team and can really hit the ball," Dale says with a wave.

I head back to Philip's car and they are waiting for me with questioning looks. "They're just a couple of my cousins. I had no idea they were playing for Madison," I explain. "They think we're a terrific team," I add.

The trip home is a time for little talk except to rehash David's grand slam. We all so admire David and his talent. We conclude that it couldn't happen to a nicer guy.

Chapter Fourteen

A Little Time Off

Although the Madison game did not end until after midnight, and after we all completed a full day's work, we gather for practice this evening with great enthusiasm. It was such a positive feeling to come from behind last night. We surely look like a quality team. Mike again arrives with Rosa in the Chevy and the Bombers wave in recognition.

David gets a lot of attention with handshakes and pats on the back. I doubt if I will ever hit a grand slam homerun, and I think the others feel the same way. Possum seems extra excited today as he drills us on the continuing importance of chatter while in the field and even offers us some new ideas.

"When I was playing, we tried to keep the pitcher aware of the defense behind him. I think too many times a pitcher blames himself for runs scored and even for fielders' errors. A good chatter can help that. I played second base and my favorite was, 'Make him hit to me, Kenny,' or Bob or whoever was pitching. I repeated the same chant with some variation many times throughout a game."

We listen with interest. I think that this is the first time I remember Possum saying anything at all about his baseball career on the field. Where and when was that?

Possum continues, "I hear your whistle out there at shortstop, Mike. It's really effective and we all know you are out there at the ready. It would be nice if some others of you might do the same thing."

At that instant, a shrill whistle sounds from across the group. It is Don, with a broad grin. "Mike just taught me that," he says.

"Sounds to me like we have another whistler. Perhaps that's enough with Don in right field and Mike at shortstop. I guess the Bombers don't need nine guys whistling," as Possum winks.

Lots of laughter with that one.

"One final idea for our next practice," Possum says. "Would each of you try to think of a new phrase or chatter in addition to the ones you have been using? You don't have to, but it might help us out a bit. I mentioned this to you before, but it takes lots of little things to win ball games and I want to try to keep making us a better and better team."

Possum shifts his weight from one leg to the other and lifts his hands with a sparkle in his eyes and the biggest smile we have ever seen.

"Now, here is some really exciting news. As some of you know, each year Wichita hosts a national tournament called the National Baseball Congress World Series. They have been doing that since 1935 and they get the best amateur teams in the nation to play there. Well, I just got a call this morning from those folks and they say they have been following us a bit

A Little Time Off

lately, and perhaps there might be an opening for us to play in their tournament, starting around August 17."

He pauses while it soaks in to all of us. Murmurs all about. This is way beyond anything we can imagine. Some of us know that the Emporia Boosters played in the Series years ago, but to have another team from Emporia like us in the Series is hard to believe.

He continues, "I don't want to get your hopes up as I think they may already have the sixty or so teams lined up. But they're looking for a few teams to fill in, just in case. That is OK with me, for sure. We'll just keep playing and winning and see what happens."

A bunch of questions come to mind from team members wondering how long the Series will last and if they will have to start planning with their jobs to find a way to get off work.

"I think with the new turnpike in operation, we should be able to drive to Wichita in just a few hours and, as usual, not expect to stay overnight. I do know, though, that some games don't even start until after midnight. Also, it is a double elimination tournament, so if we get in, we're guaranteed two games, win or lose. So, we'll just have to wait and see. Be sure to let me know if you think it is a good idea to stay in contention for a spot. I would surely like to go myself," Possum says.

I look around the circle of players and see no uncertainty at all. They are all smiles and are showing positive nods and thumbs up.

The next day's practice is uneventful after opening with a brief reminder to check out our personal schedules for possible NBC play in August. No player responds one way or the other. Possum reviews hand signals and his usual demand to "hit the cut-off man." We nod in confirmation as each subject is brought up. We have heard them so many times, but Possum seems to feel a need to remind us time and time again.

He ends practice with a request to hear chatter ideas. A few respond. I suggest that a third baseman, often closest to the pitcher, might remind the pitcher of a runner leading off first or second base. "Look over" or "take a look" might give the pitcher an idea that the runner is taking too large a lead and could be picked off.

Possum likes that one, with a smile.

Steve offers, "There he goes," or "He's going" as an alert to catcher Philip or the players covering a base on an attempted steal.

Again, Possum agrees.

No more chatter suggestions are offered.

Possum announces practice for Friday evening and repeats his usual instruction at the end of every practice, "Get some rest."

I arrive home and open the newspaper to the sports section. There is an article relating to our win over Madison. This is a rare treat. To get a game summary in the newspaper so quickly, Possum must indeed be proud of our come-back. It reads:

Brown Bombers Win Over Madison, 17-11

Running their winning streak to five games in a row, the Emporia Brown Bombers defeated Madison 17-11 in a baseball game played a Madison Tuesday night. Nine runs in the last two innings brought the Emporians from behind as they were trailing 9-8 going into the eighth inning.

Kenny Young hurled all the way for the Brown Bombers to get the mound win, although he was touched for four runs in the first inning. Ott went the distance on the mound for Madison to take the loss.

David Carter led the Emporian's attack with two hits including a grand slam homerun in the ninth inning. Three of his teammates had three hits each for runner-up honors.

Practice ends on this Friday evening with Possum asking us

A Little Time Off

to gather around him for a special announcement. "I realize this is short notice, but at my church meeting last night, the trustees asked me to invite you all to our regular service this coming Sunday morning. They have been following our team this summer and want to give the congregation a chance to meet each of you. Mount Olive is located at 601 Congress and our service starts at eleven o'clock in the morning. I know that we have a few Catholics and Lutherans on our team, but please give some thought to attending together this one time."

I glance around the group and see the Bombers to be agreeable to this invitation. It is a kind gesture and Possum would not be asking us to do this unless it is important to him and to the team. That seems reason enough for all of us to respond.

Possum announces that we will not have practice again until Monday evening and it will be a short practice. This will be the first weekend since the middle of June that we have not played. Most of the guys stay on the field after practice, quickly planning various outings with their new-found liberty. They seem unified with their commitment to attend Sunday's church service at Mount Olive.

I walk with Philip and Jesse to our cars and both show some enthusiasm with the idea of the Sunday service in Possum's church. I will not plan on working late that morning and arrange to meet the brothers at the church.

Dad and I have been working all week on shingling the roof on Frank Love's house. We always work on Saturdays and tomorrow will be no different. We will continue at Frank's house as we try to get it closed in. Then we will have a few more weeks of work with siding, painting and inside finishing.

I open this evening's paper and read the schedule for the Bombers:

Brown Bombers Book
Nine Additional Games

Nine games remain on the schedule for the Emporia Brown Bombers who have won their last five starts. Manager William "Possum" Williams announced the following schedule for the remainder of the season.

Lyndon at Lyndon	July 24
Gridley at Gridley	July 29
Osage City at Emporia	July 31
Gridley at Emporia	Aug. 4
Melvern at Emporia	Aug. 7
Reading at Reading	Aug. 12
Melvern at Melvern	Aug. 17
Reading at Emporia	Aug. 19
Osage City at Osage City	Aug. 26

It once again says that we have won five games in a row. It looks like Possum is not counting the Olpe game. It continues to be just an exhibition to him. I notice that he also did not include our scheduled exhibition game at Americus to be played on July 26. With a major-league pitcher pitching against us, I understand why he wants to keep it as a true exhibition game. This is just one more reason my respect for Possum continues to grow. He has deep values and exhibits them time and time again.

Our record of seven wins and two losses looks good right now. Perhaps the National Baseball Congress will choose us on August 17, or so. As I study the schedule, I see that if we played in the Series, we could still play the August 12 game in Reading, but would have to cancel or change plans for the remaining Melvern, Reading and Osage City games. That will be Possum's problem.

We start this Saturday morning work day with our tools out and ready to go at eight o'clock sharp. This is Dad's way and he does not tolerate any other option. We finish the roof, close in the gables and begin to install windows and outside doors.

Dad and I have an on and off again conversation relating to my plans to attend the Mt. Olive church tomorrow morning.

"Kenny, I'm not sure that is a good idea. You might find a problem being the only white guy on the team and probably the only white person in the whole congregation. I know I would never have the nerve to go to that church."

"Well, I'm a little worried, but Possum looked right at me when he invited the whole team to attend. He has always been straight-forward with me, so I think he would have said something if he thought there would be a problem. I really should go. I do not want to let the team down here either." I try to believe my own words.

"Maybe you could help me for a few hours tomorrow before you go, then. It will be nice to get this place cleaned up and ready for the week ahead."

We end the day exhausted but have made good progress. The house will soon be fully closed in and we will not be so much at the mercy of the weather.

Mom, Dad and I watch television a few hours in the evening and go to bed early.

On this early Sunday morning, before going to Possum's church, I join Dad as we sharpen saw blades, sweep the house clean and carry away trash. As Dad often says, "When we get here Monday morning, it'll be like working in a brand-new place." He seems resigned to my attending the all-black church later this morning and wishes me well.

At about ten thirty, I quickly change clothes. I briefly wish that I had replaced my confirmation suit, outgrown some years ago. I drive the two miles to Mount Olive Church. I am a little nervous with the prospect of attending a different church than the Lutheran one I have attended all my life. Nevertheless, it will be a new experience and it will be exciting to see my teammates in such a different surrounding.

I park a few blocks away as the street parking is full, and parishioners are arriving from every direction. I feel a lump in my throat as I realize that this might be a bigger deal than I had thought. Most of the men are wearing suits and ties and I wear just a white shirt with no tie and dress pants.

It is too late now; I walk toward the church while meeting Philip and Jesse on the nearby sidewalk. Both are wearing dark suits and ties.

We are quickly surprised to see Mike and Rosa approaching us from the opposite sidewalk in front of the church. What an attractive couple. Mike is wearing a dark suit and red tie while Rosa is wearing a white sun dress with white high-heeled shoes. They both are about the same height and their dark black hair is striking. I have heard that Philip, Jesse, Mike and Rosa are all Catholics. I wonder if they feel some of the same uncertainty that I do.

Just then, Harold and Clyde join us at the church entrance. Harold wears his usual overalls, with a clean white shirt, while Clyde wears dress pants and a white shirt. Neither is wearing a tie. They look as nervous as I feel inside.

Mike and Rosa lead the way as we enter the church. Jesse, Philip, Harold, Clyde and I follow. We are greeted by an elderly usher in a sharp grey suit, black tie and white shirt. His smile is broad and shows several gold teeth. Almost as a match, he wears a gold chain around his neck, with gold cuff links and a gold tie clip to complete the scene.

After quick handshakes, he asks us to follow him down the long aisle to near the front of the sanctuary. We walk past a nearly full congregation, although we are still several minutes before the eleven o'clock starting time.

Almost as a plan, on the left side of the aisle, in the second

A Little Time Off

row, I see the five other Bombers who are members of Mount Olive, already seated. I notice a little girl next to Steve, dressed in a pink dress and a frilly white hat, seated near the aisle. She smiles and waves at us as we pass by. Mike nods to the seated players as we are ushered to the right side of the aisle and into the vacant second-row pew.

Directly in front of me, Possum turns around from his front row seat and reaches out for a handshake. His smile is genuine, and I see peace in his eyes. Possum shakes each hand in our party and greets Rosa kindly. I feel my shoulders relax as he whispers that the eight men, along with their wives in the front row, are the church elders. We quickly acknowledge each of them with a nod. The congregation behind us react patiently and with smiles.

The minister is elderly, with white hair and a short white beard. He signals for the congregation to rise and the service starts with a rousing hymn, *Lord Jesus Christ, Be Present Now*. I share my hymnal while standing between Clyde and Harold. I am amazed at the volume and melody of the Bombers and the elders at the front of the room. When adding the full congregation, it is as if the roof will be lifted. I do not remember hymns in my Lutheran church sung with such vigor.

As the congregation is seated, the minister walks to the pulpit. "We wish to welcome a group of young men who have this summer cast a positive light on our community and on our congregation. Many of you will recognize several members of the Brown Bombers as our brethren here at Mount Olive, but others who are temporarily strangers. These young men are pursuing a dream that has continued throughout the summer and carry expectations of much greater success in the days ahead. Please recognize them as we invite them to a luncheon reception after the service today." The applause is deafening and some of us shyly rise with a brief wave.

During the offering, the minister announces that there will be a collection tray at the back of the church for anyone wishing to donate to the Bombers on the way out. "Perhaps you will find a calling to help our kids this way and then, maybe someday, we will feel comfortable attending a ball game at Sodens."

Is this more of Possum's usual warning, "Don't look for trouble?" The service ends after an uplifting message and several more energetic hymns. The ushers guide us as we file out of the sanctuary and downstairs to the reception room.

Within minutes the room is filled with eager men and women shaking hands and patting players backs. Don surprises Philip, Jesse and me as we stand to one side. He introduces us to his beautiful wife and three children. "I sat alone up front with the Bombers since it would be too much commotion to include the kids." He smiles at his wife and gives her a brief kiss on her cheek. They are all smiling. His children stand shyly. Once again, I think of the commitment Don is making to play with the Bombers this summer.

Steve then approaches with the little girl at his side. "This is my sister, Ida. She really likes baseball and wanted to meet you guys." Philip and Jesse kneel to greet Ida as she nods her head quietly. "Hello, pretty lady," I say. "I am so glad to meet you."

Ida smiles and says, "Me, too."

Just then, we hear an announcement from somewhere in the crowd. "Folks, we just added up the special offering for the Bombers and find a total of twenty-five dollars. Thanks to each of you. This will put the Bombers on the road for several more games. Hey, Possum, anything you want to say?"

A Little Time Off

Although we cannot see Possum over the crowd, we hear his familiar voice as he expresses his appreciation to the congregation. "OK, folks, you have put the pressure on us now. Looks like we better win or else. Thank you so much."

The crowd responds with many shouts of encouragement. I look around the room and see several small groups visiting with the Bombers. To one side of the room, David, Bob and Kenny have attracted a number of girls and are engaged in animated conversation. At the far end of the room and beyond the refreshment table, I see Clyde and Harold also with several young ladies surrounding them. Their smiles are broad and their expressions bright. Although they are not members of Mount Olive now, I see them joining soon!

Philip, Jesse and I walk toward the table filled with cookies and soft drinks and spot Rosa sitting and visiting with a group of women of varying ages. What a pleasant sight as it seems we are all being accepted to Mount Olive and with considerable enthusiasm. As we walk down the food line, several older folks join us, asking questions relating to our baseball season and what the future holds for us. The crowd slowly disperses, and I leave the church with Philip and Jesse. I notice Mike and Rosa still visiting with a small group, but do not see Harold or Clyde or the rest of the team.

Within the next hour, I find myself back at Dad's building site and ready to help get ready for Monday morning's work assignment.

Dad quickly asks, "So, how did it go, Kenny?"

"Just fine. No problem at all," I answer. "Actually, I had a great time and the people were really nice."

Dad smiles and seems to drop the subject for the rest of the day. The late afternoon winds down with memories of a truly pleasant experience at Mount Olive Church this morning and the many kind and gentle people I met. I cannot help thinking this is yet another team-building opportunity from Possum as he prepares us for the rest of the summer baseball season and, perhaps, for times after that. I wonder if he thinks of our spiritual well-being as well as our physical development on the baseball field.

Monday arrives with a full day's work planned. It is a straight forward day with six new windows and two outside doors installed and locked. Dad can rest more easily with Frank Love's house now secure for the night. As the five o'clock quitting time nears, I feel energized with the prospect of a short practice this evening and then a game at Lyndon tomorrow night. A half-dozen days without baseball is enough!

After considerable chatter relating to the Sunday morning church service and the adventures later that afternoon by many of the Bombers, on-field practice is, indeed, short. We hear that Clyde and Harold also attended a youth group meeting in the evening at the church and were encouraged to join Mount Olive. They seem very positive about the prospect.

Possum shares that the same drivers as on our other trips have consented to drive and surprises us as he hands each driver a ten-dollar bill.

"This may not become a regular payment, but the Mount Olive congregation insisted that you guys get the ten dollars at least for this trip, and maybe we can buy some needed equipment. So, I talked to the folks at Haynes Hardware and they are ordering a couple of gloves for Bob and Harold. I know that most of you have bought your own glove, but now we can

A Little Time Off

have everyone with their own so we won't have to ask the other team to share. The Bombers are all smiles with this new-found prosperity. Possum, however, gives us a stern look as if warning us not to expect any free-flowing money.

It then takes only a moment to determine our riding assignments to be the same as on previous trips for the forty-five-mile ride to Lyndon. Possum reminds us to be on time for our drive as game time is eight o'clock and we need every moment we can get for the pre-game warm up.

Since we have had several days off, Possum announces that Kenny Young will get the start, and "hopefully will be ready again for the Gridley game five days from now." Possum seldom anticipates that one of his starting pitchers will not go the full nine innings and, with Kenny as the choice, he is seldom wrong.

"Don't forget that we'll play an exhibition game against the Americus town team on Thursday, and I am planning on Smith and Ohm to pitch that game. It should be a fun time for all of us to get to meet Mr. Grimsley. Go home now and get some rest."

Before we can walk toward our cars, Clyde loudly asks for our attention. This is most unusual as we have ended practice and are not looking for any other duties this evening.

"I have been thinking about something for the last few weeks and now that everyone has a glove, I want to try it out. I hear almost every night on the radio about flying saucers being spotted all over the world. I think the fans would love to see us coordinate our glove tossing after each inning and call it our 'flying saucer throw.'

"Here is what we do. After each inning, we all run in to the middle of the infield and then I will shout 'fire' and we will then fling our gloves into the air toward the outfield from one foul line to the other. What do you think?

We all love the idea and run together as a group to give it a try. Clyde is eager to give us the signal.

"Fire!"

It is a beautiful sight, seeing seven gloves all in the air at one time fanning out across the distant grass.

Possum enjoys the scene and waves his approval. Suddenly, he calls for our attention. "Guys, I have not had much time to think about this, but it seems that we should not do the 'flying saucer' deal after each inning. Let's just do it together after the first inning. That way, it won't look like we are showing off and it will make it more special." We look at each other for a moment and nod in agreement. Once more it is good to have Possum as our leader!

Practice now ends with special enthusiasm.

Chapter Fifteen

Tension in the Ranks

On the way home from practice, I make a decision that I have been thinking about since I wore a full uniform when I pitched for the Aces last week. About a year or so ago, when I made one of my many trips to the Army-Navy store on north Commercial Street, I discovered a baseball uniform hanging within a line of men's shirts. After a brief inspection, I found it to be a complete uniform, including blue stirrup socks matching its blue trim.

It was obviously in great condition, had air-vents under the sleeves, and was exactly my size. It was startling to read the lettering across the front, *Ft. Douglas*! I know nearby *Ft. Riley* but had no knowledge of *Ft. Douglas*.

Nevertheless, I was hooked and offered the salesman the one-dollar I had on me at the time. Although marked at two-dollars, he said it had been on the rack for some time, so he agreed to my price.

During the last game, I noticed that some of the opposing players were wearing an assortment of regular baseball uniforms, including miss-matched shirts, pants, hats and socks. Except for getting Harold to wear a shirt, Possum has never said one way or the other whether he notices what our clothes look like on the playing field. However, I think many of us would like to look the part of an organized baseball team and wear regulation uniforms to replace our work clothes or whatever else we wear. It might give us a little more confidence in our play as well as in our appearance.

So, with the decision made, I get home, run upstairs and change into the *Ft. Douglas* uniform. I only have a small mirror, but my reflection is acceptable. I find a little adrenaline rush as I anticipate the response I will get when I meet the guys for the drive to Lyndon tomorrow. I will take the uniform to work and change there.

Tuesday's work day ends well. I quickly change into my new uniform and drive to our meeting place in front of the *Gazette* building. Philip and Mike are already there and, as I step out of my car, they break out in big smiles and then double over in laughter. Slapping their hands on their thighs, they continue to whoop it up. I am not embarrassed at all, until I look down and see I am wearing my old, roomy, bedroom slippers. The new, rather heavy stirrups over my socks made it uncomfortable to wear my work shoes or even my Sunday shoes.

I had planned to wear the slippers on my drive to the *Gazette* building and then leave them in the car, but instead, I step out of my car in full sight. I decide to go along with the joke and prance proudly in front of the building as other team members arrive and join the fun. The team has always seen me with long warm up pants down over my shoes and a loose-fitting shirt.

Now, my 172-pound, 6 foot 3 frame, shows starkly over my tight-fitting stirrups and size 12 ½ slippers. This makes for quite a different image, and I am making the most of it! After the hilarity calms down, the big question is, "Where is *Ft. Douglas?*" I have no answer even though I have owned the uniform for a year or so. I decide to wear my slippers in the car on the way to Lyndon and change into my spikes once we get there.

The guys quiet down as we make our drive to the game. I think the energy expended responding to my uniform and my shoes allowed for fewer jitters along the way. We will have a good night on the baseball field.

The Lyndon ball field is somewhat different than those we have played on so far, this season. The distance to the snow fence at the left field foul line is nearly 360 feet, extending to a little over 400 feet in dead center, and then to only 240 feet to the right field pole.

The four and a half-foot snow fence does little more than provide a boundary for the outfield. Our outfielders quickly note that if a ball is hit toward the fence they will continue the chase until they get to the fence and prepare to jump over it if necessary to catch the ball. That might create a rules problem and they ask Possum to clarify it with the umpires before game time.

Once again, I observe the fans filing in as we near game time and notice only a few Mexicans or blacks. I guess that is what makes us so popular—a team of all black or brown players is quite distinct from the general population in these small towns. If I can play for the Bombers, it makes no difference to me what attracts a crowd.

The Lyndon team looks like several of the other teams we have played—especially the Allen team. They all seem several years older than we are and certainly muscular and athletic. In the past, we have been able to compete very well with these teams, but there is always some uncertainty leading up to the first pitch.

Possum returns to the dugout after the pre-game meeting at home plate with the Lyndon manager and the umpires. "If you guys can jump over the fence after a ball is hit that far, and then catch it, it'll be an out. However, you cannot play beyond the snow fence before a pitch." Possum is smiling at the thought. Our outfielders look at each other with a certain hope they might get a chance for a catch like that.

The game begins, and we go down in order in the top of the first inning. Kenny immediately takes charge with two strike-outs and a ground-out to set Lyndon down in the bottom of the first inning. As we agreed before game time, we gather near the pitcher's mound and with Clyde giving the signal, we throw our gloves high into the air toward the outfield. With the lights shining down, the display is beautiful. The crowd loves it with applause and cheers. We have a new signature for our team!

The Lyndon pitcher is a left-hander, the first one we have seen this season. It is fun to see such a variation and we have heard so much about the big-league players declaring an advantage for hitters from the opposite side of the pitcher. Our entire team hits on the right side so, if this theory holds, we should be able to hit this guy a little easier than a right-hander. So far, though, as we finish the fifth inning, we do not have a single hit. The good news is that they haven't hit Kenny, either.

In the top of the sixth inning, I fly out deep to right-center field on a nice catch by the Lyndon center fielder. I check my back pocket. I forgot to put my arrowhead into my new uniform. Play on. David Carter follows with a line single over third base. On a 3-2 count, Philip hits a hard grounder to the shortstop who fumbles for an error.

Now, we have men on first and second with one out. Our number eight hitter tonight, Bob Smith, sacrifices the runners to second and third with a nice bunt down third base line.

I look at Possum in the third base coach's box and he is holding his head in both hands. He glances up with a pained expression. Obviously, he did not want Smith to bunt, making the second out.

Kenny Young is now batting in the ninth position, once again trying to conserve energy. He takes the first two pitches as balls and then hits a screamer over second base, scoring both runs. Finally, we gain the lead at 2 to 0.

As we start the bottom of the sixth inning, Kenny walks the first batter on four pitches. I play my normal position at third when I hear Possum yell at me, "Kenny, take a few steps toward the base." On the next pitch, the batter hits a hard line-drive just over the third base bag. I lunge and catch it in the web of my glove, landing on my stomach, for the first out. If Possum had not pulled me over to the base, the ball would still be rolling to the deep left field fence, and Lyndon would have scored at least one run. The walked-runner still stands at first base. I nod to Possum. He has a very serious look on his face.

The next batter hits a fly ball to deep left-center field. Jesse and Harold are off at the crack of the bat. In a split-second decision, I see Harold flash toward the fence and jump clearly over it. Then, Jesse leaps, while still inside the fence, and makes a spectacular catch before crashing to the ground. He quickly regains his feet and fires a strike to second base, holding the runner as he scrambles back to first. Harold lifts both arms, dances in celebration, and jumps back over the fence to the outfield grass. His wide smile shows all the way to the infield. The crowd roars the play.

Young strikes out the next batter on three pitches, and we are out of the inning. As we all return to the dugout, I think most of us know that Young has a no-hitter going. As has long been the tradition, no one talks about it to avoid a jinx, but Jesse's amazing catch in the outfield provides plenty of babble among the Bombers.

Both teams go down in order in the seventh and eighth innings. The top of the ninth is no different for us. We go down one-two-three but still lead 2 to 0.

The bottom of the ninth starts out with a solid single to left field by the Lyndon second baseman, and the no-hitter is gone. Now, we really need to maintain the shutout and win the game. Kenny walks the next batter. With runners on first and second, I hear Possum shouting to Garcia at short-stop, "Mike, get closer to second." Possum waves his left hand directing Garcia even closer to the second base bag. Mike complies.

As both runners lead-off base, the next batter hits the first pitch screaming over Kenny's head. Mike makes a diving catch directly over second base and almost instantly tags the base with his glove, two outs. He quickly pulls up to his knees and fires a strike to Matson at first base, catching the runner off base, for a triple play!

The game is over. We win, 2 to 0. That is the first triple play of the season for us and the first one for any team we played so far this year. In fact, I only saw one triple play last year for the Hornets. We are all relieved. I guess the absence of my arrowhead was no big deal. Our season record now stands at eight wins and two losses.

We are in the dugout shaking hands and relaying to each other highlights of the game, with some expressing disappointment that Kenny did not get his no-hitter. Possum joins us, and we see instantly that something is bothering him. "Guys, this was not our game tonight! I cannot figure out what the problem is, but it seems to me that we are losing concentration and we just can't do that with so much depending on it." He pauses as we quiet down.

"They could just as well have scored a couple of runs or more and we would be in extra innings at best. As you all know, with a loss here we would likely have no chance to play in the NBC. We have to play at Americus on Thursday and Gridley on Sunday and you guys must be ready. Practice as usual tomorrow at six." He walks off alone to his car and the drive home.

On the way to the parking lot, Mike comes over to me with a slight smile.

"Man, Possum sure knew what to do with where we were playing, didn't he?"

"Yeah, the ball hit to me would still be rolling if he hadn't called me over. Then they would have scored a run or two, and it's a whole different ball game. I saw what he did with you, too, Mike. Whew, that was a game winner for sure." We walk together to Philip's car.

The two of us once again recognize that Possum has a good nose for the game. I wonder about some of the others on the team. I will mention this in the car on the way home.

Once on the highway heading for Emporia, the topic of conversation quickly moves, for some reason, from our narrow win over Lyndon, to our successful introduction of the "flying saucer throw," to major league records of various kinds. I try to follow the major league races each day in the box scores in the *Gazette* but have not spent much time looking at old individual records. So, this is kind of surprising.

"Babe Ruth is the greatest hitter of all time," someone says.

"He not only hit sixty homers in one season, he hit 714 altogether," someone else answers.

"That has to be the greatest record there is. No one will ever hit that many again," Steve offers.

"What about the stolen base record?" Mike says. "If Jackie Robinson wouldn't have hurt his legs, I bet he could've got it."

Just then, Don Graham raises his hand to quiet down the din. "You know I looked up some of this stuff a while back. You want to hear what records will never be broken?"

Since Don is the old guy among us and previously shared the Doc Bushong story we say, "Sure," in unison.

"Yup, the Babe's records will never be broken. Guys don't stay around long enough in the big leagues anymore. They seem to get hurt pretty easy these days, so they don't play long enough." He pauses for just a second.

"But, there are a few other records that are just as impossible to beat. We might as well start with stolen bases. That mean ole Ty Cobb got almost a hundred during one season and about 900 for his career."

"Yeah, but I hear he used to sharpen his spikes to razor sharp, so the infielders were afraid to get too close to the base when he tried to steal it," Mike adds.

"You know, I've heard that all my life, but I don't see how he got away with it," I say. "During last year at E-State, I played against lots of teams and never saw anyone with sharpened spikes," I emphasize.

Tension in the Ranks

Silence.

Oh, my. What did I say? Come to think of it, I have never shared my experiences on the Hornet team. The Bombers have always accepted me for what I produce for them. I suddenly hear Dad's lament, "Don't be a big shot. Play with the team you're with."

Don picks up, "And another record is the consecutive games played by Lou Gehrig at 2130, over sixteen seasons. I have had that number memorized forever. Can you believe playing that many games without any rest at all during the season?"

We wait for Don to add to the list. After a full minute, he says, "You know, though, records are made to be broken and we're all human, so maybe" … he trails off. "There is one record that absolutely cannot be broken." He has the attention of all of us. "Want to know what it is?"

"Yeah, what is it?" Philip yells from the driver's seat. "What is the absolute baseball record of all time?" We wait while Don repositions himself in the middle of the back seat.

"In the summer of 1941, Joe DiMaggio hit in fifty-six consecutive games. His streak ended when Ken Keltner of Cleveland twice snagged backhand grounders behind third base and threw Joe out on very close plays. What most people don't know is that he hit in sixteen straight games right after that. It could have been over seventy straight except for those two plays."

I guess, for the next few minutes, we all are thinking about those numbers and quietly admiring Don for his knowledge of the history of the game. I had promised myself that I would share the moves Possum made which likely won the game for us. I look back at Mike for any sign he wants to talk about it. I see him looking out the window from the back seat, so I guess not.

"Did you guys notice that Possum had both Mike and I change our positions on the field and then the ball was hit right at us on the next pitch?" I wait for an answer.

"Yeah, I think we all did," Steve mumbles.

Nothing added, so I shift in my front seat and look down the highway. Something must have been going on for a little while with me and the team, I think. I should have known that a whole season cannot roll along without a little trouble along the way.

It is nearly one in the morning when I get home, and I am exhausted. Work day tomorrow and I sleep well. I wake up with a start as I think again about the trip home last night and still am not able to figure out the problem. Maybe there isn't a problem. We were all just tired.

Chapter Sixteen

A Big Leaguer

The team seems to practice in a trance today after last night's late hours in Lyndon. Several weeks have passed with no let-up on the pressures of winning. We think about the NBC tournament, and the fun part of the game is being taken over by the prospect of elimination from the national tournament, even before we are invited.

Although we will play our exhibition game tomorrow evening in Americus and get to meet Mr. Grimsley, it seems our primary focus is on Gridley—on their diamond next Sunday. A loss to them would be the end of it. We know that the Aces played and beat them a few weeks ago, so it would make sense that we should beat them. Nevertheless, the tension continues.

Possum suggests that if practice goes well this Wednesday evening, and if we present ourselves as a competitive team in Americus tomorrow, he might give us the day off both Friday and Saturday. We all think it is a great idea and seem a little more energized. Suddenly one of the groups playing catch erupts with laughter after Clyde shouts, "Maybe Possum should call us 'The Emporia Brown Bombers…and One White Boy.'"

I doubt that I was expected to hear that, but as I quickly look over to Clyde, he holds a hand over his mouth as if to call back the shout. I give him a frown and then try to smile at him. He turns away and resumes his warm-ups.

Practice goes on without incident and Possum winds up the evening describing a few special rules for the game tomorrow night. "Mr. Grimsley will not take a turn at batting and if his spot comes up during the first few innings, they will use a pinch hitter instead. They don't want to take any chance on getting him hurt. He plans to pitch through our order only once.

"Since we will have eleven players, I will substitute at the top of the order the two not in the line-up. That way, everyone will have a chance to hit off a major leaguer. Make sense? If not, it will tomorrow. Be sure to get to the *Gazette* about five and remember, concentrate your energy on that game, even if it is an exhibition, and behave yourselves. See you then."

We quietly leave the practice field and drive away, but I feel some sting with Clyde's comments. I wonder if the guys are still upset with my strike-out in Lebo. On the other hand, I am hitting about .330 and have given it all my best shot. Heck, even at the Aces game, where they got to me for nine runs, it should not give them a big problem. Otherwise, I have pitched pretty well for them so far this season.

When I arrive home from practice, I find Dad in the living room trying to see through lots of snow in the TV picture.

"Dad, I'm having a little trouble with the guys on the Bombers. I'm not sure they still want me there."

Dad looks at me with sad and tired eyes. "I've been thinking this might happen along the way. It seems that those guys might rather be with an all-black team. With you there, it isn't quite the same."

"I don't know what to do. It might be that we're all getting tired of each other as we either practice or play a game almost every day," I reply.

"Why don't you just stick it out for a few more days and see what happens?" Dad says.

That's exactly what I'll do. No use looking for trouble. Before going to bed, I make sure my arrowhead is in my *Ft. Douglas* back pocket.

Thursday is a special game day, and, after work, we arrive in Americus and find a very large crowd gathering around a single table set up behind third base. There sits Ross Grimsley with a smile on his face, taking pictures with fans and signing autographs. We find ourselves shyly filing into the visitor's dugout in preparation for our regular infield practice. Our trip here was a quiet one with a few individual attempts to relieve tension and trying somehow to relax. This is supposed to be a fun game for players and fans alike.

Possum meets with the Americus manager who agrees with our new found 'flying saucer throw.' Possum reminds us to throw only after the bottom of the first inning and not "over-do" it.

Game time is here and Mr. Grimsley takes the mound receiving a standing ovation from the fans. He tips his hat and takes a few warm up pitches. From the dugout, we see the ball as a straight-line blur to the plate.

Steve steps to the plate as the first batter for the Bombers. He grounds out on the first pitch. Garcia takes two strikes before popping up to the shortstop. Clyde Matson hits a drive to shallow right field for the third out. So far, Grimsley does, indeed, look like a major leaguer.

Americus scores two runs in the bottom of the first inning off Bob Smith. It seems they have some very powerful players, including two each from the Kansas University and the Kansas State University baseball teams. We agree that it is a good idea to back up a great pitcher with a competitive team—and they have done that.

Our "flying saucer throw" is again received well by the crowd. I wonder if they have already heard about it from the Lyndon fans last Tuesday night.

Our number four hitter, Harold Turner connects on the first pitch in the top of the second inning for a single to center field. Don Graham follows with a hard-hit ground ball to the shortstop for a quick double play. I am batter number six and take two blazing strikes, which I barely see. I swing at the third pitch somehow connecting for a single to right field.

I run to first base with a smile I cannot contain. I pat the arrowhead in my back pocket. Kenny Young, coaching at first base, also smiling, shakes my hand. Philip bounces out to first base for the final out of the inning.

I return to the dugout for my glove and receive positive responses from my teammates. Possum returns to the dugout. I see him visiting with Kenny Young and David Carter. We go into the bottom of the second inning.

The seventh batter for Americus grounds out to second base and is followed by the number eight hitter who strikes out on a Smith curve ball. With two outs, Ross Grimsley's number nine hitting slot is next, but another player comes to the plate for Americus. I look at Possum in the dugout and he is hand signaling, with both palms down, that this is an acceptable substitution. The pinch-hitter flies out and we return to the dugout.

Possum greets us. "Since this is an exhibition game, they agreed to let Young hit for Steve this inning and David for Mike, if we get that far. Steve will then go back into the game at second and play the rest of the game, as will Mike at shortstop. That way, you all get a chance to hit. In return, you noticed that Ross didn't take an at-bat."

That all makes sense now and is fine with us. The inning starts with Jesse and Bob each striking out. Young, however, bloops a single over third base. David follows with a long, high drive that is caught at the center field wall for out number three. That's it for Grimsley, as he leaves the mound to the roar from the crowd. Each member of our team will remember this experience—batting against a major league pitcher!

The rest of the game is unremarkable as Americus scores one more run off Smith into the fifth inning and three more off me to finish out the game. We score four runs but lose 7 to 4. Graham slugged two homeruns and Peanuts hit one. I did not get another hit but am so pleased with my old walnut bat and with a hit to remember.

As we gather our equipment in the dugout, Possum calls to us that we have a special guest. Ross Grimsley steps in and shakes hands all around. He has a few special words with Don Graham and we look on with pride. As Grimsley prepares to exit the dugout, Steve Jones offers his glove for an autograph and Grimsley obliges with a smile. Several of us do the same with others taking off their hat for a signature.

Within a few minutes, we start our walk back to our cars for the trip home. On the way across the parking lot, though, several Americus fans and a few from Emporia offer us items to sign. This is most unusual as we have not had this experience anytime during the season. We do not hide our enthusiasm and end up signing for several more minutes. Possum officially awards us with the day off both tomorrow and Saturday and with encouragement for a great game Sunday in Gridley.

The trip home is a happy one. We reflect on a wonderful experience with fans and players alike.

Chapter Seventeen

Harold and Clyde

I get home around midnight, check the newspaper and find an interesting article advertising a benefit on Saturday for the Little League teams in Emporia. Further, one of the most famous softball pitchers ever to play in Emporia will donate his time to challenge "any and all" players to hit his pitches.

Years ago, Laverne Miltz pitched for my Uncle Carl's softball team on a one-time only basis and won a very important league game for them. The story of that game has been kept alive for over ten years in our family, and I still find it exciting. For a quarter, the article says, Miltz will pitch three strikes to a batter and, with every safe hit, prizes will be awarded by various merchants in town.

For some reason, this really sounds like fun and, having never met Mr. Miltz, it might give me that chance. The contest will be held at noon on Saturday at the softball field in Peter Pan Park.

The next morning, I catch Dad as he is about to leave for work. "Hey Dad, we had a great game in Americus last night, although we lost 7 to 4. We got to meet Ross Grimsley and I actually got a hit off him. He signed my glove as well."

"Good for you," he answers.

"I was wondering if I might just work tomorrow morning and then head for Peter Pan to watch Laverne Miltz put on a pitching show. I kind of remember you and Carl's team having him for a pitcher a long time ago."

Dad perks up. "That's a good idea. I remember those days very well. If you can help me all day today, you can take tomorrow afternoon off. I might quit a little early, too. I am really tired these days."

It is about twelve thirty on Saturday afternoon when I get to the park. A big crowd is in attendance as the weather is almost perfect for a July 28, summer day. The festivities have already started as I note that Little League kids occupy the four infield positions, along with several more in the outfield. My guess is that a hit is determined by where the ball is hit between or over these fielders. An umpire stands directly behind Mr. Miltz to call a strike if the batter does not swing at a good pitch.

I grab a seat near the first base line where it appears that a sizeable number of folks await their turn to hit. A young lady sits behind a table selling 25-cent tickets for a chance. A few minutes pass when I see Harold and Clyde strolling toward the grandstand from far off near the right field pole. What a surprise! I thought I would be the only Bomber with the idea to hit off Mr. Miltz.

As they walk closer, I stand and wave toward them. They see me immediately and, with big smiles, join me. Harold looks really good today, wearing a white shirt under his overalls, which are buttoned up. I move over in my seat to make room for them and Clyde sits next to me.

"Kenny, I didn't expect to see you here," he said. "I heard about this over the radio and picked up Harold and drove over. There's a lot of talk about this guy and I'm wondering just how hard it is to hit a softball like that."

"I was thinking the same thing. I think I will give it a try. Only cost 25-cents. Hello there, Harold."

Harold nods. The waiting line is still long.

"Maybe Miltz will get a little tired later. Let's just wait for a few more minutes," Clyde chuckles.

"Sounds good to me. Harold, are you going to give it a try?"

"Yeah, I never tried to hit a softball before. It doesn't look so hard," he replies. "That sure looks like a little bat…"

"Kenny, I wanted to talk to you about the other day," Clyde offers. He hesitates for a few seconds. "I didn't mean anything by all that. It was just that our guys come from so many different directions and most of it isn't very good. Because you have a nice job and play ball in college and all. The rest of us don't go to college or have much hope to."

I am a little surprised. "I know that, and I am pretty sure I understand what you guys are going through," I answer.

Some guy hits the softball hard past second base and the crowd roars. I think it is the first hit since I arrived here. One of the officials gives the guy a free ticket and announces that it is to the Granada Theater.

"Well, we don't think you do," Clyde shrugs. "Take Harold here for instance. Did you know that his grandfather lived his whole life on a plantation in Georgia, died there when he was a very young man, and left his family without a father? Harold's dad was just a few years old at the time."

Another smash to the outfield by a really big guy lands in the glove of one of the little leaguers. The crowd applauds the catch.

Clyde interrupts, "So, years later when Harold's dad was about twenty-five and had trouble finding a job, he decided to travel to Dunlap. He had heard that it was a good place for southern Negroes to live and find work. He left his wife, Harold, here, and his other kids in Georgia and took off."

I am staring at the activity on the diamond and seeing the waiting line shorten a bit. "Harold, so how in the heck did you get up here, then?" I ask. Harold has been leaning in, listening closely to Clyde's story.

"My mom died a few years ago and most of my brothers and sisters either married or found jobs around our home town. I decided to see if I could find out where Dad is, if he is still alive.

"So, I took off hitch-hiking to Dunlap, Kansas. It took me several days, sleeping along the highways, but I made it. Then, no jobs in Dunlap and nobody ever heard of Dad. I'm kind of stuck here," he trails off.

Just then, the line thins out and we three decide to give hitting Miltz a try. Clyde steps up first with his quarter to pay the lady and I next offer to pay for Harold's ticket as well as mine. He waves his hand briefly and says, "No, I'll get it. Thanks."

Clyde is first up and swings at two pitches which are coming in on fire. "Man, when up close like this, those pitches are on you before you can even flinch," I say. On the next pitch, Clyde manages to contact the ball and it lands just over first base. The judge gives Clyde credit for a hit and awards him a free drink from the *Hamburger Stand*. Clyde walks over shaking his head. "Good luck, Kenny."

I barely see the first two pitches, taking the first one for a called strike, and swinging on the second, with the ball sailing over my bat. I have always been told that a pitched ball cannot gain height on the way to the plate. That it is just an optical illusion.

Well, I will tell people from now on that Laverne's fastball pitch starts low and does, indeed, gain height on the way to the plate. I should figure out how to throw one of those from the baseball mound! On the next pitch, I make contact, but it scribbles to the first baseman. The judge signals "out" with no prize awarded.

Then it is Harold's turn.

On the first pitch, Harold makes some contact, fouling the ball over the backstop. His look changes with a grim determination showing in his stance and, glancing back at us, in his eyes. He digs in and I know the next pitch will likely end up somewhere distant.

The crack of the bat is deafening as the softball soars well over the heads of several of the kids in the outfield. It rolls to Congress Street nearly a block away. That gets the crowd's attention and they respond with a loud roar.

The third pitch is hit to far left field, every bit as far as the first one. The crowd continues to enjoy this exhibition. I quickly ask the judge if he can try to hit three more pitches. He nods yes, and I give the lady another quarter. "This guy already has won two free tickets for free ice cream cones," the judge says, with a grin.

Mr. Miltz is smiling now, and I can imagine that he is thinking of some kind of trick pitch he might have in his arsenal.

In any case, the next two pitches are cracked directly over the center fielders and it seems that dozens of kids are chasing balls deep in the outfield. It takes several minutes to retrieve a few of those softballs before the last pitch of this series.

Harold smiles broadly as many in the crowd start to gather at the gate entering the field along the edge of the backstop. He is now very much the center of attention. The next pitch from Miltz surprises us as he tosses it some fifteen feet high and with almost no forward velocity. Harold is way out in front, but suddenly picks up the ball floating toward him, takes a couple of forward steps and gives it a mighty swing. The ball sails higher and deeper than any of the previous four.

Laverne Miltz strolls to home plate with his hand outstretched for a shake. Harold seems humbled. He nods shyly and shakes Miltz's hand. "I've never been hit so hard in my entire life," Miltz says. "So, you play with the Brown Bombers? I'll make it a point to see your next home game. I hope you can hit as hard there as you did here this afternoon."

Again, Harold nods with a smile.

Miltz turns to me and says he has enjoyed our attendance and our support for the Little League kids. I briefly remind him of his pitching years ago for my Uncle Carl's team. His eyes lighten up. "For some reason, I always remember that game. Such nice guys and I think there must have been four or five Schroeder boys and a few Rathkes."

"Yes, all my uncles," I reply. Several fans suddenly crowd around Laverne and our conversation ends.

The judge hands Harold five tickets for free ice-cream-cones from a local dairy. Harold accepts, smiling. As he turns back to the entry gate several kids and a few grown-ups gather around him. "Those were amazing hits," someone says. "So, you play for the Bombers?" someone else shouts.

Then, a little kid no more than five years old, grabs Harold's pants leg and asks, "What did you win?" Harold looks down and, with the good Lord looking over them all, he sees five kids gathered around him. Without hesitation, he bends over, stiff-legged and nearly to the ground, handing each one of them a ticket.

From the side, I see the scene and it tugs my heart. This very tall and very thin black man, with sincere pleasure on his face, is sharing with five little white kids. One of the mothers says, with a big smile, "Thank you," and they all hurry away.

"Well, Harold, that was quite a sight," Clyde says.

"So, what are we going to do for ice cream now?" I add.

It is still early in the afternoon, so we decide to visit one of the ice cream stores in town, since that seems to be on our minds right now. We travel in our two cars and meet several minutes later.

We sit in a booth in a far corner of the store and share several personal stories. I ask Clyde and Harold how they got together.

Clyde answers, "At the Bombers first practice, I met Harold and found out that he was working on a farm just a few miles from where I work, about ten miles north of town. He had walked all the way from his farm to Peter Pan Park that day. After practice, he rode back with me and I dropped him off at his place. It turns out that he had been sleeping in a storage shed there."

"Pretty comfortable?" I ask.

Harold grins and says, "No, lots of mosquitoes and other bugs, but OK."

"I live in what you might call a bunkhouse, and the bedroom sleeps two people pretty easy," Clyde adds. "So, I asked Harold if he would want to live there and walk the short distance to his own job each day. That's what we did and it's working out well."

"My boss thinks it's a good idea, too. He said he could still only pay me two dollars a day, no matter where I live," Harold grins.

"So, how'd you get here, Clyde?" I ask.

"Well, I ended up in Emporia a little over a year ago. One of my relatives who had been in the Army during the war was stationed at Ft. Riley and told me it was a good place to maybe find a job. I hitch-hiked, just like Harold did, got this far, and then found a job right away. It was just luck, I guess."

Clyde seems to want to continue his story and both Harold and I are just fine with that. The ice cream is really good, and the place is quiet.

"I had a tough time back there as I didn't live with either of my parents and just bounced around with other relatives. Toward the end, I barely escaped from members of a rival gang, and also had a little trouble with the law. I knew I needed to get out of there quick. I don't think anybody will come out here looking for me, so I am finally relaxing a bit and I really enjoy playing on the Bombers. I also have a little radio in my room and it's always playing whenever I'm there. Just ask Harold!"

Harold nods his head and grins.

"I love listening to baseball, basketball and football games, and the news every night," Clyde continues. "I heard last night that the Democratic National Convention will start in Chicago on August 13, and the Republican National Convention on August 20 in San Francisco. I can't wait to listen to all that.

Clyde pauses for a minute and then adds, "I plan to get a high school diploma some way some day. I'm not sure how to go about that, though."

Just then three or four people enter the store and walk to the order counter. They glance back at us and immediately turn around and exit. I give that little thought.

"That probably is enough about us. So, how about you, Kenny? How'd you get to here, today?" Clyde jokes.

I share my background of growing up on a little farm in the Flint Hills not far from Emporia. When I mention that we had no electricity, running water or indoor bathrooms, Clyde's and Harold's attention sharpens. Perhaps we have at least a little in common with backgrounds of hardship.

I ask both Clyde and Harold why they play the positions that they do on the baseball diamond. "I'm left-handed," Clyde answered. "And since I like to be in the action, first base is a natural position for me. I get to be involved in nearly every play on the field."

Harold, on the other hand, shares, "I like to be alone, and I like to be out there in center field where it's dark, just waiting to chase that ball."

"How about you, Kenny?" Clyde asks.

I share my walking to and from a little one-room country school and throwing rocks at fence posts along the way. "That seemed to help my arm a lot and when I got to high school, I had good luck throwing the javelin and pitching baseball. I also like third base since it takes a long throw to get the guy out and it's fun to fire it over there."

Another couple walks in the door, looks our way, and starts a conversation with the lady cashier. She gives us a look and a shoulder shrug. I am getting the message, I guess. The couple walks out.

Clyde suddenly lights up. "Harold and I have decided to join the Mount Olive church, and they say that the first step is to be baptized. Harold and I never were baptized so I guess we will do it tomorrow morning. Some of the girls we met a few weeks ago said that their mothers have volunteered to be our sponsors, and that they made all the arrangements. We need to be there a little before 11 o'clock. Heck, Kenny, would you like to come to the church to join us? We could sure use a little moral support." Clyde and Harold both give me a hopeful look.

I am surprised by the invitation, but after seeing a few snubs this afternoon, accept the invite. "Sure, I didn't plan on working tomorrow morning anyway and we have the afternoon to get ready for the drive to Gridley. Do you guys get dumped into a tank or do they just sprinkle a little water on you?"

Clyde and Harold both laugh nervously. "I don't know about that water tank deal," Harold says. "We never asked anybody about that."

"We're stuck in any case, Harold," Clyde smiles. "Let's just be happy to join such a fine church."

Nearly an hour passes while we sit in the booth, and I suggest it is time to head back home. Clyde and Harold both agree that evening chores await, and it's time to think about their baptism and the game in Gridley tomorrow. In the parking area in front of the ice cream store, Clyde hands me his free drink ticket. "I don't think I will try to cash this in. You take it if you want."

"Thanks, I sure will use it," I answer. I guess Clyde saw a problem, too.

Overall, it was a fun afternoon. Man, those guys have stories to tell. As an afterthought, I dwell a little too much on the strange behavior of the customers in the ice cream store. But, somehow, I look forward to another visit to Mount Olive tomorrow morning.

Chapter Eighteen

Gridley

After joining Mom, Dad, Willis, and Russell for a pancake breakfast in our kitchen, I check my uniform, glove and spikes for the Gridley trip this afternoon. With the Mount Olive church only a few minutes away, I time my arrival as the service begins. I find a seat on the very back pew and join in the introductory hymn.

As the congregation is seated, I note at the front of the sanctuary, Harold and Clyde sitting with two high school age girls, and two women who are likely the girls' mothers. They each have a serious look on their face and I note that Harold is not wearing his overalls today.

Midway through the service, the minister calls for the baptism party to file to the baptismal water basin. To my relief, I see that it is very small and will not fit a full immersion ceremony. I smile as I recall our conversation yesterday at the ice cream store. The ritual is brief, and the party turns to face the greeting of the entire congregation. Harold and Clyde are smiling broadly as are the four ladies accompanying them.

After the service, I wait in the front hall until I catch the attention of Clyde and Harold. They eagerly call me over and introduce me to the four women. Both young ladies are recent high school graduates, Sandra, from Emporia High School and the other, Maria, from Roosevelt High School. Their mothers are also introduced with smiling faces.

I quickly congratulate the party and remind Harold and Clyde that we have a game tonight in Gridley and I shall see them at the *Gazette* building later this afternoon. They wave good-bye and I drive back home. It is a warm feeling to see such happy faces and know that Possum's special effort has made a difference in the lives of two of the Bombers.

Since it is a Sunday afternoon, some of the Bombers arrive at the *Gazette* building a little early for the trip to Gridley. Kenny Young shows up with his usual uniform. Jesse and David have the same partial uniforms as they have worn for the last game or two, and I wear my freshly-washed *Ft. Douglas* uniform.

Two new uniforms catch me by surprise. Philip is wearing a full E-State uniform that I do not recognize. It must have been worn well before my time at E-State.

Then, Don Graham shows up in a Stony Ridge uniform. What a shock! I recognize it as a uniform worn by the Stony Ridge Mountain Boys when I was a kid on the farm.

My several Schroeder and Rathke uncles along with other neighbors at the time made up the team named after my little one-room school. Stony Ridge School is located on a flint ridge in the middle of the prairie some twenty miles southwest of Emporia. It is the highest hill around and is often lovingly called a "mountain" by those living in the area.

"Where in the world did you get that uniform?" I ask.

"One of the guys I work with said his mother had it stored in a cedar chest for years. He said if it fits, I can have it. Well, as you can see, it fits just fine. Check out the smell." He offers a shoulder sleeve.

"Cedar for sure," I say.

Just then, Clyde and Harold arrive. Harold steps out of the car and another surprise. He is wearing new Converse, 'Chuck Taylor,' basketball shoes. Now he will not have to play in his regular street shoes. The Bombers are looking more and more like a real baseball team. I assume Harold acquired the new shoes just this afternoon during a sale at Brown's Shoe Store on Commercial Street.

We jump into Philip's car and, soon, the smell of cedar fills the air. We are on our way south, down Highway-99 for the forty-mile trip to Gridley. A few miles out of town, Philip shares that he dropped in on the E-State athletic office a few days ago and asked if they had any old baseball uniforms. "The guy had me follow him to a storage room and opened an old locker. This uniform, with the number 5 on it, was stuffed in with other things and he said I could have it."

"Hey, Philip," Don calls out. "That was Joe DiMaggio's number. Lucky you."

Philip smiles. We are all pleased, once again, with Don's knowledge of big league baseball. We arrive in good time and "escape" the car from all four doors.

A sizeable crowd starts to gather even an hour before game time. Looks like a full house tonight. As I walk toward the visitor's dugout, someone shouts, "Herr Ohm, is that you?"

I am surprised to hear that word. Not since my last German class has anyone called me, "Herr."

I look around to a man, probably in his early sixties. I do not recognize him, but he extends his hand and says, "Hi, my name is Dieter Bauer. A friend of mine, Nevin Weber, from Lyndon called me last night, long distance, and told me about you."

I am baffled. "What about me?"

"He saw you last Tuesday when you played in Lyndon. We're wondering where you got that *Ft. Douglas* uniform."

"Oh, from an Army-Navy store in Emporia about two years ago." The next few minutes pass quickly as Dieter talks about his experience at Ft. Douglas.

"Right before World War One, Nevin and I were in the German Navy and we got detained in Guam and were finally shipped to Ft. Douglas in Utah. We were there as prisoners for the whole war and, since we did not have family to return to, we decided to stay inthe states.

"We each married an American woman and eventually moved to Kansas, bought little farms, and raised a bunch of kids."

"That explains a lot, thank you," I say. "I have been wondering about this uniform for some time."

"One more thing." Dieter continues. "We got to play baseball almost every day at Ft. Douglas. We joined the guards and a bunch of civilians on teams and had a good time. We really like baseball and it's fun to watch you young guys play. Good luck tonight."

We shake hands and I head for the dugout. This summer experience continues to take me in so many directions, I think.

We soon finish our pre-game field practice and gather with Possum for last minute instructions. Pitcher, Bob Smith, will be held out, if possible, for the Osage City game in two days in Emporia. Kenny Young will take the mound and is expected to go all the way. I will play third base and am surprised to be batting in the third spot.

Before our first two batters, Steve and Mike, leave the dugout to lead off the game, Possum raises his hand for quiet. "I am beginning to like the way you guys are looking with your uniforms. In fact, I just heard from a number of fans here tonight on how impressed they are with so many different uniforms. They think we must have played all over the country!"

We all chuckle with that, but I think it gives us a little boost, also.

The game is quite tense from the start. Steve and Mike get on base right away but are stranded as I pop up to third. Don hits a long fly-out to left field and Jesse grounds out to second base.

The bottom of the first inning starts out poorly. I find, once again, that I left my arrowhead at home. I picture it on the windowsill of our washroom.

The first batter hits a single to center field but is forced out at second when the next batter hits a hard grounder to Clyde Matson at first. Matson's throw is in time to get the runner at second, but the throwback to first is late. No double play. One out.

The next batter walks on four pitches. The Gridley cleanup hitter hits a long fly to center field and Harold gallops in his usual manner to collect it at the center field fence. Both runners advance. The next hitter strikes out, so we escape with no score tallied in the first inning.

For the third game in a row, we gather behind the pitcher's mound and, on Clyde's signal, throw our gloves in unison to the outfield grass. The crowd applauds with enthusiasm.

Balls are hit hard on both sides, and spectacular defensive plays dominate the action going into the seventh inning. Harold Turner makes a second over-the-shoulder catch in the outfield after gliding hundreds of feet to reach the ball. He also hit two very high drives to center field, both being caught at the fence.

The wind is blowing in hard from center field to the plate, likely keeping balls in play. The score is still tied 0 to 0, after seven intense innings.

In the top of the eighth inning, I manage a single to right field, once again trusting my warped walnut bat. Don Graham follows with a massive drive over the left-center field fence to finally give us a little cushion.

Peanuts follows with a single to left field but is left stranded as the next three batters loft short fly balls to the outfield for outs. We now lead 2 to 0.

It is the bottom of the eighth, and Possum and the rest of us are confident that Kenny can hold Gridley for the remainder of the game. It is not meant to happen. A walk, a hit batter and a double down the right field line ties the game at 2 to 2 before the side is retired.

We do not score in the top of the ninth, nor does Gridley in the bottom of the inning. We now go into our first extra inning game of the season.

The tenth, eleventh and twelfth innings end with no more scoring by either team. After two outs in the top of the thirteenth inning, Harold hits his first home run of the season. As he rounds third, Possum shakes his hand and we cheer him to the plate. We lead 3 to 2.

We now have our chance to win the game in the bottom of the thirteenth inning. Kenny is looking strong on the mound going all the way so far. We get two quick outs and victory is in sight.

As if by destiny, the wind changes direction and starts blowing straight out to right field.

The Gridley number nine batter is next up and swings late on a 2-2 count and connects for a long fly ball to right field. Don Graham catches sight as it leaves the bat and charges toward the line for the winning catch.

He leaps at the last second and the ball sails past his glove, just fair and over the fence to tie the game at 3 to 3. Our shoulders drop, but Possum continues to shout encouragement from the dugout.

Young is the first batter up in the top of the fourteenth and strokes a single. He still appears strong as he requests a warm-up jacket while at first base. Bob Smith is coaching at first base and helps him on with the jacket.

Philip is next up and chops a grounder to first base with the only play, a tag at first for the out. Young takes second with the go-ahead run.

Our number nine hitter, Clyde Matson nearly duplicates the Gridley hit in the bottom of the thirteenth, but the long fly ball is caught at the foul pole in right field. Young has plenty of time to tag up, touch second base, and run safely to third base.

We could not ask for a better set-up as our number one batter, Steve Jones, comes to the plate. He already has three hits so far tonight. On a 2-1 count, he connects for a fly ball deep to center field, but not strong enough to carry. The ball is easily caught for the final out. We now go into the bottom of the fourteenth.

Kenny Young returns for a few minutes to the dugout from third base and we all see his considerable fatigue. He takes a deep breath and, with the rest of us, trots out to the field. The first batter steps to the plate and is walked on four pitches.

Possum runs out of the dugout to the mound and has a short talk with Young. He smiles, pats Kenny on the back and returns to the dugout. Clyde and I both take a step back from our positions as we will be looking for a double play.

On the next pitch, the batter bunts the ball down the line towards me, and I see instantly that I can make no play. I let the ball roll, hoping that it will turn foul. It stops, fair on the line.

Runners are now on first and second for Gridley and no outs. Now, we are in serious trouble. Kenny manages to strike out the next batter.

The Gridley clean-up hitter is next up and hits a sharp single to right field. Graham retrieves the ball quickly and throws it for a strike to Philip at the plate, holding the runner at third. The bases are loaded. We still have hope.

Possum steps out of the dugout and waves the three outfielders in several yards since a deep fly ball will score the winning run and he is also trying to protect against a short single. However, the next batter hits a hard chopper high off the plate toward the mound and the third base runner scores before Kenny can make a play at home. We lose 4 to 3. The crowd roars.

We are devastated. Possum sits in the dugout with his hands over his face and his glasses on the bench alongside him. Many of us collapse along the bench. The crowd continues to shout in victory and none of us want to venture out yet to our cars and the drive home. I vow never again to forget my arrowhead.

No one speaks for several minutes. Then, Possum stands, shouts for Harold and Don to sit down and begins. "I'm not a quitter and neither are you," he says quietly. "We likely have lost our chance to play in the NBC series, but I tell you one thing, we won't lose another game this season. You guys have the talent to play with any team around, but you and I aren't playing very smart. That's going to change and we start tomorrow."

We look at each other. We all have a full day's work tomorrow and it's already past one o'clock in the morning. Possum continues, "I know it's tough, but we'll meet for practice at the usual time and we'll go over a few things and be ready to play Osage City on Tuesday. I am very proud of all of you. Drive safely back home."

We shuffle to the cars and head for home. Several guys doze off and there is almost no talking. When I get home at two o'clock, I throw my uniform on the washroom floor and spy my arrowhead laying on the windowsill. I cannot believe I must be ready for work in another three or four hours.

Chapter Nineteen

First Chance, Last Chance?

I cannot sleep. So, I get up early this morning to visit with Dad at the kitchen table. Mom has already left for work. I tell Dad about our heartbreaking loss and about our missing out on possible NBC play. "You don't know that for sure," Dad says. "Maybe if you win the rest of your games or some team backs out at the last minute, you might still get invited."

"Possum doesn't seem to think so. He told us to come to practice today and he will change a few things to make us play better. I guess we're all going to stick with playing out the schedule, but it sure doesn't seem like much fun," I mumble.

"You look really tired, Kenny," Dad says. "We need to finish the second bedroom flooring today and I think we can do that before noon. If you will help me with that, you can start the trim in the bedrooms after lunch. That should help a bit."

This is good news as laying hard wood floors is likely the

most physically demanding job in building a house. Dad certainly knows that and sees a chance to relieve me with a much easier assignment of trimming this afternoon. I feel a little better, have a bowl of cereal, gather my practice stuff, load my car and join Dad early on the job.

The work day goes well. I arrive at practice just when Bob Smith drives up. He waves at me. "I have been thinking, Kenny, that since we seem to always have trouble with those lousy pitching rubbers, we might change the way that we start our pitching motions."

"Where's all this coming from?" I ask.

"I just saw where one of the Yankee pitchers, Don Larsen, is doing really well lately since he started to pitch from the stretch on every batter," Bob replies.

"We could all do that, I suppose, but we'll lose some speed for sure. I know we use that form with men on base, but I never thought of not using a full windup when the bases are empty," I say.

"They asked Larsen about that and he said his control is better and he doesn't have to fight the rubber anymore. He just places the side of his right foot tightly against the rubber and pitches from there." Bob is getting excited about giving it a try, and I join him on the field.

As we warm up with short tosses, I think more and more about this idea. I recall on almost all pitching mounds of the teams we have played, the pitching rubber is unstable. Although two long spikes are driven through them and into the ground, they are often worked free after just a few pitches.

On top of that, a hole, some four to five inches deep, is often worn next to the rubber. Controlling our pitches is made so much more difficult when trying to compensate for these conditions. This problem has always been accepted by pitchers on both sides, I guess. Why not give this idea a try?

As Bob and I work with each other trying to simulate this new pitching form, Possum walks up with a look of question on his face. "What are you guys doing? You don't always have runners on base, you know."

Bob tries to explain his understanding of this guy, Larsen, of the Yankees.

"I never heard of him," Possum says. "But if you guys get batters out a little better, then do it."

Bob and I decide we are going to practice our pitching tonight, using the stretch position for every pitch. After several trials, we find that our control is, indeed, better. With Osage City tomorrow, we agree that we might try this new approach whether men are on base or not.

Possum calls us in as regular field practice ends. He is carrying a paper sack and waits until we are all settled in a circle on the ground. He opens the sack and pulls out a folded uniform top. He shakes it free and it shows a very official looking name, *Monarchs*, across the front. He casually says a friend gave it to him today and he is going to wear it the rest of the season. He puts the jersey on and it fits well.

"This uniform is just like the ones used by the Kansas City Black Monarchs and is going to be the key to our using hand-signs from now on. I will rub my hand across the *Monarchs* letters with either hand if I want you to follow my signs on what comes next. If I don't rub across, ignore whatever sign I give you. Understand?"

We each nod.

Possum then spends the next several minutes re-visiting the idea of using hand signs for certain plays during all up-coming games. As on his first try a few weeks ago, touching his chin, nose and ears in a certain order determines a steal, bunt, or take.

These will only be working signals if Possum first sweeps his hand across the letters. This added detail seems to make us more attentive to the effort this time. We agree that things need a little shaking up and this might do it.

"One other thing," Possum adds. "I noticed that you guys who are next to bat have all been doing the same thing when retrieving the bat after our batter hits the ball. It looks very clumsy when you stoop down, grab it and then take it back to the dugout—all the while trying to get to the box as the next hitter. So, from now on, the batter in the hole will be the one to get the bat and return it to the dugout. Make sense?"

We give that a thought for a few minutes and, once again, agree that this sounds like another great idea that Possum invented. Now, when our turn comes to bat, we can concentrate on hitting the ball, not chasing down a rolling bat.

As we walk to our cars, Mike joins Rosa at her car and they drive off together.

We finally get home well after dark.

For me, the next work day is about as good as it can get. Dad is working on installing the over-head garage door on Frank Love's house and I continue to work out of the wind and sun, trimming woodwork in the three bedrooms. This job requires lots of measuring and cutting, but little physical exertion.

Most of the Bombers arrive early for our home game tonight. The weather has cooled somewhat, and the word is out that a very large crowd is expected. We get our infield practice in with me to start at third base and Smith to start on the mound. Kenny Young is sitting in the dugout, still looking exhausted from his fourteen-inning stint in Gridley, and his full day's work today at a construction site south of town.

The Osage City team is taking infield practice when Possum approaches me with a look of concern. "Kenny, bad news. It seems that Bob has some sort of stomach problem and says he cannot pitch tonight. So, you are going to have to take the mound for us."

"Where is Bob? He was OK last night," I say.

"He's sitting in his car right now and says he was late getting off work and decided to eat a can of sardines for supper on his way here. Apparently, they made him sick," Possum says.

I had warmed up well with infield practice so must now adjust my focus to pitching. I pat the arrowhead in my back pocket for luck. I find Philip and we talk over our signals for today. We decide on very easy calls with one finger a fast ball, two fingers a curve, three fingers a change-up, and four a knuckle ball. I tell him to go easy on the knuckler as the last one I threw went high over the fence for a homerun.

"Are you sure you are ready for this?" Philip asks, with a smile.

"Sure, no problem. I know that this is my first start for the Bombers, but I made a few starts for the Hornets, and we will never forget the Aces game. I feel good about it."

The crowd seems extra boisterous today for some reason. Perhaps they know it is now or never for the Bombers to get a chance at the NBC series. We take the field and I walk to the mound.

"OK, all-black Brown Bombers, let's win this one," I hear shouted by someone in the stands. I wonder if he recognizes me or it is just a casual yell. I cannot think about anything else as I take my four warm-up pitches. The first batter for Osage City is at the plate.

I take my regular full windup and walk him on four pitches. Philip takes a couple of steps in front of the plate and snaps the ball to me. He is not smiling.

The next batter hits a single to center field. We now have opposing runners on first and second base. Batter number three flies out to shallow center field with the runners holding. I walk their clean-up hitter and the bases are loaded.

Batter number five hits a single to right field, scoring two. I walk the next batter. A line drive is then hit to Clyde who dives to the ground and makes a spectacular catch at first base. We have two outs.

On a 3-2 count, the final batter of the inning hits a long drive deep to center field. Harold takes off at the crack of the bat and catches it while running at full speed to the fence. Two beautiful defensive plays in a row! Side retired. We trail, 2-0.

I drop my glove behind the pitcher's mound as usual as the seven fielders gather there and, on Clyde's signal, spin their gloves to the outfield. The crowd applauds.

I enter the dugout and Possum greets me with a frown. "Young is not feeling well either and said he cannot pitch tonight. Bob just left his car and is throwing up in the trees out there. So, Kenny, you are it for the whole night."

Possum takes his usual third base coaching position as I try to figure out how to regain some control of my pitching. Suddenly, I recall Bob and me working on the stretch and decide to give it a try. My control has been terrible tonight, anyway.

We go down one-two-three, and I return to the mound. I take my warm-ups from the stretch and it feels pretty good. "Hey,

Ohm, nobody's on base, why the stretch?" The same guy yells. I do not normally hear fans from the stands, but this guy is coming through. I take the ball from Philip and face the Osage City number nine hitter.

I throw each of my three different pitches from the stretch and strike him out. The next batter pops up to third on the first pitch. The second does the same to first base. I only throw five pitches, all for strikes, and get three outs. Maybe I am on to something!

We are in the bottom of the seventh inning and, so far, no more scoring by either team. I have only walked one batter since the first inning. On the first pitch, Harold Turner knocks the ball deep over the center field wall. Score now, Osage City, 2, Bombers, 1.

Graham flies out, Carter grounds out to second and Philip singles to center. Peanuts also singles, to right field, with Philip holding at second. I am the number nine batter and hit a hard line-drive to the right fielder for out number three.

"Hey, Brown Bomber Ohm, you gotta hit 'em where they ain't," the guy is back again and shouts. He is not my worry. Steve runs by on our way from the dugout and winks at me.

Neither team scores in the eighth inning as Jones, Garcia and Matson go out for the Bombers.

Still pitching from the stretch to every batter, I retire the first two on fly-outs in the top of the ninth. Philip signals a knuckle ball on the first pitch to the third batter of the inning. It dances nicely and the batter swings and misses.

Philip again calls for the knuckler and the batter takes a called strike. Surprisingly, Philip calls for the same pitch a third time. It flutters in and drops a couple of feet as the batter swings and misses badly. I must remember this pitch! We enter the bottom of the ninth inning, score still 2 to 1, in favor of Osage City.

Harold Turner takes a 3-2 count for a long ride, once again over the center field wall, tying the score at 2. We are all relieved but hopeful that we might end the game right now.

Don Graham follows with a deep drive to right field, but it's caught at the wall for out-number one. David Carter hits one to nearly the same spot for out-number two. Philip is walked and is followed by Peanuts hitting a single to right field. Philip scrambles to third.

I am the next batter. I look down to Possum as we have done all evening and I see a confusing signal. He rubs his hand across his letters, then gives me both the bunt and the steal sign.

He steps toward Philip at third and speaks quietly to him. I must have missed something. I step out of the box and look again down the line to Possum. I see the same sign.

I have never bunted during a game before and recall that I must keep the barrel low on my walnut bat. I take my normal batting stance. The pitcher stretches and pitches a low ball and, as I turn to bunt, Philip takes off toward home.

I bunt it fair down the first base line. The Osage City pitcher, catcher and first baseman all converge on the rolling ball as I run past them safely to first base. No one is covering first to take the throw. This is the classic squeeze play as Philip scores the winning run, and I am credited with a hit and a run-batted-in. I wonder how often a squeeze play is called with two outs. We win, 3 to 2. Possum is a genius for sure! The home crowd is cheering loudly.

"Hey, Kenny. Nice game." Steve joins me on the walk to our cars. "I wrote down the 'Hit 'em where they ain't' that guy shouted to you. I think it's a funny line for my jeers list."

I'm not sure what a jeers list is. "Sounds like a good idea," I answer.

Don is walking behind us and calls out, "I just heard you talking about that guy shouting at you, Kenny. Do you know where all that came from?"

"No, that's the first time I heard it," I reply.

"Clear back in the early 1900s, a short major league player named, Wee Willie Keeler was tearing up the league with his batting. He was asked what his secret was, and he said, 'Hit 'um where they ain't,' and it got in all the newspapers and has been around ever since. That's your history lesson for today!"

"Hey, thanks," both Steve and I say at about the same time.

Don once again shows his broad knowledge of baseball history and we love it.

It has been a great evening and a terrific game. It is my first complete game win of the season. I am delighted. Now if only the NBC committee hears about this game. There may still be hope.

I start my drive on the way out of the park when I see Clyde's car still parked on the far side of the roadway near the park entrance. Two people are sitting on the fenders and two are leaning against the car. Clyde notices me and waves me over.

I see Harold and the same two girls who assisted during their baptism last Sunday morning. They must have been watching our game from the car. I park nearby and get out of my car. Clyde leads me to the group and shyly introduces me to the two girls as Harold looks on.

"Kenny, you remember Sandra and Maria from last Sunday? They are going to help us with Bible study so that we can join Mount Olive before long."

I nod in recognition and manage to answer, "I sure do. These guys are lucky to meet you ladies. You all looked really good up there by the altar."

After a slight pause, I add, "You two Bombers saved me on the pitching mound today. Harold, you with a couple great catches and a couple of home runs and Clyde, I never saw a better catch at first base to save a run or two and probably the game."

They both smile and glance at the young girls, who are also smiling broadly.

Clyde and Harold both mumble something about my good pitching, but I see their minds are now far from the game.

I drive home with a feeling that the summer will end well.

Chapter Twenty

Home Field Advantage

This is the week when we find out if we have the stuff of a great team. The Gridley town team will arrive Saturday for a return match after our most difficult loss of the season. Possum gave us off today, Wednesday, August 1. I awaken much earlier than usual. I feel that things are not quite right as I walk into the kitchen and see only Dad at the table.

"Did Mom already go to work?" I ask.

"No, she's still in the bedroom. She says she's too dizzy to get up," Dad claims. "She doesn't want me to call the doctor just yet."

I walk quickly to the bedroom and find Mom half-awake, but unable to focus. She mumbles something about feeling just fine, but she needs a few more minutes to wake up. I sit down on a nearby chair and try to make conversation. Finally, after several minutes, she seems to improve.

"I'll get up now and better get ready to go to work. I'm already two hours late," she says.

"Not today, Mom. I'll call the hospital and tell them you will be in tomorrow but are not feeling well today. I'll talk to Dad about me staying home from work for at least this morning, and we can just take a little vacation," I say.

She agrees, and I check with Dad. He says, "Fine," on my request for time off.

I call Dr. Davis' office and he tells me, "Wait for a few hours to see if she gets better. If not, give me a call back."

By noon, Mom is much better and decides to go to work for the afternoon, leaving before one o'clock. I drive to Dad's building site for work. I tell Dad that Mom is back at work and he is much relieved.

For good reason, my mind is not on baseball this afternoon, but on the future of my parents, my sister and me. I let my mind wander to the possibilities ahead for all of us. Mom is only thirty-nine years old and Dad forty-nine. They have a long life ahead, it would seem, but seeing Mom in such a dependent state this morning was quite a shock.

The afternoon goes by slowly as I continue my work assignment finishing the trim in the living room and bathroom. Finally, near quitting time, I relax a bit, realizing that I have only a month left before classes start and baseball begins at E-State.

If the Bombers make the NBC World Series, summer's end might be a good one and I will be ready for a new challenge. Dad and I stop by a little beer parlor on south Commercial Street where he buys a ten-cent glass of the "special-on-tap" and I have a Coke. His spirits lift as we visit and then head home to greet Mom, who is feeling much better.

As we arrive home, I find myself exhausted, but so happy that Possum has called off practice. Mom says she saw Doc Davis in the hospital and he suggested that he doesn't know exactly what the problem was, but nothing to worry about since she recovered so quickly. Good news all around.

Thursday's work load continues, followed by practice again at six o'clock. Possum arrives wearing his *Monarchs* uniform top. "We are a team now, guys. When we work together, we can see good things happen. Tonight, we're going to spend more time on signals, expanding a little from last time. I'm adding hit and run plays to our list and we will review the others as well."

Several minutes pass as Possum drills us on each signal and tells us to take a stance at home plate so he can see how we check for his signs. He also explains ways we can guard against the opposing team stealing our signs and using them against us.

He even insists that we pitchers along with Philip, at catcher, change our pitch signs when an opposing team member is on second base. He claims that in an instant a man on second base can relay a sign to the batter who can get an idea of the next pitch. After another hour, Possum calls an end to practice and we all head to our cars.

"Hey, Mike, where was Rosa tonight?" someone shouts.

"Had to work late, but said she will make it tomorrow," Mike replies as he rides his bicycle toward home.

The next day's work and practice go smoothly. We are pleased as a team to see Rosa once more observing practice. Some of the Bombers attempt a slight wave and nod toward her. She smiles at them.

Practice is mostly a reminder from Possum that we are to

play Gridley using our "good talents and determination to stay on the winning track." The Bombers have never been more serious and focused. I predict that tomorrow at Soden's Grove we will not be defeated.

As we are about to end practice, an old, gold-colored Buick drives up along Congress Street, and parks behind Rosa's '48 Chevy. Although trying to concentrate on Possum announcing the line-up for the Gridley game, the Bombers without exception watch as two young ladies exit the car.

We recognize Sandra and Maria and they step over and introduce themselves to Rosa. All three girls show some animation as they look toward the Bombers huddled around Possum.

Possum pauses for a minute while regaining our attention. He announces that the line-up will be the same as for Osage City, except I will play third instead of David, and bat sixth, and Young will start as pitcher and bat ninth. David Carter will coach at first base with Possum coaching at third. Bob Smith will be held out, if possible, to pitch against Melvern next Tuesday evening at Soden's Grove.

It is likely that only a few of us gathered Possum's full message, as our divided attention is on the three lovely ladies some fifty yards away. We are dismissed and, as a group, walk to our cars, mostly also parked along Congress Street.

I hear a few fragments of conversations.

"Do you think that they will come to the game tomorrow night…"

"Naw, still too likely for trouble. And besides, we got to concentrate and win this one."

"Hey Clyde, where are you guys going tonight?" Lots of quiet laughter surrounds us. Clyde smiles and waves as he joins Harold and Mike walking toward the Chevy and the Buick.

Home Field Advantage

Saturday arrives as does the Gridley team. "Hold That Tiger," plays over the loud speaker and our infield practice is straight forward. Clyde calls us into the dugout with an idea to streamline our glove throw. He asks us to flatten our gloves to better form a disc and instructs us to throw sidearm while holding the glove by the thumb. We are eager to give it a try.

The game starts with an easy one-two-three out for Gridley. We rush behind the mound and, with the "fire" signal from Clyde, hurl our gloves to the outfield. It is a stunning sight as the gloves sail in a broad arc across the sky. The crowd cheers as we run smiling to the dugout.

Steve Jones starts off the bottom of the first inning with a solid single to left field. Then, we get the first inkling that Possum is going after the lead early.

He calls for a hit and run from batter, Mike Garcia, on the first pitch. Steve runs on the pitch and Mike singles on the ground where the second baseman normally plays. Steve advances to third. We on the bench cheer loudly.

We decide to call it a run and hit, since the runner takes off on the pitch even before the ball gets to the plate. Clyde Matson flies out to shallow left field with the runners holding.

Harold Turner comes to the plate with a look like what I recall at the Peter Pan Park diamond when he hit off Laverne Miltz. On the first pitch, he strokes a high drive deep over the center field fence giving us a 3 to 0 lead. This is the beginning, I think, of a convincing win for the Bombers.

We, indeed, dominate the game, winning 14 to 2. Turner hits three homeruns and Graham hits one homerun. Steve Jones goes five for five at the plate, and every Bomber gets at least one hit. I hit two doubles to right-center field and two singles to right field, getting four hits in five at-bats. Young pitches an excellent game and Possum successfully uses every sign he invented. We look like a truly fine and competitive team tonight.

Possum holds us briefly in the dugout after the game. Still very much in game form, he tells us to rest easy tomorrow and come to a short practice on Monday, "usual time and place." I notice very little chatter about the win or any mention of revenge for the heart-breaking defeat at Gridley last week. We are evidently not looking back, but at a single goal ahead—The NBC World Series.

Chapter Twenty-One

Steve

Steve Jones is a steady second baseman for the Bombers. He makes few errors and is a reliable lead-off man, getting on base as often as any member of the team. He shows a little temper now and then, both with his teammates and with opposing players.

I notice when Possum spends considerable time on drills and instruction, Steve becomes quite impatient. He wants to be on the field working on his defense or swinging a bat.

About the only unusual thing I have noticed is that he loves to collect comments or jeers from the crowd during our games. He mentioned once that he writes them down and has a bunch of them written on a tablet at home. I have no idea how he can hear specific crowd noises while concentrating on the game, but he is an excellent second baseman, so apparently has no problem with it.

After our day off yesterday, we arrive at practice with Rosa, Sandra, and Maria watching from across the field in what is becoming a regular and welcome routine. The Bombers are looking a little more rested than usual.

That is, except for Steve. He is late for perhaps the first time this season. He is slow to join the rest of us in warming up and when he does, he snaps the ball back to his warm-up partner. He is obviously angry at something. Others notice the problem and, finally, our elected team captain, Don Graham, approaches him and calls him aside.

They walk slowly several yards away from the practice field. The rest of us start a base running drill, with Possum instructing us on the art of taking a safe lead from the base. David Carter and I are at the end of the line waiting our turn to run.

"Do you know what's going on with Steve?" I ask.

"I only know that Steve's Dad died a few years ago and his mother is not well. Since he's the oldest of several kids, he's supporting the family with his job at the greenhouse. That's all I know," David said.

Don and Steve walk back and meet Possum for a few minutes. They join us for the next hour as we continue working on infield playing situations and on reviewing hand signs. Finally, Possum calls an end to practice and asks us to gather around for a few minutes.

He starts out, "I want to share a few things with you about our friend, Steve, here. It seems that his little three-year old sister, Ida, is in the hospital with some kind of problem, and it looks like Steve might need to be with her tomorrow. Some of you may remember meeting Ida at church a few weeks ago."

Tomorrow is game day, of course, but I see sympathy on the faces around me.

"If he cannot make it to the game, we will start David at second and hold out Young for relief if Bob gets in trouble on the mound," Possum continues. "Let's give Steve our blessing and hope things work out well. See you all then tomorrow."

When I get home, I find Mom resting in her bed, but still awake. As the Director of Housekeeping at the hospital, she works very long hours each day.

"Mom, did you happen to see a little girl in the hospital today? She is about three years old."

"Oh, yes, Kenny. The cutest little tyke you ever saw. I was up on her floor with the 'Loving Arms' ladies and I got to cuddle with her for a few minutes."

Mom continues with a really big smile, "You should have seen all those little old ladies lining up to comfort little Ida. We all belong to the 'Loving Arms' club just to get a chance like this, but some complain that there aren't enough babies to go around. Anyway, I think she will be OK with just a bad cold."

"I'm going to drive to the hospital and see if Steve is there or not. I might be able to help out a little," I say.

I sit there for a few minutes while Mom falls asleep.

I know the hospital well and head up to the third floor. I ask the nurse for the room number and, as I am about to walk in, out walks Steve. "Hey, Steve, how's it going?"

"Oh, hi, Kenny. Pretty good right now, I guess. They say they're going to keep Ida overnight and maybe release her tomorrow. What the heck are you doing here?"

"My Mom works here at the hospital and is also in charge of the volunteer 'Loving Arms' ladies. She mentioned that she met your little sister this afternoon and that she seems to be getting better," I reply.

"I was heading down to the cafeteria for a bite. Looks like Ida is sleeping now. Want to come along?" Steve asks.

"Sure, I haven't had supper either."

We go through the cafeteria line and find a table near the south windows. Steve seems more relaxed than at practice and with good reason, I think. "You know, Steve, I'm sure we'll be in good shape tomorrow with Melvern. I heard that the Aces beat them a few days ago."

We both work through our pork tenderloins with few words. Finally, I ask, "How are you going to get Ida home tomorrow? Do you have to work all day, or can you get some time off?"

"My boss, Wes, at the greenhouse has been really nice to me and, by the way, loves baseball. He said that either I can take off some time to drive Ida home or he and his wife would be glad to do it. Problem is that I don't think Mom will go for that at all. She's a little too proud for her own good."

"I know that feeling, for sure. My mom's the same way."

"When Dad died a year or so ago, Mom sort of lost it for a while. We had just moved into our house after living with my aunt for a couple of years. I attended Roosevelt High School but didn't finish when Dad got sick and couldn't work. He was working for the same greenhouse where I am now," Steve slowly speaks.

After a short pause, Steve continues, "Before my mom got married, she was a wonderful jazz pianist. She actually played at a club at Eighteenth and Vine in Kansas City. Have you ever heard of that area, Kenny?"

"No, I only know about the Kansas City Athletics Park on Brooklyn Street. I always remember that since the Brooklyn Dodgers were one of my favorite teams and now the A's are on that street." I am a little embarrassed by these ramblings.

"Anyway," Steve continues, "Mom taught me to play the piano a little before Dad died and I really liked it. But, things changed after that."

"So, how many brothers and sisters do you have?" I ask.

"I have two brothers and two sisters, and I'm the oldest. Ida's the youngest. I think we can make it OK if I don't miss any work. Dad at least had a car and it runs well.

"My main worry is to make sure my brothers and sisters get to school and do well once they are there. At least we have integrated schools here in Emporia. I have a friend who lives in Topeka, and he said with the recent Brown versus the Board of Education law that things are looking up for his kids to enroll in a regular public school instead of their segregated school. Even so, I think our integrated schools here in Emporia can do a whole lot better for the black and Mexican kids."

I see an unusual sadness in Steve. I search my mind for an answer.

"I know when I was in high school there were several times when I saw unfair treatment of you guys. One time right after James Cole broke his arm, he was yelled at by the teacher because he was not writing out his assignment.

It turned out that he'd broken the arm of his writing hand and couldn't write. That didn't seem to make a difference as the teacher kept after him for a few more days.

Then James dropped out and I never saw him again. I guess prejudice is everywhere and it's going to take years to get over it."

Steve looks at me, shakes his head and smiles softly.

I have no further advice for Steve, so try to change the subject. "Why don't you plan on taking the day off baseball tomorrow and get Ida home and get things back together?" I suggest.

Wrong idea.

"I'll not be missing that game, for sure," Steve nearly shouts as a few of the folks in the cafeteria look our way.

I pause for a minute. "You know, Steve, I wouldn't either. What a stupid thing for me to say. We either play this game or we don't."

Steve smiles a little and whispers, "I'm not sure other people feel this way."

We both glance around the cafeteria but see no one looking back at us.

Steve asks me to check with Possum at the barber shop tomorrow during my lunch hour, and tell him that he'll be at the game tomorrow unless a major emergency happens along the way.

I agree and Steve heads back upstairs while I drive home.

Most of us arrive at Soden's Grove about an hour early as usual. Steve does not show up as we get closer to game time. Our infield practice has Matson at first, David at second, Mike at shortstop, me at third, and Philip catching. Bob Smith will start on the mound with Kenny Young on the bench and coaching at first base.

We start the game without Steve and, after a scoreless top of the first, once again dazzle the crowd with our 'flying saucer' throw. We surge to a 3 to 0 lead by the end of the third inning, with David Carter as the star hitting his first home run since his grand slam in Madison.

As we enter the bottom of the fifth inning with the score still 3 to 0, Steve shows up in the dugout. He has his glove in his hand but shows no anxiety whatsoever.

"Hi, guys," he calls out. "Just wanted to make sure you were doing what you're supposed to. Nice to see the lead." He looks up to the scoreboard.

We are happy to see him, but not ready for what comes next. "I'm going to watch the game from the bench," he says, smiling. "Looks like you are doing just fine."

Possum nods his head and seems to somehow take this as a very positive sign. "Let's go get em," he says. "Three runs aren't nearly enough."

We end up scoring seven more runs as David Carter hits his second home run, and Bob shuts Melvern down with only three hits and no runs—a beautiful shutout.

During our times in the dugout, Steve's teammates show concern and they approach him with pretty much the same question, "How is Ida doing?"

We find out that she is at home and doing very well. "Mom is taking good care of her."

With a 10 to 0 victory behind us, we have four days before traveling to Reading next Sunday. Possum gives us tomorrow off, but practice will be as usual on Thursday and Friday for sure and maybe Saturday as well. In any case, all is well today with the Bombers.

Chapter Twenty-Two

Reading

Practice begins this Thursday evening when Possum tells us he found an old box of baseballs in a second-hand store on east Sixth Avenue. He says he bought them for a dollar, and when he got back to the barber shop today, Fritz Brown wanted to buy them for the team. "No argument, there," Possum says.

Once again, Rosa, Sandra, and Maria watch practice from their usual positions near their cars. They seem in constant conversation, but with occasional and welcome glances our way as we work on the practice field. Their nearness seems to give the Bombers a more dedicated, yet relaxed approach to the practice at hand.

We start our warm up as Possum calls for Don to join him for a few minutes. They walk to the side of the practice field and huddle together in conversation. I see Don nod his head and return to our group to continue the warm up.

After a few minutes, Don walks toward Harold, and they are soon standing back to back, as they make quiet conversation. An unusual sight, for sure.

Over the next several minutes, Don duplicates this action with Clyde and Bob, all the while acting in a casual and off-hand manner. Since Don is our captain, none of us question him.

Possum suddenly shouts, "Time for a little hitting practice!"

This surprises us as it will be a different activity from our usual practice sessions in the past. With no extra baseballs, we have had very limited opportunity to face a pitcher during practice, but now we have a new luxury!

The softball field at the far end of our practice site has a nice backstop, so since no one else is on the field, we trot over there with a few bats and about six old baseballs from Possum's box. Possum offers to throw batting practice for us.

We take our hitting positions very close to the back stop so that we don't need a catcher. The last thing we want to do is to get Philip hurt or worn out. He is the only catcher we have used all season.

This arrangement works well as Possum has a nice easy delivery and throws several medium-speed pitches to each of us. This is great fun. We spend the next hour shagging grounders and fly balls from the bat of each player as they take their turn at the backstop. We all agree that our hitting will improve with a little more practice like this.

Friday evening practice starts out the same way as yesterday with enthusiastic batting practice. However, after a half hour or so, cars start to arrive, and we soon find that games are scheduled for the softball site this evening as well as for all day tomorrow.

Reading

We hear a few, "Get off the field. Don't you guys know this is for softball?"

"You guys don't even belong here."

We hear that kind of stuff all the time; no Bomber reacts one way or the other. We simply move to our regular unused section of the field, review Possum's hand signs, and then take a serious look at our game plan for Sunday afternoon in Reading.

"The weather man says it will be way over one-hundred degrees tomorrow and Sunday, so I'm thinking that we shouldn't have practice tomorrow," says Possum. "Maybe we can all get some rest and be ready to go then on Sunday." None of us argue.

As Possum is about to call the end of practice for today, Kenny Young calls out, "I'm wondering why we always meet at the *Gazette* building before our trips out of town. I live way south, and it would be easier for me, at least, to meet at our practice field here at Peter Pan Park. I bet there are other guys who feel the same way."

Possum looks a bit weary as he asks us to sit down around him. He slowly begins to answer, "With a bunch of black guys with their cars, bikes, and other stuff all waiting for a ride out of town to our next game, I chose the *Gazette* building as the safest place to be while we're waiting.

"You guys may not know this, but the original editor of the *Gazette*, William Allen White, was the guy who kicked the Ku Klux Klan out of Kansas in the early 1920s. He also hired me to work as a paper carrier when I was only fifteen years old, and I've been working for the White family, off and on, for all these years.

"I'll tell you one thing. No one is going to mess with us when we're near the *Gazette* building. So, that is why we meet here!" Kenny Young nods with understanding, as do others.

"Any other questions?" None of us move. Possum waves us off for our trip home. "Now get some rest," he calls out.

The Bombers seem to drift off, quietly subdued in their thoughts as they have once again been reminded of their position within society. I hear no conversation as I get to my car.

I drive home wondering if Possum anticipated this moment and used it to reinforce the dedication and resolve of his team. So, likely, Possum continues a well-thought-out plan for about everything the Bombers do. I am thankful for that and happy to be a Bomber.

I work with Dad on Saturday as Frank Love's house is progressing well. I spend most of the morning installing locks on the bathroom door, the door to the garage, and the back-screen door. In the afternoon, I work on building shelves for each of the three-bedroom closets.

Dad is getting anxious to complete this job and to finally settle with Frank. He is also considering buying a building lot on Logan Avenue. He suggests that we have just enough time to get a new house closed in before winter. It looks like I will have a job through Christmas at least.

As Possum predicted, Sunday is a scorcher. The temperature is about 105 degrees according to the bank thermometer as we gather at the *Gazette* building for our trip to Reading.

Around noon, we take off down Highway-50 east for the thirty-mile drive. Our car windows are wide open, but the heat is incredible. No conversation is attempted as we reach our destination.

The Reading diamond is located on the far eastern side of Reading in an open field with no nearby trees. Philip drives into the parking lot a few minutes ahead of our second car. We pile out and start to walk to the diamond.

What a strange sight! We do not see a single person anywhere. The area is absolutely desolated. A slight hot breeze carries a dust cloud across the sandy infield: otherwise, no movement at all.

"Something's not right here," I say, to no one's surprise.

We join players from the second car as Possum drives up, alone as usual in the third car. He exits his car, and we expect some kind of explanation. He looks as mystified as we are.

"Where is everybody?" Steve shouts.

With no opposing team and no fans at the ball field only a half-hour before game time, a mix-up is evident. Possum hesitates for a minute or two before he commands, "You guys stay here. I'll find out what's going on." This command does not go over well. The heat is suffocating and the surroundings so dismal that we wonder what we are doing here on this Sunday afternoon.

Soon, Possum returns with a fire we do not often see. "They said they postponed the game until this evening at eight o'clock because of the weather. They said they sent a postcard to me a few days ago. I didn't get it."

Possum continues, "I'm not sure what we should do. The manager said there'll be a lot of people here tonight, so he should be able to pay us maybe 20 dollars or so to play the game. I think the real problem, though, is if we don't play, then we must forfeit. The NBC guys would probably find that out."

It takes a few minutes to soak in, but we look at each other and know that we have little choice. If it were not so darn hot! "Why don't we just stay around here until game time?" someone asks.

"Where do we stay?" Jesse shouts. "No one wants the bunch of us Brown Bombers roaming around this town. They probably won't wait till sundown to enforce their stupid sundown laws!"

"We're better off just driving back home and finding a cool place to take a nap and then drive back here for game time. Let's do that," Possum says.

With considerable grumbling, we start our travel back home. Just as we leave the parking lot, two cars from Emporia arrive. We recognize Mr. Hodges as the driver of one car and Mr. Griffitts, the other. Several additional passengers occupy both cars. "What's going on?" shouts Hodges from his open car window.

"We have to play tonight instead of this afternoon," Philip answers with disgust. "We had some kind of mix-up on the schedule."

Mr. Hodges and Mr. Griffitts confer for a few minutes, deciding to return to Emporia.

"Thanks for driving out here," Philip shouts toward the two cars. "Maybe we'll see you all this evening."

No response.

After our arrival back in Emporia, most of us settle at Peter Pan Park, scattering to different picnic areas under shade trees. We find no cooling anywhere. I find a spot under the grape arbor and stretch out on a picnic table. With temperatures like this, no other park visitors are here. We seem to be as alone as we were in Reading.

David Carter shows up at our six o'clock departing time and tells us he is not going to make the trip. He feels terrible. We tell him to get home and take care of himself. Bob says he does not feel well, either, but will drive with the team to Reading.

The ten of us, and Possum, travel a second time along Highway-50. There is little talk among the Bombers. We arrive, have a gentle warm up and skip infield practice. Our plan is clear. Hit the ball hard, win the game, and go home.

A large crowd gathers and several offer Steve more addenda for his 'Jeers List.' We are surprised to see not only Mr. Hodges and Mr. Griffitts returning, with their cars full of people, but several other fans from Emporia, as well. Philip and I spot Mr. Rose with four or five of his friends.

"Remember, Kenny, he was our coach at Peter Pan Park years ago," Philip says with a smile.

I nod and smile back. "I don't remember seeing fans from Emporia in any of our previous out-of-town games, do you?"

Philip shakes his head.

Overall, the crowd seems good-natured. I feel, somehow, the word is out, and they are rooting for us in anticipation of a possible invitation to the NBC World Series in Wichita.

We have scored twenty-four runs in the previous two games, and we are determined to add significantly to that total in this one. Kenny Young starts on the mound and allows one run in the bottom of the first inning, after which we hurl our gloves to the outfield. The crowd responds with cheers.

Kenny pitches well for seven innings, allowing only the one run. We score at least one run in each inning. Suddenly, the air cools and a large black cloud comes up from the west.

Within minutes this surprising change in weather produces large drops of rain as the crowd scatters to their cars. We gather up our equipment and run for our cars as well. It seems obvious that this game will be called with us leading, 10 to 1.

As we look out over the field from our car windows, we see three or four light bulbs at the top of the light poles explode with bright flashes. This likely is caused by rain falling on hot, lighted bulbs.

This unsettled weather pattern adds to the already very strange day. But, as quickly as the storm arrived, it passes to the east. Precipitation amounts to just enough to wet the grass in the outfield but has little effect on the sandy infield.

Possum and the Reading manager confer for a few minutes and decide to finish the game. A small number of fans remain and return to the stands with newspapers and rags to dry off the seating. It seems to me that they do not want the evening to end just yet.

Possum approaches me as we enter the top of the eighth inning. "Kenny, I am going to let Young go back out there for the bottom of this inning, but I want you to be ready to pitch if he gets into any kind of trouble. No use taking chances with such a good lead. I want you to go play in right-field, and we will have Don take over for you at third."

That seems a little strange to me. It will be my first experience playing in the outfield this season. We score three more runs and go into the bottom of the eighth inning now leading 13 to 1. I trot the three-hundred feet to near the right field fence and look back toward the infield. What a ghostly apparition.

The baseball field has only three light poles, one placed behind home and the other two along each foul line behind first and third bases.

On a good night, very little light is cast to the outfield, but now, with the loss of several light bulbs, it is eerily dark. Thousands of moths swarm around what is left of the lights at the top of the poles.

It is like I am standing apart from the rest of the world, viewing action at a great distance. A sea of tiny lights peppers the crowd from the cigarette and cigar smokers still in the stands.

I am barely situated in my right-field position, swatting a mosquito, when Kenny Young's first pitch is hit in my direction. It lands to my right and begins a roll toward the fence. I do not make a good angle and find myself chasing the ball as it screams past me.

It forms a startling "rooster tail" as it spins water behind it from the rain. I finally catch up to it and throw to the cut-off man. The batter stands on third base with a triple.

Possum is immediately out of the dugout and motions for me to run in from my outfield position to the mound to relieve Kenny. We simply make a trade in positions where Kenny goes to right-field. "I put you out there, so you'd be rested for pitching if we needed you—not to be chasing the ball to the fence," Possum smiles. "Let's get them out and end this thing."

I assume my new stretch position and fire in my first pitch, a fast ball, which is hit high over the left-field fence. The score is now 13 to 3. I glance into the dugout and Possum shows no emotion at all. I retire the next three batters in order and we enter the top of the ninth inning.

We get a few men on base but do not score. With no further discussion, I return to the mound for the final half-inning and retire the side after only one hit. The final score is 13 to 3, and we now have an 11-3 win-loss record.

We were spectacular at the plate tonight, with two homeruns each from Harold, Steve and Don. The rest of us had at least one hit during the game, including one homerun by Jesse.

The crowd seems to leave on a positive note, having witnessed our very fine baseball team with talented players—and with a possible future of greater accomplishments.

Before our departure back to Emporia, Possum shares that the Reading management paid him twenty-five dollars for the game. "That way, each of you drivers will get paid five dollars for each trip today. Looks like an OK deal to me."

We feel much better on our trip home with a few wise-cracks relating to Philip needing to wear his mask, chest protector, and shin guards behind the plate on this hot evening, and then driving all the way back home.

"Hey, Philip. Did you know that some people call your catching stuff "the tools of ignorance? How bright is that?" someone laughs.

"Any time you guys would like to try it, just let me know. I'd love to be strolling the outfield in the cool air. The problem is you couldn't get along without me," Philip smiles confidently.

We nod in agreement.

We know that we are nearing the end of the season. We have a full five days before our next scheduled game with Melvern, unless we get an early invitation to the World Series in Wichita. Even then, we might still have to play that game next Friday evening in Melvern. Then, if no invitation comes through, we have just a few more regular-season games.

Finally, when we get home around 1 a.m., the temperature drops to the low seventies, and I look forward to a pleasant night for sleep. No practice tomorrow, Possum said!

Chapter Twenty-Three

Melvern

Dad and I work on Frank's house this Monday. Dad shows his very special talent as he starts building the kitchen cabinets. I have watched his cabinet-building over the last several years and know for a fact that I could never duplicate such an effort. It seems an almost spiritual challenge, squarely met.

I continue working inside the garage, hanging and finishing sheet rock and framing the door into the attic. I notice in the afternoon that heavy clouds are forming in the western sky, and rain is predicted for the next few days.

I wonder what we would do if the Melvern game were rained out next Friday. We need to stay on the winning streak but, hopefully, a rain-out would not diminish our chances for a shot at the World Series.

The sky broke open late Monday evening and rains continued Tuesday and Wednesday. No practice and lots of good work is done on the Love house these last two days. Dad says that we can start painting the outside early next week and then complete the inside painting the following week.

"After that, just a few touch-ups and we'll be done. Then we can settle with Frank. I think I will buy that lot on Logan Avenue and get the diggers going on the basement." Dad is optimistic about the future as he often is during the work day.

Finally, the skies clear this Thursday morning, and Philip drops by with instructions from Possum for practice this evening. It has been a nice few days with just work and little else going on. I am ready, however, to get back to baseball and seeing the guys again.

The regular dirt softball diamond at Peter Pan Park is too wet to have batting practice, but we complete our usual warm-up and review of play-situations on the grass field to the east. Everyone seems enthusiastic with prospects of a likely final game in Melvern tomorrow evening. Mike arrives driving the Chevy, but the Buick does not show up. We all agree it is too wet for the three ladies to wait around to watch a practice.

Out of the blue, we hear Clyde informing no one in particular that the Democratic Convention in Chicago just nominated Adlai Stevenson for President and Estes Kefauver for Vice President for the election in November.

"I can't wait for the Republican Convention next week in San Francisco. It'll be no surprise that they'll nominate President Eisenhower, but maybe we'll have a different vice-president than Richard Nixon." This is typical of Clyde who finds an interest in politics more than any of the rest of us. I hear no response.

Possum ends practice with several announcements. The first one is rather startling as he says, "Guys, I've had several contacts with players who would like to join our team for our possible appearance in Wichita. One of them is supposed to be a really fine pitcher and another, a super outfielder." Possum waits for our reaction.

Don speaks out immediately. "We already have a good pitching staff in Young, Smith and Ohm. They've done a nice job all season. I see no weakness in the outfield, either—especially in right field." That brings out laughter.

"Yeah, but what about the other outfield positions?" Mike yells. Again, more laughter, especially directed to Peanuts and Harold.

Philip adds, "My car only holds six guys and with twelve smelly arm-pits and twelve stinky feet, enough is enough."

More giggles.

"I drive with only ten smelly arm-pits and ten stinky feet, but my '47 Chevy is smaller than Philip's car, so we can't hold anymore either," Bob says with some seriousness.

Don continues, "We've come all this way and we're where we want to be. We've a chance for the big time so let's not change anything. Let's go all the way to the finals with our eleven players." That is as close to a pep talk as we have had all season by our captain. We all agree with smiles on every face.

Possum confirms, "I knew that would be your answer. I will let those other guys know that we are set for the rest of the season and won't need any more help."

Just before the end of practice, Clyde calls out to us to stick around for a few more minutes. "I have an idea on how to improve our glove throw. Instead of all throwing at once, let's try to throw quickly one at a time so it looks like a Fourth of July Roman candle."

We gather quickly to a single area on the field and practice a few throws. One at a time, in order from right to left, and after Clyde's signal, we fire our gloves into the distance. We are delighted with the result. This will be a fun exhibition for the Melvern fans!

The sun rises on the day of what might be the final regular season game for the summer of 1956. The temperature has moderated, and the forecast is for clear skies this Friday evening for playing our game in Melvern.

My workday is uneventful, although climbing up and down on scaffolding under the eaves of the house takes its toll on my calf muscles. Dad said we had to get the vent holes cut to give the attic air during these very hot days. Otherwise, this is not hard work with light tools.

We gather as usual at the *Gazette* building with all Bombers showing up on time and then make the forty-five-minute trip to Melvern. What a beautiful sight as we enter a newly-paved parking lot. People seem to be milling around in every direction.

A guy at the ticket gate says, "With this brand-new stadium and the word out that you guys are likely getting an invitation to play in the NBC World Series next week, fans are flocking in."

We did not know that ours would be the first game in this stadium nor did we know of the NBC invitation. Two surprises!

Perhaps Possum knows more than he is telling us for some reason. We wait for him in the parking lot while changing into our spikes and gathering gloves, bats and balls. Possum drives in.

"Hey, Possum," Don shouts. "People are saying we got the invitation to Wichita. What's the deal?"

Possum walks to our cars. "I'm not sure yet. I got a phone call just before I drove here. It seems that we and one other team are on the list for the last position in the tournament.

Our record isn't quite as good as theirs. I think they are from Rhode Island. If we play though, they tell me that it would be about nine in the evening on Sunday. I think our best hope is that the Rhode Island team won't be able to get out here that quick, so we can get in. That's all I know."

"Should we talk to our people at work, then, on when we should get off?" Mike asks.

"Yeah, let them know tomorrow if you can. I'm sure we wouldn't play again as soon as Monday, so I don't see any reason to miss work on Monday. We should get home by two or three that morning after our first game, so go to work if you have to. I'll know when we play next, once they call me. You'll also want to let your bosses know that you'll miss a day or two later next week since it's a double elimination."

A pause.

"How do we know what to pack? Do you think we'll stay overnight at any time there and what are we supposed to wear?" Clyde asks nervously.

"I don't want any of you going out and buying any new shoes or anything. Wear what you have that's comfortable. The same uniforms you have been wearing, for goodness sake. Kenny, you might want to buy a new pair of shorts, though." Possum looks away and smiles.

Some of the guys look at me and some of them look at Kenny Young, all with laughter.

"Look guys, we've got to win this game tonight or nothing else matters," Possum says, as he stuffs his notebook in his back pocket and waves us toward the diamond.

On the way to the field, a man carrying a trombone approaches me. "Hey, what do you know about *Ft. Douglas*, on your uniform?"

"Oh, I bought this at an Army-Navy store in Emporia," I reply.

"I was stationed there in Utah during World War Two," he says with a broad grin. "I'm playing tonight in a little five-piece band we got together just for this special night."

"Are you anything like the Sym-Phony band for the Brooklyn Dodgers?" I ask.

"How do you know about that?" he seems surprised.

"When the Dodgers won their first World Series last year, that little band was all over the movie newsreels and radio. They're pretty good," I reply.

"We're probably not as good as them, but they gave us the idea."

"Good luck. I'll be listening for you." We shake hands and he trots off.

We fan out over the field near our dugout with warm-ups that seem a little more intense than usual. We take regular infield practice and the crowd is a noisy one. Suddenly we hear the live band and spot the group of five guys playing music near the Melvern dugout.

They do sound pretty good.

Back to the game.

We have a full roster of our eleven guys this evening, so it should be an easier game to manage than the one last week in Reading. Possum lists our starting line-up as it has been for some time now, with Kenny Young on the mound, and with David Carter and Bob Smith on the bench or coaching first base.

We start off well with Steve's lead-off single. He follows with a steal of second base, as the players in the dugout also catch Possum's steal sign. Mike and Clyde both fly out, but Harold smacks a double and Steve scores. Graham grounds out to end the inning. We lead 1 to 0.

As I jog out to my position at third base, I marvel at the finely groomed infield and the bright lights. The playing field is surrounded by six light poles providing excellent lighting over the infield and well into the outfield. The stands are partly covered and well-lighted.

This is a first-class facility, for sure. I am hoping for no bad hops on grounders tonight. I pick out just a few very small pebbles and throw them to the side. I check my left back pocket and feel the little arrowhead. Good luck tonight.

Just then, the little band strikes up "Hold That Tiger." Oh my. That song has found us again, even here in Melvern.

Two loudspeakers are positioned on each light pole over first and third bases. Other speakers are situated high in the stands above the crowd and near a brightly-lighted press box.

With the crowd at such high energy, I imagine Steve is picking up some pretty good jeers to add to his list. I don't hear anything further as I concentrate on each pitch from Kenny and keep Possum in my view for any assistance he can give me on my positioning. We retire Melvern one-two-three in the bottom of the first inning.

As we rehearsed in our last practice, we meet near the pitcher's mound. The crowd roars as they must be anticipating our flying saucer routine. At Clyde's "fire," we toss our flattened gloves high into the air one after the other. The crowd loves it with more cheering as we run to the dugout. This new routine is a hit!

As the number six hitter, I lead off the top of the second inning. On my way to the plate, I hear the announcer, "And batting sixth, the third baseman, Ken Ohm." It startles me somewhat as I do not recall ever being introduced over a loud speaker either in Junior Legion baseball or at E-State. I promptly fly out to center field.

We are now in the bottom of the fourth inning, still leading 1 to 0. The first batter pops up over my head in foul territory. I take off to where I think it should land and find a four-foot wooden fence directly in front of me. Fans are leaning over it and waving and hollering at me, "Be careful. Be careful!"

I spot the ball and lunge over the top of the fence and catch it in the webbing of my glove. I thank the nearby fans and tip my cap to them. They get a kick out of that. I head back to my position. One out.

The next batter hits a line drive directly at me and I snag it for out number two. Batter number three in the Melvern line-up walks and is followed by a single from their clean-up hitter. The next batter hits a high pop-up to me for the final out.

I recall hearing that this feat ties a minor and major league record by recording all three outs by one player in one inning. A very strange statistic, but I smile at the thought. There are probably tens of thousands of players who share this record.

I lead off the top of the fifth inning with my first hit of the game. It is a single to right field and my walnut bat continues to support me to a low .300 average. Philip and Peanuts both follow with base hits and I score the second run of the game.

Kenny Young flies out to shallow right field for out-number one. The top of our order, Steve Jones and Mike Garcia, each ground out to end the inning with us holding a 2 to 0 lead.

Both teams go down in order in the next two innings. It is now the top of the seventh inning. With two men out, Harold hits a towering drive over the center field fence. Don Graham follows with a homerun over the left field fence. We now lead 4 to 0. Surprisingly, the crowd stays.

Perhaps they sense a Melvern rally, as the first two batters in the bottom of the seventh inning match Harold and Don with back-to-back homeruns. The score is now 4 to 2 and Possum walks to the mound to visit with Kenny. Bob Smith is warming up near our dugout with David Carter catching. Possum decides to leave Kenny in and the next three batters are quick outs. We are relieved, but feel tension mounting as this game, once again, is a must win.

Neither team scores in the eighth inning. We start off the top of the ninth inning with Steve Jones, our lead-off hitter, getting his third single of the day. Possum gives Mike Garcia the bunt sign and it is executed perfectly, with Steve reaching second base, but Mike is thrown out at first.

With one out, Clyde hits a single hard into center field, scoring Steve easily. Harold Turner walks, but Don Graham hits into an inning-ending double play. Our lead now stands at 5 to 2.

We go into the bottom of the ninth with the whole season hanging in the balance. The crowd roars as the Melvern lead-off batter comes to the plate. "Go Melvern! Go Melvern!" they shout. On a 3-2 count, the batter strikes out swinging. Kenny Young looks pretty good from my viewpoint at third base. The next batter hits the first pitch for a lazy fly-out to left field. Two outs.

The crowd's chant dies out as Kenny pauses and walks off the back of the mound. My attention is on the next batter and Kenny's next pitch. The batter pops up to Philip behind the plate and the game is over. We win, 5 to 2.

We run off the field with great relief. Possum is not in the dugout. We wait for several minutes until we see him walk from the official scorer's table in the press box to meet us in the dugout. With a typical big Possum smile, he quickly shakes hands all around, asking us to sit down.

After a few seconds and then taking a deep breath, Possum says, "Guys, we just heard from the NBC. This new stadium has a telephone and the NBC guys had asked to be called with a report of our final score this evening. They got our winning score and they just called back. We're going to the tournament!"

Our shouts are deafening. We are going to the big time. Just then, the announcer booms over the loud speakers, "Folks, we just got news that the Bombers received an invitation a few minutes ago to play in the NBC World Series this year in Wichita. Let's give them a hand." The crowd erupts with cheers and the little band plays a Sousa march.

We are surprised by this spontaneous support from fans of an out-of-town team. It looks like we will have a little extra reason to play for more than just our own home town. Several Melvern players enter our dugout, shaking hands, with smiles and with many and varied comments. They seem almost as pleased as we are.

It is at least a half hour later, and we are still accepting good wishes from many Melvern fans, as well as several Emporia Bomber fans. We hear a quiet chant, "Bombers, Bombers, Bombers," and recognize familiar faces for the first time this evening. They insist they did not want to distract from our play, so tried not to make their presence known. Now they are all smiles. Tonight, we see a traveling fan base!

Possum calls for us to gather around him before we leave the parking lot. "We play at nine in the evening on Sunday against the top-seeded team. They are from Fort Wayne, Indiana and are an excellent team for sure. I think they are called the Dairymen. Since it is double elimination, we'll play at least two games, win or lose. We should leave for Wichita at about five o'clock Sunday afternoon. So, let's have a short practice tomorrow at six, and I'll try to have more details then. By the way, I want to hear exactly what you work out with your bosses for missing some work time this coming week."

A short pause.

"Oh, one other thing. I don't know if any of your families want to travel to Wichita for such a late game but, if they do, let me know tomorrow and I will try to arrange for tickets. They apparently have special seating for the families of players and need to know about possible numbers."

After a short pause, Possum waves a good-bye. "See you tomorrow then."

The trip home is on a cloud!

Chapter Twenty-Four

A Long 40 Hours

This Saturday morning's get-up time seems earlier than usual. I think the whole Bomber team is exhausted from hard daily work and from late nights after away games. Nevertheless, another work day is here, and Dad and I get off to the building site at about seven o'clock.

We are in the process of finishing the woodwork in Frank Love's house. Since it is Saturday, and Mom does not work at the hospital today, she helps to fill nail holes and do some sanding before applying the final varnish. For some reason, she really enjoys this part of house building. She says, "It is fun to see your face reflected from the shiny, finished woodwork."

Dad and I have other preferences, and we build forms for the concrete driveway. Dad expects the drive to be poured on Monday morning, and I plan to be there to help. Perhaps I will have exciting news of a Bomber victory.

At noon, during our lunch break, I ask Dad if he would be interested in driving to Wichita for our game tomorrow night. His look tells me the answer. "I would love to, but Mom and I are so tired right now. We both have to work on Frank's house tomorrow and then regular work again on Monday. Maybe if you win, we can get there later, but I don't think so."

I knew the answer before I asked, but I can see that the game would be a place Dad would like to be.

Our regular quitting time of five o'clock arrives, and I feel relieved to get through the day. I drive to practice with hopes that Possum will not keep us long, so I can go home and get some sleep.

The events coming up tomorrow seem like a dream. Can it be that we will take the field against what might be one of the finest town teams in the United States? I mull this over and over again.

Possum usually arrives for practice well after we are fully warmed up, but tonight he is the first one to the park, and with nervous energy.

The Bombers all seem to show up at the same time, by usual means. Steve Jones lives close by and often runs to practice, while Mike Garcia used to ride a bike but now drives with Rosa.

The rest of us get to practice one way or the other by car. Sandra and Maria arrive several minutes later in the gold Buick. The instant we all get there, Possum calls us to sit around him on the grass. He has his notebook prominently placed in full view, and quickly gets down to business.

"First of all, what do your bosses say about possible absences from work this week?"

No one volunteers as each player looks to others for a first response. Clyde starts out, "My boss, Morris, has no problem with missing in the middle of this week. He seemed quite interested in our playing in the big time. Harold and I also talked to his boss, and he felt the same way. So, we are clear to play. I am not sure about getting paid for those days though. I doubt it…"

Possum interrupts, suggesting, "Guys, this is our once-in-a-lifetime chance. Try not to worry about the money part. Anyone else find out anything?"

No one responds.

"Well, then, does anyone have a problem with missing a couple of days?" Possum waves his hands, a little frustrated.

Mike finally says, "The guys at the bank are worried that they cannot get cover for me on Tuesday and Wednesday or the rest of the week either. But they said they would try their best. I can make it to play tomorrow night but will have to work on Monday. That's all I know for sure."

"We'll plan on you tomorrow for sure, Mike. That's the main thing for now. We sure need you at shortstop. OK, then, anybody else?"

Again, no response.

"Then, I guess, that means all of you are committing to playing each game we're scheduled for this next week."

Again, no reply.

"Now, for the next item. Will any of your families attend the game?"

The only response is a shake of heads as a "no."

"Make sure they know that they are welcome and that we can make arrangements for tickets if they can get to Wichita for this game or the next one.

"OK, then, I want to change our riding assignments a little for tomorrow afternoon. It turns out that Richard Solis will umpire the late game after ours tomorrow night in Wichita, so he and his brothers Philip and Jesse want to ride together in Philip's car. Clyde, you will ride in Bob Smith's car and I am going to ask our captain, Don, to ride with me," Possum says with a smile.

This is a first! Possum must be taking this game even more seriously than usual. Maybe he has a special strategy to share with Don on the way down to Wichita. As I look around, I see faces full of nervous hope in our playing a competitive game tomorrow.

Possum goes over our signs which he does not change from the previous several games. He also hands ten-dollar bills to both Philip and Bob. "Remember, it costs a little to drive on the turnpike, so this will help with that, as well as with gas."

Possum pauses for several seconds before continuing, "If you guys want to buy something to eat before the game from the concession stands, that would be OK with me." He reaches in his pocket, pulls out a wad of cash, and hands each of us a five-dollar bill.

What a surprise! Good news keeps coming.

For the next half hour, we throw softly and play pepper. Possum calls us together for what we hope will be only a few final announcements before we can be on our way home.

"Our competition," Possum says, "is from Indiana and they have been a very strong team for several years. Since we're the last team to qualify, we get the top-seeded team. It's a normal way of setting up play in the first rounds. If we win, we get a few days off, probably until Wednesday, and will play another team considerably lower in the rankings than Indiana. If we lose, we will have to play sometime late on Tuesday. I am sorry I cannot be more definite, but that's all I know for now."

Possum continues, "As far as our travel is concerned, you

A Long 40 Hours

guys can wear regular clothes. You'll each have a spot in the locker room to change into your playing clothes. Just pack your stuff in a bag to carry along. I know that most of you are concerned about the expenses for these trips to Wichita. I understand that the tournament folks will pay out shares of the ticket receipts after the tournament is over. They gave me a rough idea and it looks like we might get as much as a day's pay for each of you if we draw good crowds."

That brings many smiles from the team.

Possum pauses for a moment. He holds up one hand.

"Guys, I have something else to say. I know you have all heard of players sharpening their spikes to try to intimidate the infielders. The story of Ty Cobb and his sharp spikes cutting up basemen is a sad one. Respectable ball players will not tolerate such action. I want you to know if that would happen on my team, the player would be sent home and not play another game for the Bombers. Do you all understand?"

No reply.

"One other thing I need to mention," Possum continues. "Would you think about whether our flying saucer throw is something we should maybe not do at the national tournament? It might seem a little amateur to some folks there. No need to decide now, but let's talk about it when we get to Wichita for the first game."

Once again, the guys seem very tired and show no response.

Practice ends.

I arrive home and check out the newspaper for news of our victory in Melvern and our invitation to the tournament. Nothing appears. Once again, I assume Possum has been too busy to drop a game report off at the sports desk. I bet if we beat Indiana, we will get some good coverage.

Mom and Dad are in the living room watching the snowy TV screen and I share a little of the Bombers plans. I had talked to Dad earlier about days off during the middle of next week. He was receptive, although somewhat concerned about getting the outside painting done on Frank's house.

"Possum said we'd likely get Tuesday off if we win but would have to play on Tuesday if we lose. My guess is not to plan on me working on Tuesday. If we win, though, I'll be here for sure."

Dad shows a big smile on that one. "Let's just win and be done with it. We can always catch up with the painting later. Don't even plan on working on Tuesday, in any case. Also, sleep in tomorrow. I have decided not to work tomorrow either."

"How many guys on your team are going to Wichita?" Mom asks.

"If you count Possum, there will be thirteen. Richard Solis is riding along with us this time. He is going to umpire another late game. We will have six in our car and five in Bob's. Don is going to ride with Possum."

"I will make 3 sacks of ham sandwiches for you guys to take along. They'll be in the ice box, so don't forget them," Mom says.

"That'll be really nice, and I know the guys will appreciate it. I'm heading for bed. See you sometime tomorrow."

I sleep soundly, with game day arriving for me when I wake up at about twelve noon on this Sunday. I take a long bath and then eat a breakfast of pancakes, bacon and eggs. Thanks Mom!

Dad manages to tune in to the major league game of the day on TV. As is usual, the Yankees are playing. Today, they are in Detroit and their pitcher is Don Larsen. Good.

I can check out what Bob has been saying about pitching from the stretch. I watch a few innings and become more and more convinced that this will be a helpful switch to my pitching style. I decide that will definitely be my technique from now on.

The afternoon passes quickly as I pack my *Ft. Douglas* uniform, spikes, walnut bat and glove into my car and am ready for the short drive to the *Gazette* building. I double check the arrowhead in the left-rear pocket of my uniform. Mom reminds me of the ham sandwiches, stacked in three separate paper bags, and I load them also.

Although I arrive fifteen minutes early, most of the team is already there and ready to travel. Richard Solis has loaded his gear into Philip's car, and with the usual chest protectors, knee guards, face masks, bats, gloves and balls, the trunk is packed.

Possum hands out a road map to Philip and to Bob with directions to Lawrence Stadium in Wichita. I hand David a sack of five sandwiches and tell him to wait until they get on the road to open it. I see Don getting in the car with Possum and hand him a sack of two sandwiches. At precisely five p.m., we caravan away.

The long wait is over!

Chapter Twenty-Five

Turnpike Tussle

The new Kansas Turnpike is a dream. Two lanes both ways and no reason to stop until we reach Wichita exit number fifty, some eighty-five miles southwest, down the road.

No sooner have we checked through the turnpike toll gate, when aconversation begins among the three Solis brothers. Mike, Steve, and I find ourselves listening intently as we discover that the Solis grandparents arrived directly from Mexico in the early 1920s. The brothers' father was only nine years old at the time. He accompanied his family as they picked sugar beets through Nebraska and into Minnesota, battling for survival during the heart of the great depression.

"When I was about five years old, we moved to California. A short time later, our parents separated, and our grandparents came out to get us. We returned to Emporia and have pretty much been here ever since. It turns out that it was just a few years later when I met you, Kenny, for the first time at Peter Pan Park. Those were fun summer mornings playing baseball with Mr. Rose," says Philip.

I nod in agreement. The wind whistles through the open windows.

Richard changes the direction of the conversation to his special passion for the game. Since he is a professional umpire and is well paid for the job, we are ready to hear his view which might be new to us. He shares a little of his umpiring history, starting as a softball umpire at Peter Pan Park when he was only sixteen years old. Then he played Junior Legion baseball in Emporia for two years before finding regular assignments as an umpire for both the Legion program and for the two college baseball teams, College of Emporia and Emporia State.

"I was also called to umpire a couple of town team games a few years ago, and they were really fun. The competition was very good. I loved watching some players who might have played in the big time if they'd had a chance. I accepted more and more offers to umpire in the little towns around here which, I guess, got me the offer to umpire in this year's NBC World Series."

It is great fun to hear his story and to ride along with a real official for one of tonight's games.

Many of us have questions. Steve asks, "How much do you make at a town team game and do you have to find a second umpire, each time?"

"I take whatever they offer me. It can be five or ten dollars and sometimes it's nothing at all. I don't mind, though, since I like to do it. Most town teams have perhaps one or two men who regularly volunteer for the job as the second umpire to call the bases. In a lot of my games, I've heard announcements just minutes before game time calling for a member of the crowd to be a base umpire. Most of the time, the call's answered by volunteers ranging from older men to some who might be in their middle teens."

I imagine Philip and Peanuts have heard some of this before, but they seem to listen closely to their brother.

"Do you ever have to umpire the whole game by yourself?" I ask.

"Sometimes, when umpiring in the pasture-lands of the Flint Hills, I am the only umpire. What I do then is to stand behind the pitcher to call balls and strikes and to be closer to the bases. When baseball first started in the 1800s, umpires were always behind the pitcher."

We all smile at that one.

"Do you have lots of trouble with players arguing your calls?" Mike asks.

"Not really. I get an occasional second look by a batter on a called strike or a shrug from the pitcher on a call he doesn't like. But, I think most players realize the game cannot go on without an umpire."

"I've noticed that base umpires have to work at getting in the right position to make calls. With only one base umpire, they have to run almost as fast as the base runner. As a second baseman, I see them flying by on many plays," Steve adds. "I think my biggest problem with the base umpire is when men are on base and he has to stand right in front of me at my second base position, so I can't see the batter very well."

"They should always be alert so as not to block your view. But, remember most are volunteers and have no idea where they should be on the field," Richard says. "So, try to adjust yourself to get in position."

"I notice you're dressed in all-black for tonight's game. I've seen all kinds of clothes on umpires, but you really look sharp," Mike says.

Richard is a little embarrassed and smiles. "All the umpires in the NBC are supposed to wear black or dark blue. I think you'll find three umpires for each game, by the way."

That surprises us. It also brings our attention back to where we are headed and perhaps a little anxiety starts to show. This really is the big time!

Richard continues, "Plate umpires rarely have shin guards and often have to shake off foul balls from the bat or from wild pitches or passed balls. It can really hurt sometimes."

"Do you have to buy all your umpiring stuff?" Steve asks.

"At first I borrowed extra chest protectors and masks from the teams who were playing. I eventually bought my own. Someday I'm going to buy a pair of shin guards." Richard continues, "This payday will be the best I have ever got to umpire a game. They pay us twenty dollars a game and we rotate around the bases and at home plate from game to game. The home plate assignment is by far the most work, but on the other days it's pretty easy money."

We are surprised. Most of us work for about eight to ten dollars a day and, for the most part, at very hard labor. But, as we listen to Richard, we are so happy for him. He apparently loves what he does, and we know he does a great job.

Philip interrupts saying, "My speedometer says we are halfway. Only about forty-five more miles to go.

"Let's hit the sandwiches," I say.

"So that's what you have in those paper bags?" shouts Steve.

"Yes, I didn't want to say anything until we got on the road. Mom made six for us. One each. Here you go."

I hand them out. They look terrific, with thick slices of ham, lots of butter, lettuce, mustard and mayonnaise. That ought to hold us till we get to Wichita. Then we can use the five-dollars Possum gave to us to get a hotdog or something before the game—and then maybe something after the game, too.

Several minutes go by with no one talking.

"Are there any other professional umpires other than you in Emporia?" Mike breaks the silence.

Richard takes the last bite of his sandwich. "The only professional I know is Fritz Schrader. He sometimes umps college games around here as well as a few Legion games."

"He's my uncle," I interrupt. "I know that he umpired one or two of my games in Legion ball and one in college just this last season."

"I don't think he has time to ump very much as he works for Hopkins Manufacturing. He is an older guy, probably almost 50," Richard adds.

"I've got to tell you guys a story about him. I don't think I even told it to you before, Philip," I say.

Philip shakes his head and looks only slightly interested.

"I'll never forget that day, a few months ago. I was the starting pitcher for E-State against C of E and Uncle Fritz was the home plate umpire. I recognized him right away before the first pitch and waved at him and he barely nodded. I got out of the first inning OK, after walking two batters, but really struggled in the second inning. I threw pitch after pitch and they were called balls every time. I thought it was because Uncle Fritz didn't want to show favorites. Finally, my second baseman trotted in to talk to me and I asked him what he thought of the pitches. He said they looked like balls to him. Before it was over, I had walked seven, hit two batters, and threw two wild pitches.

They scored six runs without a hit, and I only got one out before Coach Sisson sent me to the bench."

Each player in the car is looking for a response from another. None comes.

Finally, Philip says, "Man, that would have to be the worst inning ever pitched in history."

I smile as does everyone else.

"Was all that in the paper?" Steve asks.

"Yes, unlike coach Possum, coach Sisson got the results of each E-State game into the *Gazette* the very next day," I answer. "The worst part is we tied the score later in the game before we finally lost it. Coach Sisson didn't talk to me after the game, but when I checked the box score in the paper, I was given the loss. I still cannot see how that would be in the rules."

Richard answers, "Oh, yeah. The official scorer can make that kind of ruling if he thinks a pitcher anywhere along the line clearly loses the game for his team."

Peanuts adds, with a chuckle, "Seems to me you deserved the loss, Kenny."

Philip quickly changes the subject. "Be on the lookout for exit fifty. We should see it in just a few more miles."

Just then, a loud noise erupts in the left rear of the car. Philip quickly slows down and pulls to the side of the highway. "I think I know what it is," says Philip. "I have a loose bumper that's held with baling wire and it probably came loose."

He stops and gets out of the car with Steve. Four of us stay in the car. I look back through the rear window and see a white pick-up truck slowly coming to a stop several feet behind us.

Out from the pick-up jumps a large guy with a full beard carrying what looks like some kind of tire iron. "I think we got trouble!" I shout.

All four of us step out of the car and quickly join Steve and Philip. At the same time, several passengers in the pick-up also approach. The big guys shouts, "What are you guys doing here? You have no business around here!"

Steve makes a sudden lunge toward the guy with the iron and is grabbed by Richard and pulled back. "Stay right there all of you and don't move," Richard says to us.

He turns to the big guy. "We're a baseball team heading for Wichita. Another two cars with our players are just a few minutes behind us. We don't want any trouble. We just have to tie down our bumper and be on our way."

Some of the pick-up guys look back down the highway likely looking for the rest of our team. The big guy points at me and shouts, "Hey, four eyes, why are you running around with this kind?"

My heart beats fast and I can feel it in my temples as my blood starts to boil and my fists clinch.

I take a step and Richard grabs me with his other hand, now holding Steve and me. The other Bombers react with controlled anger. Richard continues to encourage the visitors to get into their pick-up and leave us alone.

I think we six men make quite a sight as we bunch together in a line with Richard at the center. Steve continues to mutter with words not clear. I glance to both sides and see Philip and Jesse carrying baseball bats from the open trunk.

The big guy turns back to the truck and calls back to us, "Just make sure you're out of here in a hurry. You're not welcome here." They all quickly load into the truck and roar past us, crossing a barrow pit and into an adjoining pasture. While continuing to shout obscenities and waving their arms, they soon disappear into the hills.

Philip quickly reties the bumper and we are back on our way.

"Do we tell Possum about this?" Jesse asks.

"Nope, I don't think those guys will be any more trouble, and Possum has enough to worry about," Richard answers.

No more words are spoken until Philip reminds us to look for exit fifty.

There it is! We turn off and look at the road map to find where we are. Just seven more miles and we will be at the stadium. My legs feel weak and I am still shaking a little.

Chapter Twenty-Six

Lawrence Stadium

We drive into the parking lot and a guy comes by with a lumberyard apron around his waist. He looks like he is selling tickets for something. "Park over there near the red Chevy," he says. "It'll be two dollars."

Philip looks out his open window. "We are the Brown Bombers from Emporia. Do we get a free pass to park?"

The guy walks slowly toward our car. He looks in and sees five brown guys and me. "Where is the rest of the team? It takes nine guys to play baseball." He smiles with his humor.

Philip answers, "Two more cars will be here in a few minutes. We have thirteen guys all together."

Bob's car arrives, followed by Possum's. Possum sees us and parks next to us. As soon as he turns off the engine, he gets out and approaches the guy selling tickets. "We are the Brown Bombers baseball team from Emporia and need to find a place to park our cars and get to the locker rooms," he says.

Possum is in no mood to be delayed.

"Yes, sir. The players are all to park over near that far building." He points to the spot some one-hundred yards away. "You can see some cars already there. Good luck to you guys tonight," the man says.

Possum waves for us to follow as he gets back into his car. We all park near a sign that says, "Players Entrance."

The Bombers are in the big time for sure! We exit our cars when Possum tells us to leave our equipment bags and join him.

Richard collects his suitcase and other equipment from Philip's car trunk and waves goodbye to us. He said he will be housed in a hotel with the other umpires for the rest of the tournament. He will not be riding back home with us tonight.

Several players, as well as Possum, find me for a quick, "Thank you to your mother for the sandwiches," comment.

We walk, a bit stiff-legged, to Possum's car.

Viewed from the outside, most of us agree that Lawrence Stadium is the biggest we have ever seen. Steve says he heard it seats over ten thousand people.

Just then an incredible roar erupts from the crowd. Something exciting is obviously happening inside the stadium. I can feel my adrenaline kicking in and, as I look around at my teammates, it seems they are having the same reaction.

Possum gathers us for a briefing on plans for the rest of the evening. We stand nervously near his car.

"Although game-time is nine o'clock, we'll get at least a half-hour to warm up after this game ends. So, we want to be ready to go by eight thirty in any case. Now listen everybody, Don here, has an announcement," Possum says with a big smile.

Possum motions to Don who carries four boxes and is also smiling broadly.

Possum continues, "Mr. Davis, the car dealer in Emporia, bought a few uniforms for those of you who don't have one. The rest of you will wear what you have been wearing for the last several games. In fact, we're somewhat famous by our range of uniforms and we don't want to change now. I want everyone to be proud of whatever you'll wear tonight."

That suits all of us as we have had many nice comments about our many uniforms. But, I must admit, we will look a little better with each team member having at least some kind of baseball uniform.

Don asks Harold to take one of the boxes. Harold opens it with a wide smile.

Clyde is called next with the same reaction.

Finally, pitcher Bob Smith is handed box number three. He fumbles some with embarrassment. "I'm not sure why I get one of these, but thanks."

"Now for the next box," Don says.

Don lifts the lid and pulls out a bright red baseball cap with the letters *BB* on the front, and hands it to Bob. A second identical cap, but this one white, is handed to Harold. A third blue cap is then tossed to Clyde.

"Red, white and blue. Rather patriotic don't you think, guys?" Don says.

Steve replies, "I guess we'll still be known as a bunch of guys with non-matching outfits."

Our expressions show happy agreement.

"I have a few more surprises before we get to warm-ups but will hold off until then. I'm going to check in at the player's entrance and be back in a few minutes. You all just wait here," Possum says.

As Possum walks off, we start our usual babble.

"Man, those uniforms look really nice…"

"They're going to make mine look kind of dingy…"

"I wonder what else Possum has for us, he sure is…"

Possum returns with name tags hanging on strings. "Put these around your necks and wear them until we go to the locker room in about thirty minutes. These tags will get you into any game for this whole tournament, so hang on to them.

"The guys are going to let us into the stadium where there are some empty seats to watch some of the game going on right now. The Deming Washington Loggers are playing a team from southern California. I think the Loggers won the whole thing a few years ago and are seeded number two behind the Indiana team this year. Put those new uniforms in one of the cars and be sure to lock the doors. Let's go."

We follow Possum through a side gate and, as it opens to the playing field, we take a deep breath. The view startles us. The greenest green any of us have ever seen! Bright lights are shining from several light poles high overhead, even though the sun is still up this evening at seven forty-five.

We feel very special, and the tournament folks here are taking good care of us. They hand out a free fifty-cent program to each of us. We find our team listed, but no photographs since we were invited at the last minute. Possum and our whole team are named along with our 12-3 season record.

We find seats along the left field line near the foul pole. "Hey, guys, it's only three hundred and eleven feet to the wall here!" Harold shouts.

We look at him and motion for him to calm down. We don't

want people to think we have not been here before. However, we cannot help but survey the impressive surroundings with the large and noisy crowd and guys selling beer and peanuts in every direction. Finally, we settle in a bit and check the scoreboard to find the Washington team leading 11 to 2.

I whisper to Philip, "Both teams look really good from here. It's hard to believe the California team is losing so badly. It's also hard to believe our record is only twelve wins and three losses, while these guys have each won over thirty-five games this season."

"I'm glad we get to watch some of this game. Do you realize we're going to be on this field in about an hour? We've got to get our minds on the game coming up. This should help," Philip says quietly.

I nod in agreement but am unsure how we can do that. Too many things are going on right now. I notice that the Deming team has at least a couple of black guys and the California team has several blacks and a few Mexicans. I decide not to comment on that.

With an inning left to go in the game, Possum waves us to follow him to the locker room after we pick up equipment and uniforms from our cars.

The locker room is designed for about twenty-five people, so we have plenty of room to stretch out. The noise level is suddenly diminished. In fact, no one is talking at all. Possum stands to one side as we shuffle with our uniforms and lace up our spikes.

I have not seen Harold, Clyde or Bob for several minutes. Suddenly, they exit from the shower room and they are a sight to see. They stand there in full white uniforms, with blue numbers trimmed in red on their back. The fronts have stylized lettering showing, *Bombers*. Harold, especially, with his white hat, new uniform with the number nine, and white, size fourteen Converse shoes, presents an image that we find almost stately.

Clyde, with number seven on his back and Bob, with number three, wearing their new full uniforms are also well modeled. So that is what Don was doing at our practice some days ago. He was getting sizes from these guys so that uniforms could be ordered. It has been a well-kept secret until now.

Possum obviously directed the three guys to dress in the shower room and exit together as part of this very special moment. As I look around the room, I see us together as a tight group, recognizing ourselves as a baseball team deserving to be playing for a national championship.

Possum interrupts our mood with a call to attention. "Guys, I have another surprise for you." He opens the locker room door to the outside hallway and motions for several men to enter. Clyde's boss, Morris, leads the way, followed by Wes, the owner of Steve's greenhouse, then Harold's boss, each with broad smiles.

Mr. Davis, the car dealer and a couple executives from Mike Garcia's bank follow closely. When the last two men, Mr. Rose and Mr. Hodges, walk through the door, we cannot not help but applaud them all.

Possum's eyes are shining as he says, "These guys and several more pitched in to buy these new uniforms and a couple more bats and also these." He opens a large square red box and pulls out a smaller red box. He opens it, un-wraps white tissue paper, and holds up a brand-new baseball.

"A full dozen in all," Possum says. "No more playing catch with more than one guy." He motions toward the visitors lined up along the lockers with a wave of his hand.

"Thanks to all of you for these wonderful gifts. We will make you proud."

Pause.

"Right, guys?"

We smile and wave to our benefactors with several "Thank you's."

It is hard for us to respond more fully. It shows that several folks in Emporia have recognized our fine season and now have come to support us. We might have felt some pressure with all this but I, for one, feel quite relaxed and confident. As I look around the room, I see the same attitude all around. The visitors are smiling broadly.

Someone peeks in the door and announces that we are clear to go to the playing field for warm-ups. He also announces that the Loggers just won, 15 to 6.

It is time!

Play ball!

Chapter Twenty-Seven

Game One

We gather at the locker room doorway. Possum takes his place at the head of the line and leads us down a hallway entering the back of the visitors' dugout. We know that we will be the visiting team regardless of how many games we win—since we were the final team, number sixty, to be included in the tournament. That is fine with us.

The view from the dugout is unlike any we have encountered all season. The dugout is positioned so that when sitting on the benches, the field is at eye level. Screens protect us from foul balls. Steps are at either end of the dugout and lead up to the playing field. Possum tells us to be seated. With only eleven players, we again find ourselves in spacious surroundings.

"As promised, gentlemen," Possum begins, "please unwrap a half-dozen of our new baseballs from the box Don is carrying. We will save the other six until the next game. Let's all act like the professionals you are. OK, let's hit the field with our regular warm-up drills."

A few things come to mind. We had never before been called gentlemen or professionals and never before had brand new baseballs just for warm up. This is indeed a special occasion.

We stroll onto the field and play catch to warm up. I find myself with Harold, while our starting pitcher, Kenny Young, starts gentle tosses with Philip.

Possum is writing in his notebook and is likely listing the starting line-up for the evening. I think it will be pretty much the same as it has been during the last few weeks of the regular season. No need to change things now.

It is a good thing that we had a few minutes in the stadium watching the last game. The reality of actually being on the playing field is breathtaking, but we are acting like we do it all the time. I notice each player is stealing sideways glances at the expanse of the stadium, and the crowd settling in to view our game.

Music is playing over the loud speakers and includes a number of popular singers, including Elvis Presley, Buddy Holley and several others. At least it is not "Hold That Tiger!"

Since this is the fourth or fifth game of the day, Possum tells us that they will not play the National Anthem. However, we will be introduced one at a time and take positions along the foul line in front of our dugout, between third base and home. The Dairymen will line up on the opposite base line in front of first base. Apparently, the announcer will have a few words to say about each team before the game starts.

The Ft. Wayne team takes infield practice first and looks powerful. Their throws snap from one base to the other with speed and accuracy. "They don't look so tough. I think we can

Game One

take them," Don says to no one in particular, as we watch from the dugout.

"Sounds like a captain talking," Mike offers.

Possum calls us together to announce the starting lineup. "Steve Jones, at second base will lead off, Mike Garcia will play shortstop and bat second, with Don Graham in right field, batting third."

"Man, Possum is formal tonight," I hear Clyde whisper.

Possum continues, "Harold Turner, you'll play center field and bat clean-up. Jesse Solis, you'll play left field and bat fifth. Ken Ohm will play third and bat sixth. Clyde Matson will be at first base and batting seventh, with Philip Solis catching, at eighth. Kenny Young will pitch, batting ninth. We expect Kenny will have great support tonight."

"Oh, one other thing; The folks here have asked us to do our flying saucer throw only after the bottom of the sixth inning. Apparently, they heard about us and want to show off our style to the crowd. After you throw your gloves, run out to retrieve them. They don't want any left on the field. Any objections?"

We give a loud cheer and nod in agreement.

With that, we see the Dairymen leaving the field and Possum waves us to take the field. We trot out to our positions and follow our normal routine with Possum hitting grounders to each of us in the infield and fly balls to the outfield. David Carter is catching for infield practice. Down the first base line, Kenny is heating up his pitching to Philip. Bob Smith is getting comfortable in the dugout preparing to pitch in relief if Kenny gets into trouble.

We return to the dugout after our infield practice and immediately the public-address announcer welcomes the two teams with a few words. He briefly describes our playing history this season and then begins the player introductions. As the visiting team, we are introduced first. Each player, one by one, runs to the foul line in the same order as Possum read the lineup.

The Dairymen are introduced but show a full twenty-five-man roster. They extend from home plate all the way past first base. It is a nice sight all with matching uniforms and with postures of confidence.

Both teams return to their dugouts for a minute or two before the Dairymen are introduced and run out as a team to their fielding positions. The game is now underway.

The usually confident Steve Jones shuffles to the batter's box, digging his cleats into the fresh, smooth surface. He stares out to the Dairymen pitcher, who might be the tallest pitcher we have faced this year—certainly as tall as Harold. Steve pounds the first pitch to the right of the shortstop who makes a fine stop and fires to the first baseman for the first out. If we all can hit the ball that hard this evening, we have a good chance to win.

Mike Garcia works the count to two balls and no strikes before lifting a long fly ball to left field for out-number two. Possum shouts to our next hitter, Graham, "Look at a few, Don!"

Possum obviously wants us to work the pitcher a little more. Don, indeed, reaches a three-ball, two-strike count before hitting a line drive to the Dairymen second baseman for out-number three.

It is our turn in the field and we run to our positions with serious purpose. While Kenny throws his four warm-up pitches, I find myself at third base in the spotlight of heavy banks of lights surrounding the playing field. This lighting seems even brighter than from sunlight on that hot July 4 afternoon at Soden's Grove.

Game One

The ball Kenny is throwing seems to sparkle on its straight-line trajectory to Philip's glove. There will be no excuse tonight for losing the ball in the darkness. With the grass infield, my usual inspection for rocks in the fine dirt of the base paths is easy. I cannot find a single pebble and smooth the few spike marks from the first inning. I pat the arrowhead in my left rear pocket for luck.

Kenny dominates this first half-inning with two batters grounding out to Steve at second base and striking out batter number three. We made it through the first inning with no damage and enter our dugout with confidence.

Harold Turner batted clean-up for the last several games and has earned that position with regular and powerful hitting. To start off the top of the second inning, he hits a two-ball, no-strike count deep over the left field fence. We lead 1 to 0. We gather around the dugout steps to welcome him after his homerun trot. Everybody smiles. It seems that we are in a battle that could be won.

Peanuts and I both ground out to shortstop for the first two outs of the second inning. Clyde connects for a long fly-out to center field for out-number three.

Kenny mows down the Dairymen one-two-three in each of the next three innings, with no hits allowed. We now maintain a 1 to 0 lead going into the top of the fifth inning after going down one-two-three in both the third and fourth innings.

Jesse starts out the fifth inning with a solid base hit to center field. I follow with a clean single to right field. We have a threat going with Clyde at the plate. He smashes a sharp grounder fielded by the shortstop, who throws to second for one out and on to first for a double play.

Jesse advances to third with two outs. Once again, we are

hitting the ball hard. It is just that we are hitting them directly at Dairymen fielders!

Philip hits a long fly ball to the left field fence where it is caught at the warning track for out-number three. We go into the bottom of the fifth inning, still leading 1 to 0.

Kenny Young gets off to a rocky start, walking the Dairymen clean-up hitter. Batter number five for the Dairymen hits a double off the wall in right-center field, scoring one. It is the first hit allowed by Kenny and we lose the shut-out as well. Winning the game is what matters at this point. The fifth inning ends with the score tied at 1 to 1.

Once again, we go down one-two-three in the top of the sixth inning, even though we are at the top of our batting order.

In the bottom of the sixth inning, the Dairymen score one run on a walk and a double to left-center field. The inning ends with a spectacular catch by Harold Turner as he catches what might have been a home run by leaping over the top of the fence. He saved two runs on that play.

We quickly gather at the pitcher's mound and, with a loud "fire" from Clyde, spin our gloves into the bright lights to the outfield grass. The crowd roars as we then sprint to retrieve our gloves and return to the dugout.

We are now behind 2 to 1, with Harold leading off the top of the seventh. Once again, with the count at two balls and no strikes, he hits a towering drive well over the left field fence close to where his first homerun landed. We are now tied at two each, going into the bottom of the seventh inning. After Jesse grounds out to first, I pop up to third and Clyde grounds out to second.

The Dairymen do not score off Kenny in the bottom of the seventh inning. He struck out nine batters so far. Possum does

Game One

not seem to be planning on a pitching move at this point in the game. Bob Smith throws lightly in the bullpen to David.

The eighth inning starts out well for the Bombers with both Philip and Kenny stroking singles with no outs. Possum gives the bunt sign and Steve sacrifices both runners to second and to third but is thrown out at first base. A hit now and we can take the lead.

Mike strikes out. Don walks to fill the bases for Harold, our hottest hitter. The count goes to two balls and two strikes when Harold hits another high drive to deep left field. After a long run, the left fielder makes a fine catch to end the inning.

Shoulders temporarily drop, but then we pick up. We are still tied at two each. I see no "give up" as we run onto the field and enter the bottom of the eighth inning.

The first Dairymen batter hits a double down the right field line. The second hitter smashes a long drive to right center where Harold overtakes it on the dead run. The runner at second has time to tag up and run to third base. Only one out. Possum decides to walk the next two batters.

The bases are loaded for the Dairymen's number five hitter. He hits the first pitch to deep center field. Harold catches it while running at full speed to his right and, as the runner on third tags up, throws a strike, on the fly, to Philip at home.

The runner charges into Philip resulting in a sound heard throughout the stadium. Philip tumbles head over heels. While on his back, he holds up his glove with the ball firmly in the pocket. The umpire signals "out." The capacity crowd rises to their feet with a deafening roar.

As Harold enters the dugout, we all smile and compliment him. He is playing a superb game and everyone knows it. The score is still tied. I look at Mike and shake my head. "Harold must have pegged that throw well over three hundred feet, on the fly. A pitcher on the mound couldn't have been more accurate with that throw!"

Mike nods in agreement.

The top of the ninth inning starts out with a clean hit to center field by Peanuts. I follow with a bloop single just over the head of the first baseman. As I hit the ball, I felt a tingle in my hands off my walnut bat. I stand on first base and see Philip pick up my bat and look at it on the way to the dugout.

Clyde places a perfect sacrifice bunt and Jesse and I advance one base. Philip follows with a shallow fly-out to left field. Jesse cannot score; Two outs. Kenny Young connects to deep left field where the Dairymen fielder once again makes a nice run, catching the ball for out number three.

We comment to each other, in passing, about the coincidence of both long balls to left field being gathered at the end the last two innings. We must shake it off and look to shutting down the Dairymen in the bottom of the ninth.

The top of the Ft. Wayne batting order comes up this inning. The lead-off batter hits the first pitch for a short fly ball to right field. Don reacts instantly and gets a great jump on the ball. With a horizontal dive, he snags to ball before it hits the ground.

From my third base position, I can see the top of the white ball shining from the webbing of Don's glove. When we were kids we called that an "ice-cream-cone" catch. The crowd gives the play a standing ovation. One out.

The second batter hits a soft drive just out of reach of Mike's outstretched glove and is safe at first base. Possum waves both Clyde and me to play closer to the foul lines to prevent a long double which would score the winning run. Batter number

Game One

three swings at a 3-2 pitch for a hard single to center field. Harold rushes for the rolling ball but cannot make a play at third. The hitter at first holds.

With Dairymen on first and third bases, Kenny strikes out the clean-up hitter for out number two. The next batter has been hitless for the game but is by far the fastest man on their team.

On the first pitch from Kenny, he chops a high ground ball off home plate. I rush for it with full speed as does Kenny. Kenny gets to the ball, spins and throws to first base with a safe sign from the umpire. The runner on third base scores the winning run. Possum storms out of the dugout with arms waving.

"He was out! The ball beat him by a mile," he shouts.

The umpire turns away with his arms crossed. Possum knows it is no use arguing further. He calls the Bombers in and we accept defeat. Final score Dairymen 3, Bombers 2.

The sad thing we all remember is that this was almost the exact same play that beat us in Gridley several weeks ago. How could lightning strike twice on such an unusual play? We must shake it off and try to focus on the next game. Possum contacts each of us with a handshake and a pat on the back.

Kenny Young limps a little as he takes a seat at the far end of the dugout bench. He looks exhausted. David catches my eye and, raising his eyebrows, looks away.

I drift toward the stack of bats and see my walnut lumber with a large split from the handle up through the barrel. I pick it up and will take it back to Emporia. I will need a different bat before the next game, sadly.

For several more minutes, we try to regroup emotionally as we sit quietly on the bench. Possum takes this time to meet with a tournament official and then signals for our attention.

"It turns out that the losing team playing right before our game tonight will be our competition on Tuesday. It's a team from southern California and the game will be played late again, starting around nine o'clock. So, we'll leave Emporia the same time as we did today, but here's where plans are going to change a little."

What does Possum have up his sleeve this time? We've seen this look before, serious and determined.

Possum continues, "A team from Missouri lost earlier today and had two major injuries along with some kind of virus with several other players. They've had to cancel their remaining game. The reason this is important to us is they will be leaving their boarding house early tomorrow for their trip home.

"One of the NBC ambassadors just contacted the lady owner of the boarding house for us to stay there after our game on Tuesday evening. She agreed for the regular rental price for each room. I told the ambassador we will take them up on the offer. So, contact your bosses tomorrow to get Wednesday off. If you must get back for work Wednesday, let me know. We can work something out on getting you back to Emporia."

No one else says a word.

"The further good news is that over the last several days, we have received several more dollar donations from our friends in Emporia. This allows us to stay here in Wichita overnight on Tuesday and pay for meals Wednesday. The NBC ambassador also told me that we drew one of the largest crowds ever for a first-round game. This means that we'll get a little larger pay-out than what we expected. I think folks wanted to see a really good all-black team and we were it." Possum has a look of satisfaction we have not seen before.

Possum continues, "If we win on Tuesday, we'll decide on a

plan of action at that time. So, get home tonight, have a good work day tomorrow and pack for an overnight on Tuesday, win or lose. Work out what you can with your bosses concerning working on Tuesday before our trip back here, as well as possibilities for Wednesday."

We change quietly into our street clothes and walk to our cars. "By the way," Possum calls out to us, "The folks here really like our flying saucer throws, so asked us to do it again on Tuesday after the bottom of the sixth inning. Also, no practice tomorrow. See you all on Tuesday."

We load Philip's car with his catching stuff and the rest of our equipment bags. As I toss the walnut bat into the trunk, I think I catch a little sympathy in the eyes of some of the players.

Chapter Twenty-Eight

Monday, the Day Before

We arrive home in the early morning hours with a work day ahead for all of us. This is a day to do well at our work site and to recover emotionally and physically from the difficult defeat. We now know that we can compete with the best amateur teams in America.

My six o'clock wake-up time arrives too soon, as usual. I step down the stairs to see Dad in his morning routine and Mom delaying her work day for a change. I am carrying my still-wet uniform and my broken walnut bat. I briefly describe the game last evening, and Mom and Dad listen intently.

"The guys really enjoyed the ham sandwiches. We're driving to Wichita again tomorrow afternoon, so we could use the same kind if you want to make some," I say.

"I still have part of that big ham in the ice box, so do you want the same number of them?"

"Just make one less than last time since Richard won't be going with us. I'm going to put my uniform into the washer. This time I'll wash it alone. No more pink underwear."

Mom smiles.

I show Dad the broken walnut bat. As he holds it, he views it from several directions. "It sure did the job, didn't it?"

"Yes, but what do I do with it now?" I ask.

"Well, when some guys catch a big northern pike up in Minnesota, they put it on a board and hang it over the fireplace," he answers with a smile.

That brings a laugh from each of us.

"I'll just take it to the basement where I got it in the first place." I say.

I put my uniform into the washing machine and place the bat on the same shelf I got it from several weeks ago. We have been on quite some journey, I think. I pat the barrel with my hand and turn off the overhead light.

Dad meets with Frank Love today to make final arrangements to close out their contract. Even before the meeting, Dad is on the phone calling a dirt mover to start digging for the basement on the new house he is planning on Logan Avenue.

He says he wants me to work on this house as many hours as I can while keeping my other jobs going. He seems more tired than usual, but the stress of closing one house job and starting another is certainly taxing.

"Kenny, let's meet at about ten o'clock at the Logan Avenue lot. We can get the house basement plan lined out before the digger gets there tomorrow."

If I had known of this late start, I would have slept another hour or so. I have time, though, to get my uniform washed and dried. I dab a little Shinola on my leather spike shoes and polish them to a nice glow. I have to start thinking about a different bat than the walnut one. I hope that one of the bats we just got from Mr. Hodges will work.

I arrive at the new building site and find Dad already there. He says Mr. Love agreed to finish off the final details for his house. Dad shows me the check paying for the work done. "I will cash it this afternoon, but while I am thinking about it, I want to give you this twenty for your trip tomorrow."

It is a new and crisp bill.

This is a real surprise as Dad rarely has cash in his pocket, so he must have been planning this for some time. "Possum caught me last week and asked if I would be able to donate some money to help the Bombers on their tournament expenses. I told him I would give some money to you and you could give it to him if you wanted."

"That will work just fine," I answer. "Thanks a lot."

"By the way," Dad says with a smile, "That money is also from Mom and Bonnie."

"I'll thank them when I see them later today."

We walk together to a spot on the new lot nearest the street. Dad has driven a wooden spike into the ground which reveals the location of one corner of the house. He begins to unwind a length of string from around a foot-long piece of lath.

"Kenny, take this string and wrap it around the stake here and walk out about six feet, parallel to the street. Then, drive this stake into the ground at that point. This will give us a good start for square corners."

He hands me two stakes along with a hammer.

This is the first time I have helped Dad to lay out dimensions for a house basement. When we finish the first corner lay-out, we have three stakes with string stretching exactly six, eight and ten feet from them, forming a triangle. Dad says, "This idea works every time and guarantees exact square corners."

I glance at the dimensions and recall one of the formulas I learned in my freshman mathematics class. It is called the Pythagorean Theorem and states simply that the sum of the square of the sides of a triangle is always equal to the square of the longer side—if the triangle has a ninety-degree angle. So, there it is. Dad uses this ancient formula to insure square corners for his houses.

I share the theorem with Dad, but he only nods and says he knows it works every time no matter what it's called.

We continue until noon, working to mark each of the four corners of the house. Dad and I sit under a nearby tree eating sandwiches and drinking our cokes. Dad suggests taking only a half-hour for lunch so that we can quit a little early. This suits me fine. I will use the time to get my mind set for tomorrow's travel and game in Wichita.

"Dad, I was wondering if you can get along without me on Wednesday as well as tomorrow. It seems we have a chance to stay overnight tomorrow and we might even play again on Wednesday, if we win."

Dad thinks for a moment, then says, "I'd say this is perfect timing. It'll take a few days for the digger to get done here. After that, though, it will be full time work until winter sets in. So, plan to work again here on Thursday or Friday depending on the results of your games."

I am relieved but not surprised. Dad continues to support my desire to play baseball, even if I lose wages in the process.

We finally finish staking and positioning the four corners of the new house and then take several minutes walking over the property. Dad does not say anything at first. Then, he seems to switch to a philosophical mood.

"I think on this house I'll try a few new things. We have space across the lot for a double car garage. I really think the day will come when many families will have at least two cars, especially if they have a few kids.

"I was also thinking about making the kitchen more open to the living room. There's no reason the wife has to cook in an enclosed room while the rest of the family watches television in another room."

All I can do is nod in agreement. It seems Dad is searching for even more of a statement.

"This may be my last house to build. I really want something to stand a long time and people will see this house, years later, and know that Frank Ohm was the builder."

"I think they already do, Dad. I have heard lots of folks point out houses you've already built, and they seem to be impressed knowing you were the builder."

"I guess so. I think this one will be extra special, though," he says with a smile.

My sister, Bonnie, and her husband bring little Monica over for a visit this evening, and it is an exciting time, especially for Mom. I glance at the sports page of the *Gazette* and see no story on our game. Since we did not complete the game until after midnight, I did not expect that it would be covered. It will likely be in tomorrow's paper when we are on the way back to Wichita.

Willis and Russell study quietly in their rooms and I sit at the desk in my nearby bedroom. I glance at my two remaining baseball cards stuck on the cork board with straight pins.

My 1948 Bowman Yogi Berra rookie card and my 1952 Topps Mickey Mantle card are all I have left of my original collection.

I gave the rest of my cards to cousin Larry when I entered college. I had decided to use my time wisely with no distractions other than classes and varsity baseball.

I sleep well this Monday night, even with the prospect of a road trip and playing an excellent baseball team from California. From Allen to Americus to Bushong to Gridley to Lyndon to Madison to Melvern to Olpe to Osage City to Reading, we now look to a team from Los Angeles!

Chapter Twenty-Nine

Hazel's Boarding House

No work today and I awaken much later than usual. My first thoughts are that this may be the most important day in the baseball lives of the Brown Bombers. We are playing a team that flew on an airplane all the way from Los Angeles to get to Wichita, and we only have to drive the eighty miles or so to play them.

This free day gives me time to think of "little things," as Possum says, to maybe gain a little advantage in tonight's game. I am alone at the breakfast table reading a note from Mom.

She reminds me of the ham sandwiches in the refrigerator and wishes me and the Bombers good luck in tonight's game. The sandwiches surely worked out well on Sunday and will help save a little meal money again today.

I consider options to my trusted walnut bat and decide to choose the heaviest one in the Bombers collection for tonight's game. I am confident an adjustment can be made for any differences.

I check my glove and find the laces tightly knotted. My spike shoes look good with their new polish and my freshly-washed *Ft. Douglas* uniform also looks good. I check that the arrowhead is in my uniform's back pocket.

My overnight packing consists of fresh, non-pink underwear, socks, towel, razor, comb, soap, a white t-shirt for sleeping and an extra shirt for tomorrow during the day. Possum said we will adjust the schedule if we win tonight. My guess is that we would drive home to regroup before the next game.

I think I am ready and it is only two o'clock in the afternoon. Suddenly, a new thought comes to mind.

Possum talks a lot about looking neat and presentable both on and off the field. I think he hesitates to be more specific since most of the team cannot afford much more than what they wear in their daily lives. I decide to show a little more class than I usually do by wearing my Sunday dress slacks and lace shoes, a short-sleeved white shirt and my dark blue knit tie. That will likely get a reaction out of the guys.

It is finally time to drive to the *Gazette* building to meet before our trip to Wichita. I am excited as I imagine the reception I will be getting from my teammates with my "up-town" clothes.

I arrive and see several Bombers already milling about in front of the *Gazette* building. It looks like we have all had the same idea. The guys look terrific. Philip and Peanuts have white shirts and dark ties like mine.

I step out of my car and see Bob and Kenny wearing striped sport shirts with button-down collars. Man, do they look nice! Steve and Mike have brightly colored shirts, as does David.

David has some new Converse "Chucks," similar to Harold's. Harold has discarded his over-alls, with nice looking slacks and a white-collared shirt. Clyde is smiling and showing off a patterned shirt featuring tiny fish.

David has a newspaper under his arm and has been waiting for just the right moment to share it with the team. "Take a look at this, he says," opening to the sports page featuring a short story on our game against Ft. Wayne.

We pass the paper around and are pleased with the coverage. We are hopeful that it will result in some Bomber fans attending our game tonight.

It is already five fifteen and neither Possum nor Don has arrived yet. This is unusual, but we have plenty to talk about with our unexpected, team-effort dress-up.

Emporia Bombers in Narrow Loss to Indiana Team in National Tournament

The Emporia Brown Bombers lost to The Ft. Wayne Indiana Dairymen 3-2 Sunday night at Lawrence Stadium in Wichita. Harold Turner hit two home runs to account for all the scoring for the Bombers. They play again on Tuesday at 9pm in the second round of this double elimination tourney.

A few more minutes elapse when we see Possum's car approaching from the north. He steps out the driver's side and Don out the passenger side. We are astonished.

Both Possum and Don wear tight-fitting black shirts, with black slacks, and with black, polished street shoes. Both show exceptional muscle which is not surprising for Don, but Possum normally wears loose-fitting clothes, so this new look is striking.

Further, Possum has let his whiskers grow into a short, but prominent, white beard. Add that to his rapidly graying hair and he appears like a different person. We applaud him with laughter and smiles.

Possum shows no embarrassment as he starts with, "I received a call at home an hour ago from the officials in Wichita, and they told me that an earlier game lasted through the fifteenth inning. So, we can expect as much as a two-hour delay in our starting time tonight."

"I have another bit of news," Possum continues. "Don and I met earlier today and drove to the College of Emporia athletic department. We wanted to see if they had any extra uniforms like Philip found at E-State. We were really lucky when they gave us two complete uniforms from years past."

Don approaches carrying both uniforms. He hands one to David and one to Peanuts. Both guys had been wearing uniform tops with non-matching pants, but now, as with the rest of the team, will wear full-matching tops and bottoms and stirrup socks. Both guys respond well with smiles and pack their new uniforms in their travel bags.

With that, Possum gathers us around him with the obvious intent to direct our planning for the next few days. "Since our game will start late tonight, we will drive directly to our boarding house where we will be staying tonight. The house is only a couple blocks from the stadium. Bob and Philip, I want you to drive to the stadium parking lot and meet Don and me there before going to the boarding house. We'll get situated and get a little rest before going back to the stadium and be there for a good warm-up before game time. Anything else?"

I jump in with a quick, "I have ham sandwiches again that Mom made just like the ones the other day."

I pass out the sacks to Bob and Don and keep one for the riders in Philip's car. Each team member shares a "thank you."

Once our drive is underway, the conversation centers on the dress of Possum and Don. Possum, especially, receives numerous comments.

Hazel's Boarding House

"Man, I had no idea Possum was built like that," Philip says, smiling, from the driver's seat. "Can you imagine getting those muscles from shining shoes?"

"I don't think I would want to tangle with him, if he was mad," adds Clyde. This comes from the biggest and maybe the toughest guy in the car!

"He sure looks like a leader. I don't think we could have wished for a better coach and boss. He seems to get respect from everyone he meets," says Steve.

The car is quiet except for the wind blowing in from the open windows and the noise from the car engine.

We are halfway to Wichita and I hand out the sandwiches. Each guy accepts with another "thank you" to Mom.

We pass the location of our recent encounter with the white pick-up truck. I think each man notices, but there is no comment. We do not want to re-visit that scene.

We are the first car to arrive and find a space near the entrance of the stadium parking lot. Soon Bob and Possum drive in and find us immediately. Possum steps from his car and speaks to Philip and Bob explaining directions to the boarding house. We follow him.

We park in front of a three-story white house with a large sign on the front lawn reading, HAZEL'S BOARDING HOUSE. For most of the team, this will be a first visit to a commercial residence. We gather our overnight bags, leaving baseball equipment in our cars and, with Possum and Don leading the way, walk to the front entrance.

The door opens, and we are greeted by a tiny, black lady with a broad smile and sparkling eyes. "Hello, gentlemen, I'm Hazel LaCount. Come on in." She steps back as we walk in. Harold takes off his hat. The rest of us quickly do the same.

The front hall opens to a large parlor with several antique chairs with flowered seats. To one side sits a tiny white piano. The next room shows several round tables with red and white checkered table cloths. This is obviously where Hazel serves breakfast as part of the room rent. I wonder if she has any idea how much this team might eat for a breakfast in this kind of setting.

"It's so nice to have you here for tonight. We've seven or eight rooms available, so you can decide among yourselves how to assign sleeping arrangements. A couple rooms have a double bed and the rest have bunk beds sleeping two people in each room," Hazel says with a continuing smile.

Mike jumps in, "Possum, I don't know how much money we have to spend for rooms tonight, but I think the team would be fine with you having a separate room, with the double bed, and the rest of us can divide up."

The team gives nods of approval to Mike's idea. We are relieved to have him speak up. Possum nods his agreement.

"The rooms are on the second and third floors so, if you will follow me, we can go up and take a look," Hazel says. "The bathroom is located at the end of the hall. It has a couple of shower stalls, and there are plenty of towels and washcloths in the cabinets."

We tour the rooms and find them very clean with fresh sheets and pillow cases and thank Hazel for her hospitality. Hazel looks at me on her way down the stairs and asks, with a twinkle in her eye, "So, you are a Brown Bomber, also?"

I nod and smile. What can I say?

I see David and suggest that we room together. He says, "OK."

Don shouts out that since Mike and he are Korean War veterans, "We can room together with bunk beds. Heck, we slept that way a lot in the service."

Everyone soon is settled in a room, with Bob Smith taking the other room with the double-bed. Possum suggests we get some rest for at least the next two hours since we now have the chance to do so. None of us argue, although we still feel the excitement of another new adventure.

David and I toss our overnight bags onto an antique couch and, David in the lower bunk and I in the upper bunk, doze off immediately. A knock on the door at nine thirty awakens us.

Possum goes from room to room telling us that our game time has been set for midnight. We are all to meet in a half hour in the parlor and will then drive to the stadium for a bite to eat before suiting up for the game.

It seems that each of us took advantage of nap time, and we now show a serious look of refreshed determination. Possum hands a five-dollar bill to each of us to pay for supper at the stadium.

The time is counting down for our next opportunity to show the world the character of the Brown Bombers. We are ready.

We arrive at the stadium and head for the concession area. Hot dogs and hamburgers with Cokes and 7UPs are picked from the menu with enthusiasm. We look over the playing field and Philip shouts out, "Hey look, guys, Richard is umpiring behind the plate!"

We jump up to get a better view and there he is in his dark suit. Peanuts points out that Richard is wearing shin guards. This is really a fun time for all of us. We feel a kinship with a high-powered umpire, and he is a fellow Emporian.

Philip and Peanuts are both grinning broadly as they watch several pitches called by Richard. I recall our drive with him to

Wichita the other day and feel like I know him well and am so proud of him.

We eat leisurely as the game in progress is only in the fifth inning. We have a few hours yet before game time. David and I sit at a picnic table near the concession stands when we hear a commotion nearby.

We see both Possum and Don surrounded by adults and kids alike, signing autographs. "Those folks must have recognized Possum," David says. "He looks pretty special today, I tell you."

Just then we see Harold, several yards away, also signing autographs.

"Harold looks pretty sharp, too," I add. "We're not quite so famous, I guess. No one seems to have noticed us."

We both smile with that.

Possum finally breaks away from the crowd and directs us to the visitor's locker room. We enter looking like professionals—quite unlike our first entrance a few days ago. We migrate to individual lockers that were ours during our last game and start to dress into our uniforms. Each player seems to be immersed into his own thoughts. Few words are spoken.

Once again, the two guys carrying new uniforms disappear into the shower room. Several minutes later, they emerge wearing their College of Emporia uniforms. They model them proudly.

David has red letters across the front of his uniform and Peanuts has blue letters, both with C of E showing brightly. David has the number ten on the back of his uniform and Peanuts the number one on his.

We now all wear full uniforms, but we maintain our unique team reputation of having widely different styles and colors. The tradition continues.

After a short pause, Don shouts out, "Hey, David, you have the same number as little Phil Rizzuto of the Yankees, and Peanuts, the same as Pee Wee Reese of the Dodgers. Peanuts and Pee Wee make quite a combination."

The players respond with laughter.

The locker room activity is interrupted when the main door opens and in walk the gentlemen who greeted us before our last game. Mr. Davis, bosses for Clyde, Harold and Steve, two executives from Mike's bank, Mr. Hodges, Mr. Rose and a new visitor, Mr. McFarland, the Aces coach, all show smiles.

The room once again resounds with applause. Here it is nearly midnight and we get a personal visit from a number of folks from Emporia. I am especially pleased to see the Aces coach and wave to him. He walks over and puts out his hand for a shake. The rest of the team and visitors are busy in conversation.

"Really nice to see you. Thanks for coming by," is my greeting.

"Good to see you, Kenny," he says. "Here is a little something that I owe you."

He hands me a five-dollar bill. "Just put it this in your back pocket. By the way," he says, smiling. "You can keep the Aces uniform you wore that day. I understand it's now pink and has your number ten, the same number you wear at E-State."

I am hoping I do not show embarrassment with my reply. "Thanks very much. I doubt I will ever wear it again, but it'll be a nice souvenir."

Coach McFarland laughs, then continues visiting with other players around the room.

We get the announcement that the game outside is now in the bottom of the ninth inning and Possum gathers us for a final pre-game talk. The Emporia visitors line up along one wall and listen quietly.

Surprisingly, Possum is brief. "Guys, this is it. Our season comes down to tonight. We deserve to be here and do not forget that. We can play with any town team in the nation. Big city guys are no different than we are. We're a team that has stayed together and played together this entire season and that will count for a lot. Just relax and play your game and things will turn out well. The line-up will be exactly as it was in game one. Kenny will start, and we plan to finish with a win. We remember his excellent fourteen inning stint in Gridley and we are going to give him great support tonight. Don will take out the new balls for our warm-up. Good luck, gentlemen."

We nod to Kenny with confidence.

A few minutes later we are called to the field and wave goodbye to our guests. Without another word, we walk down the tunnel to the visitors' dugout.

Chapter Thirty

Game Two

We warm up playing catch for several minutes while the California team, called the Surfers, takes infield practice. At ground level, they all look like seasoned baseball veterans. Steve mentioned earlier that he heard one or two of them played in high-level AAA baseball.

Their uniforms are pin-striped white with bright blue lettering. Their matching hats show LA letters. They certainly look like they belong here in championship play.

As I play catch with David, I visually pair each of our players with some of the opponents and find that we compare physically but are a much younger team. That may be to our benefit.

Their player roster number a full twenty-five allowed by the tourney rules. Even though we only have eleven players on our roster, we have fared well this season and there is no reason not to expect another good performance tonight.

It is our turn for infield practice and we run out to the field with confidence. There is not a pebble in sight around third base.

The large crowd erupts as we begin fielding ground balls and returning fly balls from the outfield. This crowd response surprises us. I had not noticed the same response with the LA team.

It looks like we captured a nice following here in Wichita. Maybe they are anticipating our flying saucers in the sixth inning!

Music plays loudly with what the announcer calls "rock and roll." It gives us a bounce in our step, for sure.

As we run in from the field, a fan, with a beer in one hand, leans over the dugout and shouts directly to David, "Hey, nickel, nickel. Hey, nickel, nickel. You are ninety cents short of a dollar." Then he laughs loudly.

We all hear the comment and enter the dugout to find Steve grinning. "Sounds like I have another entry for my jeers book," he says.

David and the rest of us are bewildered.

"What was that all about? I ask.

"He's referring to David's number ten. I've heard that one before. A guy once called a player with number twenty-five, 'nickel, nickel, nickel, dime, you are seventy-five cents short of a dollar," Steve shares, happily.

"Well, I'm glad that's all he said," is my reply.

We settle in the dugout ready for game time.

The umpires are announced, and we find Richard Solis assigned to the third- base spot. Philip and Peanuts and the rest of our team find it hard to hide our pride.

After a fine introduction to both teams, the LA Surfers run to the field to start the game. Our lead-off hitter, Steve Jones,

Game Two

shuffles the dirt in the batter's box and takes his stance for the first pitch. It is a called strike and the game is underway.

Steve and Mike Garcia both line out to the shortstop for the first two outs. Clyde Matson hits a shallow single to center field. Our clean-up hitter tonight, Don Graham, flies out deep to the left-field wall for out number three.

I take my position at third base to start the bottom half of the first inning. I approach Richard with a nod and a smile. He nods back with no words spoken.

Kenny, once again, looks confident on the mound. After the usual four warm-up pitches to Philip at catcher, the first batter hits a pop-up to Clyde at first base. The Surfers second batter drives a hard single to left-field just beyond my glove at third base. Batter number three hits a ground ball to Mike at shortstop, starting a double play by tossing to Steve at second base, who then throws to Clyde. Side retired.

I am the second batter in the top of the second inning and survey our stack of bats. I find one that shows a number thirty-six on the knob, and it seems to be the heaviest. That will be my choice tonight. I pat my left pocket and the arrowhead.

Harold Turner, our centerfielder, steps to the plate to start the inning. While I am standing in the on-deck circle, the same guy, with another beer in his hand, starts to chant toward me, "What do you get when you mix seven black guys with one white guy?"

He answers his own question, laughing loudly, "A bunch of Brown Bummers."

Before I can react, he adds, "Then what do you get when you add three Mexicans? A bunch more Brown Bummers." Now he is doubled over with laughter. Just then an usher, in a red jacket, escorts the guy out of the area.

I have no idea what the guy is saying nor why and am not interested. I see Harold lift a high fly to center field for out number one.

This new bat feels very light as I dig in at home plate. The first pitch is a fast ball outside. I feel I can hit another one like that if it is over the plate. The next pitch is down the middle and I swing, connecting solidly.

The ball sails off my bat deep into left-center, hitting the wall, half way up. I scramble to second and slide in for a double.

I dust myself off and glance to Possum in the third base coaching box for a signal. He shows none.

Philip follows with a ground out to second base as I advance easily to third base. Peanuts connects for a long fly-out to right field. The side is retired as I am stranded on third base, no score.

Kenny strikes out the first two batters in the bottom of the second and forces a ground ball out by the next Surfers batter. The inning is filled with Bombers chatter and with sharp whistles from Don and Mike.

The top of the third inning starts well when Young hits a single to center field. Steve catches a sign from Possum and sacrifices with a successful bunt, getting Young to second. One out. Mike grounds out to the shortstop with Young holding at second. Clyde flies out to center field and we end the inning.

Kenny trots in from second base and meets Steve carrying Kenny's glove. They chat for a second. I take my position at third and I think I notice a grimace on Kenny's face as he takes the mound for his warm up pitches. I ignore it.

The Surfers hit the ball hard in the bottom of the third inning, but only score one run. Our defense plays well.

Don Graham leads off the top of the fourth inning with a

pop-up to the first baseman. Harold follows with a towering drive well over the center field wall to tie the score at 1 to 1.

I carry my new bat to the batter's box and swing at two pitches on the inside corner of the plate. The next pitch is eye high and I swing and miss for strike three.

On the way back to the dugout, I realize I need to take those high pitches for balls. Still, I am getting to like this new bat.

Philip walks after a 3-2 count, but Peanuts grounds out to end the inning.

The first California batter, in the bottom of the fourth inning, hits a high fly to deep right-center field. Harold is off at the crack of the bat and makes a spectacular catch high off the wall. Don, nearby in right field, tips his hat to Harold.

The next batter hits another long fly, this time to left-center. Once again, Harold makes a superb, diving catch in front of Peanuts who is backing him up. Harold gets up from the ground and grins at Peanuts.

The final batter of the inning for the Surfers hits a line drive to me at third for the final out. At the end of four innings, the score is 1 to 1. Harold receives loud applause and shouts from the crowd as he enters the dugout.

Kenny leads off the fifth inning, as he did in the third inning, with a lazy single over second base and into center field. Bob Smith, coaching at first, helps Kenny into his warm up jacket even though the temperature is in the high 70s tonight.

Possum does not show the bunt sign at he did in the third inning, giving Steve the go-ahead to hit away. Steve hits a hard grounder to the right of the shortstop who barely throws out Kenny at second. Steve is safe at first.

I wonder if Possum sees something wrong with Kenny and chose not to force a tough play with a sacrifice. In any case,

Kenny walks slowly to the dugout as Mike strolls to the plate. On the first pitch, Mike strokes a single to right center-field and Steve makes it to third. Only one out.

Clyde Matson has not been hitting well lately but catches a fast ball for a long fly-ball out to center field, scoring Steve after the tag-up. Mike holds at first as the throw from center field goes to second.

We are leading 2 to 1 and our guys are all standing and cheering behind the screen in the dugout. We are in this game and there is no doubt.

Don hits the first pitch hard near the right field wall. The right-fielder makes a fine play, diving to his right to make the catch. Possum claps his hands at our effort as the side is retired.

The bottom of the fifth inning starts with a lead-off walk to the number six hitter for the Surfers. Playing to tie at home, the California manager calls for a sacrifice bunt which works perfectly for the next batter. The man on second is in scoring position when the next batter walks on four pitches.

It looks to me that Kenny is in obvious pain. I look at Possum who nods and trots out from the dugout to the mound. After a brief visit, Possum heads back to the dugout leaving Kenny pitching to the number eight hitter. He strikes him out after a 3-2 count.

With two outs, the next batter walks and the bases are full of Surfers. I notice the runner on first taking a very large lead—even with the bases full.

"Kennylookover, Kennylookover," I quietly call, with my own attempt at a whistle. He takes his stretch and quickly throws to first catching the runner off base for out number three. It worked! We escape, still leading, 2 to 1.

I get greetings on returning to the dugout, and Possum smiles at me before he takes his position at the third base coach's box. We start the top of the sixth inning.

Harold leads off with a hard single to left field. I follow with a hit to nearly the same spot. The Surfers' coach comes out and replaces their starting pitcher. The crowd gives him a nice round of applause.

The new pitcher gets Philip to pop-up to third base. Peanuts hits a slow bounder toward third base and beats it out on a close play at first. Everyone is safe.

The bases are loaded for Kenny Young. Kenny walks to the plate with a noticeable limp. He works the count to 2-2 before hitting a hard-line drive to the second baseman who steps on the bag before I can get back safely. It is an inning-ending double play. Our lead stands at 2 to 1.

The bottom of the sixth inning starts out badly with Kenny walking the California lead-off batter. I notice on each pitch, a slight grunt from Kenny. The second hitter lofts a shallow fly-ball out caught by Harold. The third hitter slams a fly to deep right field for a double—scoring the base runner. The score is now tied at 2 to 2. The clean-up hitter reaches a count of two balls and two strikes when Kenny falls to the ground in pain.

Possum runs out to the mound with hands outstretched motioning for our team to stay where they are on the field. He helps Kenny to a standing position and motions Philip and me to the mound.

"I'm going to have you pitch to this guy and take Kenny out," he says to me. "This hitter and the next one are looking for a fastball every time. Try one of your round-house curves or a knuckle ball, and I think they will take the bait."

Bob Smith is waved in from the bench to take over third base for me. Possum and Young walk slowly to the dugout.

After the allotted several-pitch warm up, where I do not show a curve ball, the umpire calls for play to resume.

Philip calls for the curve and I deliver a soft, round-house. The batter is way ahead on his timing and swings and misses. That is strike three and now we have two outs. The number five hitter swings on the first pitch, a knuckle ball, and dribbles it to first base for the third out. We get out of the inning, tied.

The fielders sprint to the mound and on Clyde's signal, I join them for the saucer throw. This time eight gloves soar deeply into the outfield. The crowd stands and cheers loudly. We run together to collect our gloves and return to the dugout as the crowd continues their applause.

We now go into the top of the seventh inning. Possum approaches me with a look of concern on his face. "Kenny, we will keep you in for one or two more batters and then bring Bob to the mound. You did a great job out there." He walks off to take his position in the coach's box.

I find Kenny at the end of the bench. "What seems to be the trouble?" I ask.

"I think it happened at the end of our last game when I slipped throwing to first. It's my left hip and it really hurts," he says.

"Well, take it easy. We are going to win this one," is all I can say.

The top of our batting order is coming to the plate this inning. Steve and Mike both fly out to center field. Clyde smacks a 3-2 count pitch deep to right field where the Surfers' fielder makes a great catch for out number three.

My first pitch in the bottom of the seventh inning is tagged for a triple down the left field line. Possum runs out of the dugout and signals for Bob to change places with me. Bob takes his warm-ups as I return to my position at third base.

Game Two

Bob strikes out the next batter on three pitches. After a 2-2 count the next hitter pounds a high fly to left field. Peanuts makes a nice catch, but the runner on third base tags up and scores.

The Surfers now lead 3 to 2. The next two batters go down on ground balls to Steve at second base with easy throws to first.

We return to the dugout for the top of the eighth inning where each Bomber is showing confidence with lots of chatter. Steve leads off the batting order with a hard-hit drive to left center field, caught on a diving play by the Surfers' fielder.

Mike follows with a line drive out to third base for out number two. We are hitting the ball hard, but they are not falling in safely. Clyde connects with a high fly to the left field wall, gathered in by the Surfers' left fielder for out number three.

We enter the bottom of the eighth inning with Bob on the mound. The third-baseman for the Surfers is the first batter. He drops a bunt down the first base line and beats it out, with no play. On a 2-2 count, the next batter hits a hard ground ball to Mike at shortstop who throws to Steve covering second base. The base runner slides in hard with his left leg high, exposing flashing spikes. As Steve attempts to throw to first for a double play the shirt on his throwing arm is caught in the spikes of the runner. Both players hit the ground hard. Before anyone can react, Possum storms from the top steps of the dugout with a fire I have never seen.

Rather than to get into the fight, Possum tackles Steve and hugs him tightly while walking him back toward the shortstop position. Meanwhile, the runner is up with fists clenched looking for action. Don Graham storms in from right field and grabs the runner in a bear hug.

The California coach runs out to the scene directing his players away from second base. A few minutes pass as the crowd roars. Steve shows his right bicep bleeding from a small scratch.

Both players stand staring at each other from a distance while still wrapped up by Possum and Don. Don has an intense smile on his face as he speaks forcefully, "Calm down, calm down!"

Both players relax and are freed. They stand quietly.

Possum and the Surfers' coach confer with each other and with the umpires for several minutes. From my position at third, I hear the umpires deciding on whether to throw the two players out of the game. I see Richard within the group, but not talking.

"No, no," Possum shouts. "There's no harm here. Let them both finish the game."

The Surfers' coach agrees as do the umpires. Steve walks slowly back to his second base position. The base runner returns to the dugout and the batter is standing, safe, on first base. One out.

Just then, Mike calls out to Possum as he collapses to the ground grabbing his left leg with his hands. Possum waves in David Carter to the shortstop position and Possum and I carry Mike to the dugout. Mike is in considerable pain, but Possum says it is just a muscle cramp and to rest on the bench. "It'll be fine."

After some delay, the game resumes. Bob strikes out the next batter, but has trouble finding the plate on the following Surfer and walks him. With runners on first and second, the batter hits a single to right field scoring a run.

We now trail 4 to 2. The final batter of the inning flies out on

Game Two

another spectacular catch by Harold in center field. The crowd loves it and gives Harold a standing ovation on his way in from the field. Harold smiles softly as he trots into the dugout.

It is our last at-bat here in the top of the ninth inning. Don Graham hits the first pitch high over the center field fence for his second home run of the tournament. As he rounds third, I notice the third baseman give him a nod. Don nods back. We are still in this game.

The crowd is standing, cheering and applauding. Harold follows with what looks like another home run, but the left fielder leaps high to catch the ball just before it goes over the wall. Out number one.

I follow with a long fly ball to the same left fielder who again makes a nice running catch. Philip is next up and hits a single to right field. Peanuts hits a smash that is knocked down by the third baseman and is safe at first. Bob Smith, batting in Kenny Young's position, walks on four pitches. We have the bases loaded with two outs.

Steve Jones comes to the plate and watches several pitches until reaching a 3-2 count. The next pitch is a fast ball hit hard to the right fielder who makes a spectacular diving catch for the final out and the game ends. The crowd's roar quiets quickly.

We are stunned. The dugout seems to slump. Philip, Peanuts and Bob join us from the field. Steve slams his bat into the rack. Possum is leaning, with arms outstretched to the dugout wall. His head is hidden between his shoulders. We wait for someone to make a sound or a move.

Finally, Possum straightens up and walks to the center of the dugout. "That was a wonderful game, guys, and you should all be so proud of how well you did. Just an inch here or there and we would be on the other side of the score. But, we are not and that is that. After you take showers and dress in your street clothes, I want you to drive over to Hazel's and I will join you later. Don, you stay with me, please.

"Oh, and there's one other thing. Be sure to keep your name tags," Possum adds.

We take showers and dress quickly. Mike moves gingerly, but says he is feeling much better, "just as Possum said I would."

As we leave the locker room, via the Players Entrance, we are greeted by several dozen fans with programs, paper, pencils and pens. We are each approached for autographs and receive numerous compliments on our play. We are surprised by this response, and it helps us push back the postgame blues.

On the way to our cars, the public-address announcer comes on. "The final line of the Bombers, Surfers game is for the Surfers, four runs, eight hits and no errors, and for the Bombers, three runs, seven hits and no errors. The winning pitcher for the Surfers is Woods and Ohm takes the loss for the Bombers."

"What, again?" I shout.

The players around me show slight smiles but have no comment.

We gather around Philip and Bob and pile into their cars for the very short drive to Hazel's Boarding House.

Chapter Thirty-One

Possum's Story

We approach Hazel's and find a most unusual sight. It is nearly 3 o'clock in the morning, and the house is brightly-lighted in all three stories. We walk to the front door and Kenny knocks.

We are greeted by Mr. Davis from Emporia who wears a big smile and shouts a welcome to us all. "Come on in, guys. What a terrific game! We are so proud of you."

We follow him to the parlor where several men, all of whom we met in the locker room a few hours ago, are either seated or standing with drinks in their hands. They quickly make the rounds to each of us with handshakes and complimentary remarks.

Mr. Davis points us to the dining room where we find a long table, with a white tablecloth, overflowing with food. Lunchmeats, cheeses, fried chicken, breads, fresh-looking lettuce salad, potato salad and many different desserts—all greet us.

In the far corner on the floor sits a wash tub filled with ice and a wide variety of drinks. Bottles of Orange, Grape, Root Beer, and Colas, along with several brands of beer, sparkle from the overhead lights.

In walks Hazel with a big smile. "Welcome, boys," she says.

Kenny, who must be assuming leadership in the absence of Don, replies, "Miss LaCount, what are you doing up so early this morning? You surely didn't have to do all this for us."

"I'm always up within an hour or so, anyway. I wouldn't miss this for the world. Besides, I hear that you boys played really well tonight. We are so proud of you."

We mumble in near unison, "Thank you, Miss LaCount."

Mr. Davis invites us to take a plate and start down the food line. We do not hesitate. Without Possum around, it seems like we are on our own as a team for the first time. The Bombers dig in with enthusiasm. I feel that we are just now losing our adrenaline rush from game time and are finally relaxing.

Mr. Davis speaks for the sponsors. "As Miss LaCount said, we are so impressed with the wonderful game you played tonight. We are proud to be from Emporia and watching our boys play ball." After a short pause, he continues, "The only guy here who might not be eighteen is Harold, so the rest of you are welcome to a beer if you wish."

Most of the Bombers pull soft drinks out of the ice tub, with just one or two opting for a beer.

Several minutes pass with intense focus on the fine food. Finally, Possum and Don arrive at the front door. They walk in with a sparkle in their eyes as they spot the food table. Possum fills his plate and grabs a beer from the ice tub. Don follows.

By now, most of the Bombers are in the process of re-filling their plates, some already going back for thirds. Miss LaCount comes and goes, refilling the serving platters.

Possum finally asks for our attention. "First of all, I want to thank Mr. Davis and all these other fine gentlemen for making possible our trip and our stay here in Wichita. With every boss allowing our guys to take off work this Wednesday, we are going to relax for a few hours and then get some sleep. Let's not plan on driving back to Emporia until the middle of the afternoon."

The response from the players is very positive. I notice an even more relaxed and comfortable mood across the dining room.

Possum continues, "Mr. Davis has asked me for your attention, as he has a very special announcement."

Mr. Davis is smiling broadly as he stands before our group. He has in his hand a roll of bills bigger than any money we have ever seen. "By combining money donations from people in Emporia, and from the first-round box-office receipts, we have a crisp fifty-dollar bill for each of you."

He starts handing out the bills with Don first in line. Mr. Davis begins by singling out players, but finally says, "Not one of you is less important than any other member of this team. I've been following you guys for the last several weeks, and in almost every game I found a different player who made the difference. Heck, Kenny, I would have to say you made a really big difference in the Aces' game, for sure." Mr. Davis winks at me.

With this, the Bombers are laughing and giving me all kinds of attention. I try to react but come up with only a slight smile. Suddenly, I remember the five-dollar bill in Philip's car in the back pocket of my wet uniform, and then I manage an even more sincere smile.

Mr. Davis continues, "If there ever was a team effort, yours' is the one. The fact that you prospered with only an eleven-man roster is further confirmation of your great talent and commitment. Finally, coach Possum has shown us his amazing understanding of the game and how to coach and play it. I have to say, once again, congratulations to all of you."

I see most of the Bombers eyeing their new fifty-dollar bill. I carefully fold mine and place it in my pocket.

Possum thanks Mr. Davis and strolls over for another beer.

Steve's boss, Wes, takes this opportunity to call for our attention from his chair beside one of the dining room tables. He begins, "Several of us have been talking about a little recognition for the Bombers and have come up with the idea of a parade down Commercial Street, with you guys on flatbed trucks. As they say, we want to 'Strike while the iron is hot,' so we're thinking about planning this for next Saturday in the late afternoon after work.

"As usual, Saturday afternoons and evenings are prime times for lots of people to be on Commercial, and this will give the folks in Emporia a chance to recognize you for your fine play this season and during this tournament. This will also give us a few days to get things together and get a little publicity out there for you guys. What do you all think?"

Again, this evening and night have been full of surprises, but this one is beyond what we could have imagined. The crowds at our games have been pretty good, but the idea of the whole town coming to see us is unimaginable. How could we not agree to this?

Don responds, "I'm sure I speak for all of us when I say this is a wonderful idea and we'll be there on Saturday if work and family permits it."

Possum's Story

Before Don can speak further, Wes raises his hand with a smile, "Don, let's invite all your families, your friends and anyone else you would like to join you to ride the trucks. Heck, I have a large flatbed and your boss at the lumberyard has a couple, so I know we can make a nice parade out of this.

The sponsoring gentlemen from Emporia say their goodbyes as they have to get back yet this morning since, "We have to work tomorrow!"

We smile at that and wave as they step out the front door.

Things are quiet for some time as we each have our own thoughts and are trying to put this all into perspective.

Possum may be on his third beer, or maybe not. He breaks the silence, "You know, men, it has been a long time. Twenty-one years ago, maybe twenty-one years ago tonight, I played right here in Wichita. I was over forty-nine years old at the time. That's even older than you, Don."

Possum smiles and pauses. The Bombers look at each other around the room with no words spoken. Don is looking on, nodding in agreement.

Possum continues speaking very slowly, "I was a second baseman for a team from down south. I had been playing for a Kansas City team, but we had already finished the season. This team from down south had already won two games and were about to play the best team in America. They were from Bismarck, North Dakota and you know who was pitching for them?"

Have some of us heard this story before in Fritz's barber shop? I do not remember Possum saying he was there.

"Yup, Satchel Paige. He'd struck out some thirty batters in their first two games before meeting this team I was on. They had contacted my Kansas City coach looking for a guy who might replace an injured player on their team. My coach said I could do it, but I lived in Emporia and I had some jobs there, including working for the *Emporia Gazette*."

"They actually called the *Gazette* to get ahold of me," Possum speaks softly. "I had just started a shoe-shine business in the Broadview Hotel, had to close it down for a day or two, and also get someone to throw my *Gazette* papers. I did that and hitched a ride to Wichita just in time for the game."

Possum is looking around the room assuring himself that everyone is listening. We certainly are.

"We were the visiting team and I played second base and batted eighth. Satchel was as good as they said he was. In the first two innings, he struck out five of the six batters he faced. It was the bottom of the second inning and the Bismarck team had a guy on first base."

Possum pauses again, this time a little longer as if forming a picture in his mind so as not to miss a detail.

"I think there was only one out. The batter hit a hard grounder to our shortstop and I ran to cover second base for the double play. I caught the toss, tagging second with my left foot and started to throw to first for the out. The base runner, though, came at me with spikes flying. He caught my left leg squarely and ripped my pants and tore a long gash in my leg. I dropped the ball and fell on the guy and we started to throw a few punches."

Whether Possum was giving us more than he needed to get our attention or were these details he had to share? I don't know. Possum pauses again with sleepy eyes.

"Other players were on us in a hurry and our fight was over. I tried to get up but had a horrible pain in my leg. I looked down and blood was everywhere. In fact, there was a puddle of blood

Possum's Story

on the ground near the base. Some guy had a rag of some kind and was pressing in against the gash in my leg. They had to carry me off. I heard an umpire say that the runner and I were both being thrown out of the game."

More delay in the story. No sound from the room.

"I got to the dugout and the blood kept coming. Some guy in the crowd came down and offered to take me to the hospital. Our coach agreed. He looked really worried. I told him to find out if the player had sharpened his spikes. If he had, he should not be allowed to play anymore. That's all I was thinking.

"We got to the hospital and they put in one hundred twenty stitches and it took me several weeks to walk well again. Here's the thing, though. I never cared that I got spiked or that I had all those stitches and all that pain. I would have been up to bat the next inning against the greatest pitcher of all time, maybe forever, and I missed my chance. Did you know he struck out seventeen that game and a total of sixty for his four games in the tournament? Those are records that will never be broken."

The Bombers are quite alert, but Possum is nearly asleep. Don speaks for all of us, "Possum, we're so sorry that happened to you. That sure makes a great story, though."

"Possum kind of smiles. He rolls up the left leg of his pants. A number of gasps and groans fill the room. A heavy, irregular scar runs from the ankle bone to just beside the knee of his left leg and is prominent even across the room.

"It's more than just a story," Don says, above a whisper.

Possum gets to his feet and slowly heads upstairs to his room. The Bombers sit quietly for several minutes.

Soon a buzz starts within the dining room. Observations of many kinds are made.

"No wonder he has no use for sharpened spikes."

"I know now why he didn't want anyone thrown out tonight when Steve got into it. He couldn't have hit against Paige anyway with his injury."

"You can see how much he loves the game and its history."

"It's hard to believe that we may be the only ones to know this part of the story in all of Emporia or anywhere else."

"I wonder if he wants us to share it with anybody else."

"Let's ask him tomorrow when he's feeling better."

Steve strolls to the little piano in the corner of the parlor and sits at the bench. He slowly and quietly plays a beautiful melody some of us recognize but cannot name. We sit captured. After several minutes, he closes with a soulful smile.

Although we all find ourselves exhausted, we are surprised and inspired by this unexpected performance. "Where did this come from?" Don asks. "And what was that you played?"

Steve, still showing a gentle smile, answers, "Mozart's concerto number twenty-one. It's one of my favorites."

We look at each other around the room and shake our heads in wonder. This is a side of Steve that we do not recognize. I recall Steve mentioning to me several weeks ago about his playing the piano, but nothing like this!

After several more minutes of pats on the back and compliments to Steve, we slowly file to our upstairs bedrooms. At the same time, we encounter some of the regular boarders coming down the same stairway for their early morning breakfast. They are smiling.

"That piano was the nicest alarm clock I've ever heard," one remarked.

Miss LaCount appears from the kitchen and looks to be ready to provide for the next group of guests as she clears our food table and replaces tablecloths and silverware.

Possum's Story

We sleep soundly until awakened about two o'clock in the afternoon with several voices speaking with excitement. Don comes by our door and tells us to get dressed and come down to the dining room as quickly as we can.

We dress and rush downstairs to see two guys dressed in sport shirts and wearing St. Louis Cardinals caps as they sit along one wall. Nearby sit Possum and Harold and a few other Bombers. They are all wearing smiles. Within minutes the entire Bomber team is assembled in the close quarters of the parlor.

Possum calls for our attention and introduces the two men. "We have here Mr. Brewer and Mr. Samson who are scouts for the St. Louis Cardinals baseball team. They dropped by to meet us and especially, Harold here. They have a few words to say."

Mr. Brewer rises, "Good afternoon, gentlemen. Mr. Samson and I would like to congratulate all of you for your outstanding performance on the field these last few days and also recognize your outstanding season. Just two runs, total, separated you in the games played against two of the finest town teams in America. Mr. Samson would also like to say a few words."

Mr. Samson rises, "We have been visiting with Mr. Turner for the last half-hour or so and are making him an offer to join the Cardinal organization."

A loud cheer goes up from the Bombers with enthusiastic waves to Harold as he sits shyly, with hands on his lap.

Mr. Samson continues. "As you guys know, Harold had an outstanding two games with three home-runs, a very high batting average, and he made some catches out there in centerfield that we see only occasionally even in the big leagues. This offer, I am sure, is a surprise to all of you and certainly to Harold.

We have not asked Harold to say yes or no, but what do you guys think he ought to do?"

"Sign, for heaven's sake."

"Go for it, Harold."

"Be sure to write us when you get there."

Mr. Samson continues a little more seriously, "Without going into detail of the financial arrangement, we just want to say that we would like Harold to plan on attending spring training with our other prospects next February in Florida. In the meantime, he can make arrangements to finish out his job here and do a little running to stay in shape."

"We're heading back to the stadium to watch a few more games this afternoon but wanted to meet all of you. You certainly have something to be proud of with your performances this summer. Harold, you have two weeks to make up your mind. We'll stay in touch. By the way, we wish that Don Graham were about fifteen years younger."

Mr. Samson points a finger at Don and says, "Don, you're an excellent player and likely would have come a long way in professional baseball."

Don shakes his head, "I wish I was fifteen years younger myself."

My thought is that since Don is such a fan of the history of the game, he knows he would not have had a chance, as a black man, to play professional baseball fifteen years ago.

Both scouts shake hands all around and are gone.

The Bombers jump up and gather around Harold, patting him on the back and pushing and shoving him with laughter.

"So, what are you going to do?" Peanuts asks.

"I'm not really sure. What do you guys think?"

Before anyone else can answer, Clyde says, "Of course, he'll sign. He has no other choice. He will represent the Bombers all the way to the top."

I see a tear in Clyde's eye.

Chapter Thirty-Two

Commercial Street Parade

On our way back to Emporia, there is no loss for conversation topics. Harold, who is riding in Bob's car, is still getting considerable attention relating to his signing a professional contract. Possum, with his amazing story of conflict and injury, has earned even more of our honor and respect.

"Don, you're the expert. How much money do you think Harold will get for signing with the Cardinals?" Philip shouts toward the back seat.

"I don't really know, but I read where some of the first-time signers can get as much as a couple thousand dollars. The good part is that they get all expenses paid to go down to Florida for several weeks during spring training," Don answers.

"I would sign right away, if it were me," Mike offers.

"Boy, did Harold have a super couple of games. I bet he'll do well in the big time. Heck, I'd sign just to go to spring training and not worry about how much money I would make," I add.

"Harold needs to get as much money as he can right now. This could be a turning point in his whole life," Clyde says wistfully.

The subject rapidly changes to Possum and his injured leg.

"Man, that must have hurt to get your leg ripped apart like that," Steve says. He strokes his upper right arm with his left hand. "My little scratch still hurts."

"Yeah, and my leg is still sore and it's not nearly as serious as Possum's," Mike adds.

"We have a regular ambulance service here with all you injured guys," Philip laughs.

"Possum's a tough guy, all right. I guess that's not a big surprise," Don says.

After some quiet moments, Clyde shouts for Philip to turn on the car radio. "The Republican Convention is supposed to nominate a President and Vice-President today. Maybe it'll be on the radio."

We groan, as once again Clyde is thinking differently than the rest of us. After some adjusting of the radio dials, Philip catches the end of a newscast announcing President Eisenhower and Vice-President Nixon were nominated for second terms this afternoon.

"No surprise on Eisenhower, but I'm a little surprised by Nixon," Clyde announces to an indifferent group.

Arriving from an out-of-town game when it is still daylight is an unusual experience for the Bombers. We drive to the *Gazette* building and find a small crowd waiting for us. Because of our late game early this morning, we know it is not a newspaper story, so we are uncertain how these folks learned of our arrival time.

We are the first car here, so we are getting considerable attention and are being asked for autographs from several fans. Even without Harold, our carload is the center of interest and we have a good time writing our names on small pieces of paper and visiting with some of the people.

Just then Bob's car arrives and Harold steps out. Most of the crowd quickly runs to him with pencils, pens and paper. We are suddenly alone. We do not mind at all. This is a wonderful experience. Harold is smiling broadly and chatting happily.

Possum's car arrives, once again with Don as a passenger. The fans drift over to them. This is another nice sight with Possum getting the attention he deserves. Don is also signing autographs.

After several minutes, Mr. Davis, the car dealer, drives up in a shiny black car. He steps out with a big grin and greets us all. "I contacted the radio station early this morning and they had a nice piece about you Bombers. In their story, they asked fans to wait by the *Gazette* building late this afternoon to show their support. Looks like a good number showed up."

Possum walks over to shake Mr. Davis' hand and continues with a short visit. Meanwhile, the team members are occupied, as more fans press for autographs and engage in conversation.

More minutes pass by. Suddenly, Possum raises a hand asking for our attention. "Gentlemen, I have an announcement or two for you before you head for home. Mr. Davis, here, just told me that they have nearly completed plans for a parade down Commercial Street this coming Saturday afternoon starting at five o'clock. Also, they are inviting all family members to join us as they will have several flat-beds available.

"Members of the Chamber of Commerce will have transportation for everyone to get back to the starting point of the parade on the E-State campus. All you players need to do is show up and we would like for you to wear your uniforms. Those have been one of our trademarks all season long and I am sure the crowd will enjoy that. Our trucks will be lined up along Twelfth Avenue in front of the Norton Science Hall on the E-State campus, so meet us there."

After a short pause and after conferring with Mr. Davis, Possum continues, "We've all been invited for a late afternoon supper at the home of Mr. Davis, here, next Sunday. Several of our sponsors will be there and we will have a surprise program that I know none of you will want to miss. You may certainly bring family and other guests, if you wish. Just let me know in the next couple of days, or even at the parade on Saturday, if you can attend."

With that, Possum waves for us to head home and to have "a nice couple days" before we get back together.

This Thursday is a regular work day for the Bombers. Some of us have missed two days and it will surely show up on our next paychecks. The fifty-dollar bill will help though.

Dad and I spend the day digging a shallow ditch for the footings for the basement walls in the new house. It is very hard work because our shovels are resisted by the heavy clay soil. We manage to finish about half the digging, leaving the rest of the job for tomorrow. Dad is quite optimistic with the hope of this being one of his best house-building projects.

No practice this evening and my drive home is leisurely. For an unknown reason, I take a short detour past our practice site in Peter Pan Park. I drive back home and retrieve the newspaper from the porch. I open the paper and am surprised by a front-page story in the right-hand column.

It seems that I only make the papers when I get a loss, but I am feeling much better about this fine season. Somehow, I know that this summer of 1956 will provide memories for a lifetime.

I walk into the kitchen and Willis, Russell, Mom and Dad greet me with smiles and a series of "well-dones." I visited with Mom last evening and Dad all day today, but a special sit-down supper like this is unexpected.

> **Emporia Brown Bombers Lose Final Game in the NBC World Series, 4-3.**
>
> The Emporia Brown Bombers ended their season with a narrow loss to the California Surfers Tuesday night in the NBC World Series in Wichita. With the score tied in 2-2 in the seventh inning, the Surfers scored on a sacrifice fly to take a lead they never relinquished. Harold Turner and Don Graham both hit home runs for the Bombers. The winning pitcher was Woods and Ken Ohm takes the loss for the Bombers.

I find myself a little overcome. I stiffen up a bit and can think of only one response, "So, what's for supper?" That brings more smiles and we all sit down to a fine meatloaf and potatoes meal and energetic conversation.

"We've been hearing about the game in Wichita all day today during the news on the radio. I heard your name mentioned a bunch of times," Mom says.

"Yeah, something about Ken Ohm taking the loss," Willis chuckles.

We all laugh at that one.

"We're supposed to have a parade down Commercial Street Saturday afternoon, and everyone's invited to join us on flatbed trucks. Would any of you be interested?"

I already know the response of Mom and Dad who, last night, said they would be working, but I am hoping that Willis and Russell might join me. Mom and Dad briefly remind me of their commitments, but the two boarders both say they will be delighted to join the team on the flat-bed trucks.

I ask Mom to let Bonnie know of the parade and that she and her husband and Monica can join us Saturday if they want to. Mom agrees to call Bonnie.

We finish digging and then building the forms for the footings on the new house, this Friday morning. Late in the afternoon, Dad and I assist with unloading the pre-assembled wood forms for the basement walls as they arrive from a local dealer.

We work later than usual this evening. Dad says that tomorrow will also be a tough day as concrete will be poured for the footings and we will begin to assemble the wall forms around the perimeter of the basement. Dad assures me, though, that I can leave early to get into my uniform before driving to the Twelfth Avenue parade location.

We arrive home after work exhausted but satisfied with the work accomplished today. After a hot bath, I retrieve the *Gazette* from the front porch and am surprised to find another front-page story.

We cannot complain about lack of publicity these days. Two very fine articles in two days will surely give recognition to the Bombers and to Coach Possum.

Dad promised a hard work day today and it surely is. The basement forms we are using have been used many times and

Downtown Parade Saturday
For Emporia Brown Bombers

The Emporia Brown Bombers will be recognized with a parade down Commercial Street at 5pm on Saturday. Fresh from a fine showing at the National Baseball Congress World Series in Wichita, members of the team, along with Coach William "Possum" Williams, and their families, will ride from 12th avenue to the railroad tracks on south Commercial. Everyone is welcome to show this team our appreciation for representing Emporia so well during the Series.

have old concrete and creosote saturated throughout. The texture and the smell make for a very unpleasant job for the installation. The day does end for me, however, at about four fifteen in the afternoon. Dad continues working.

I drive home for a very quick bath and a change into my *Ft. Douglas* uniform. My street shoes will have to do as my spikes will not work on a flatbed truck. I arrive on Twelfth Avenue a few minutes before five o'clock and see dozens of people milling about.

There are seven or eight trucks lined up along the curb in front of Norton Hall. I spot Possum several yards away and trot over to him. He directs me to a truck about half way back. I notice a smiling Willis and Russell already on the flatbed and a big surprise.

Bonnie, with little Monica, is on the truck as well. Chairs have been set up on most of the trucks. I greet Bonnie who tells me her husband is working this afternoon, so it seems we will have five people on our flat bed. I am delighted to see each of them.

At five o'clock sharp, several police cars drive around the corner of Eleventh Avenue leading the Emporia High School Band. The musicians position themselves, with the police cars leading the way, followed by our first truck. It carries Kenny Young and his dad and Mike Garcia, alone.

The second truck has the Solis brothers, Philip and Jesse (Peanuts), and their smiling grandmother. I recall that their brother, Richard, is still umpiring in Wichita.

The next truck hosts Clyde and Harold and, as expected, both Sandra and Maria stand with them. I notice Clyde and Sandra holding hands. Our truck is next in line and the engine rumbles nicely. I see David Carter walking nearby.

"Are you on a truck yet, David?" I ask.

He shakes his head.

"Run over here quick and I will give you a hand up," I say.

David joins us on the truck bed as we start our slow drive. I look back and see Don, with his wife and three kids on their truck. What a nice-looking family!

The truck following Don's has Steve, along with his mother and brothers and sisters. I see little Ida dressed in a white, lacy dress. They are all smiling broadly.

On the last truck, Bob Smith and Possum are already waving to the crowd. I, for the first time, look down Commercial and see a large crowd of people lined up on both sides of the street.

Our trucks move very slowly as we approach Tenth Avenue. We stop for a minute or two and I find several fans clapping and cheering toward David and me.

"Kenny Ohm, what are you doing on a black team?" I hear someone shout.

"They were the only ones who would have me," I shout back.

Lots of laughter from the crowd, along with cheering, and yells of "Yeah" are in reply. That inspires me to tip my cap. Russell and Willis laugh and recognize classmates and others in the crowd. Bonnie is smiling.

We continue to similar crowd reactions until we reach Seventh Avenue, when we stop again. I look ahead and see Harold, Clyde, Sandra, and Maria on the truck now stopped at Sixth Avenue.

I notice for the first time that Harold wears a bright red St. Louis Cardinal cap. I listen carefully and hear a person over a loud speaker introduce Harold as an outstanding player who just signed with the Cardinals. With that, the crowd erupts with a roar.

David and I look at each other and both feel, I think, a great pride in what Harold has accomplished. The announcer follows with brief words about Clyde and his value to the team as a first baseman and as a fine hitter. Sandra and Maria are beaming.

Our truck resumes its slow movement, and then we also stop at the intersection of Sixth Avenue. This has obviously been the routine for the several trucks in front of us and I am wondering what the announcer might have to say about us. David looks a bit nervous.

"Coach Possum has called David Carter the finest utility player he has ever seen," begins the announcer. "Coach says he has played nearly every position on the team and has always been ready to give the team the boost it needed."

The crowd applauds. David responds with a wave of his cap.

The announcer follows with, "And Kenny Ohm here has had an outstanding season both at the plate and in the field as a third baseman and pitcher. You might say he has the most unusual record of any pitcher in recent history. His record for the Bombers was one win and one loss, but he also has the distinction of the pitcher who gave the Bombers a win by pitching for the losing team."

The crowd loves this and erupts in cheers and jeers. I can only tip my hat and smile. I had never put it in so many words, I say to myself, but that must truly be an unusual accomplishment. Our truck moves on toward the end of the parade near the railroad tracks.

We near the end of the route, when I see several Bombers and others on trucks before ours, leap to the ground, and trot north on Commercial Street. David and I realize that the last truck on the parade route is about to reach its stopping point at Sixth

Avenue and it carries Possum and Bob Smith. I make sure the folks on my truck have rides back to the starting point of the parade, and then join David for a sprint to Sixth Avenue.

We get there as the announcer finishes his salute to Bob Smith. "Bob pitched almost as many innings as Young did and he played a number of infield positions as well."

The crowd applauds.

The announcer than directs his attention to Possum. "I cannot say enough about Possum and his leadership of the Bombers this season. Perhaps the best evidence is that he started out the season convincing eleven guys to stick with him and to expect a good, winning ball club. That is exactly what happened. You have seen these eleven players today and know that they have lived and breathed baseball this entire summer, ending up playing in the national championships."

The announcer motions a guest to the microphone. "I want to introduce you to the mayor of Emporia who has a special recognition for coach Possum."

Mayor Wagner takes the microphone and asks Possum to step down from the flat bed and join him. He shakes coach's hand and says, "This plaque is in recognition of your contribution to the Emporia community this summer, and I want you to know that we are so very proud of you and this Bombers team."

Every one of the Bombers is gathered around Possum as he takes the microphone. "I can only say thank you to all of you who have turned out today and also a thank you to a truly great baseball team who can play with any town team in America. I'm so proud of you all."

Most of the crowd along Commercial Street has gathered around this last truck filling the intersection of Sixth Avenue.

They respond with a loud cheer. We lift our caps to them. Many in the crowd remain seeking autographs and visiting with the Bombers.

While we are nearby, Possum reminds us of our supper invitation at the home of Mr. Davis tomorrow afternoon at about three o'clock.

As I walk toward my car, I see Clyde running toward me.

"Kenny, Harold and I will officially join Mt. Olive tomorrow morning at eleven. Most of the Bombers who are members will also be there, but we are hoping that you might come by as well. I know you were at our baptism, so this would be kind of nice for us."

For a quick second, I recall Mom and I are planning to attend our church tomorrow morning but decide that we can just as well go to the early service, and then I can make the Mt. Olive service at eleven. "OK, I will give it a try. Thanks for the invite."

Clyde hurries off to join Harold, Sandra and Maria.

Chapter Thirty-Three

Jeers from the Crowd

Mom and I agree to attend the eight o'clock Sunday morning service, making it possible for me to attend the membership ceremonies of Harold and Clyde at Mt. Olive. We are recognized by many of our own congregation, some of whom were in attendance yesterday for the Bomber parade. Pastor Stoeppelwerth greets Mom and me after the service with a handshake and lets us know that he was in the crowd at Sixth and Commercial for the introductions of the players and Possum.

"It was so impressive to see such a large crowd for a team that was little-known until late in the season and then, of course, with play in the national tournament. We are really proud of you guys," pastor says.

I find it surprising once again that my whiteness is not singled out and that most folks simply accept me as part of the

Brown Bombers. It certainly reflects the team's exceptional baseball talent and that our coach is highly respected.

I drive to Mt. Olive and find a place in the last pew in the back. Before I can get comfortable, Don approaches from his seat in the front and asks me to join him. I walk after him with a little discomfort and find the member Bombers making room for me in the second pew.

The service is inspiring as Harold and Clyde, with their sponsors, become members. They show a certain sincerity and enthusiasm that I have seldom seen elsewhere. By the end of the last hymn, I find myself also inspired with the surroundings and the message.

The Bombers file out of Mr. Olive and we remind each other of the get-together this afternoon at three o'clock.

We all arrive at about the same time for the gathering at Mr. Davis' house on Livingston Street. I notice that not a single member of any of the Bomber families is in attendance. This, somehow, does not surprise me.

We have learned over the past several days to dress casually for events like this and we all show up looking well-rested and fresh. The table spread greeting us recalls that of Hazel's dining room. Mr. Davis is joined by several of our sponsors who have supported us during the last few weeks.

After time for seconds and thirds in the food line, Mr. Davis asks us to take a seat. "One of the surprises I promised you is to hear from your teammate, Steve Jones."

We look at each other. What might this be about?

Steve reaches under his chair and pulls out a small stack of papers. He is shaking a little as he walks to the front of the room.

Jeers from the Crowd

He looks nervously over the crowd, "Possum and Mr. Davis caught wind, somehow, about my interest in comments or jeers from the fans during my many games over the years. As most of you know, I started collecting samples of them clear back when I played Junior Legion baseball and even before that in grade school. They asked me to share some of them and so, here goes.

"I have to tell you that I was in a play in junior high and some of the people there said I should be on the stage more often. I do not know if that is true or not, but I want to try to imitate the fans as I remember them as they shouted out the jeers. Incidentally, I have collected several hundred of these, so I just picked out several of my favorites last night. So, no more talking. I will start out with those directed at pitchers. So, Young, Smith and Ohm, pay attention," he says with a smile.

Steve suddenly relaxes and seems to be pleased to share some of his collection with us. He cups his hands on either side of his mouth to give the impression of yelling, and then he points to us.

"Nice pitch. It's not that fast, but it's straight and right down the middle."

Before we can react, Steve shouts out several more.

"I've seen better curves on a racetrack."

"I've seen better curves on your grandma."

"I've seen better curves on Olive Oyl."

Steve is getting more animated as we respond with soft laughter and smiles.

"I've seen more control on two rabbits on their first date."

"No, really, throw a fastball."

"Feel free to mix in a strike once in a while."

Steve suggests that we just threw a pitch short of the plate.

"You have a great fifty-foot six-inch curve ball."

"You're supposed to be a pitcher not a bowler."

Steve is now pausing just long enough for us to react to each jeer. His next set is for hitters.

"He couldn't hit the ground if he fell off a horse."

"He couldn't hit water if he fell out of a boat."

Steve points out that this next one is one of his favorites.

"He couldn't hit sand if he fell off a camel."

Everyone likes these jeers. Our sponsors near the side wall are laughing right along with us.

Steve continues.

"We know you can catch the ball, how about hitting it?

"You swing like a rusty gate."

"I've seen better swings in a park."

"If you get a hit, go to first base and turn left."

By now, the room is fully attentive. We are seeing a side of Steve we haven't seen before. Heck, he could be an actor.

Steve says that this next one is for me after I struck out in Lebo and broke my bat. He said he heard it from a very happy Lebo fan. Steve takes a deep breath and shouts.

"It's not the bat's fault!"

The guys in the room love it.

I just wave and say, "Go to the next one, Steve."

Steve is grinning broadly as he next sets his sights once again on our hitters.

"You couldn't drive anyone home if you were in their driveway."

"You haven't driven anybody home since the junior prom."

Then Steve turns to night games.

"Hey, Dracula, wake up your bat."

"I thought bats could see at night."

Now more for hitters.

"Hey, batter. You couldn't hit the side of a barn."

"You couldn't hit a bull in the butt with a shovel."

"If you're not going to swing the bat, you could at least walk back to the dugout faster."

Steve next shares one he heard in Melvern after Clyde struck out on a called strike.

"First guy says, 'Can I help you?' Second guy says, 'No, thank you, just looking.'"

Now, Clyde gets the razz-berries. We all join in as Clyde shakes his head in agreement.

Steve directs the next ones to those of us who struck out on only three pitches.

"Good morning, good afternoon, good night."

"Is it hard to hit the ball with your hands around your throat?"

"Did Possum have the strike-out sign on?"

We look to Possum who has a broad smile and mumbles, "No, but they swing anyway."

"Pitch him underhand."

"Swing hard! Just in case you hit it!"

Now, Steve starts to pick on the fielders.

"Tell your mom you need a new glove."

Steve next targets Harold, Peanuts and Don.

"Look in the other hand, you may have a sandwich."

"You couldn't catch a cold."

Steve smiles at Mike and Clyde, reminding them of a few bobbles during the season.

"Better lay off the Brylcreem."

"Granite hands!"

"Throw the glove the next time; you can get a hold of that."

Steve mentions missing Richard this afternoon and that we know he is doing a fine job with his umpiring while still in Wichita. Steve says he has a few umpire jeers if we want to hear them.

A unanimous, "Yes!"

"Could you see the plate better if you had a hamburger on it?"

"You're missing a good game."

"You should buy a ticket."

"You are an embarrassment to the color blue." He misses another call, "Hey Pink, you are not any better now, either."

"How do you sleep at night?"

"I've heard better calls at a square dance."

"I've got better calls from my ex-wife."

"I thought only horses slept standing up."

"Just because it's a night game, doesn't mean you should be asleep."

I can see that Philip and Peanuts are going to share some of this with Richard the next time they see him.

Steve now directs his jibes at Philip, our catcher.

Philip perks up.

Steve says he heard this one in Gridley when Philip walked to the mound to visit with Young.

"Tell 'um whatcha know…That's enough!"

Later, in the same game, Steve heard this one when Philip, Possum and Clyde joined Kenny on the mound.

"Put your heads together and make a rock pile."

This one brings more laughter than any of the others. I wonder if it is because it includes Possum.

Steve targets Possum on the next ones, when he goes to the mound to talk to our pitcher.

"Leave him in. We aren't not done with him, yet."

"Wind him up again, coach!"

Once again, the Bombers and the sponsors love it. Steve says he has just a quick two or three more jeers.

"You've been on the bench so long, you have enough splinters to build a house."

"You glued to that bench?"

"I've seen better arms on a chair."

"Save us some time and just throw it into the gap."

We stand up and applaud Steve. He smiles and gives us a wave. It is obvious he has been having a good time.

Mr. Davis rises. "Thanks, Steve. That was really fun. It seems that about everyone in the room got a little jeer. That's the way it should be. With that, then, I have an announcement that I'm so excited about. It just came with a telephone call this morning from the officials at the NBC."

"Coach, if you would join me for a minute," Mr. Davis motions to Possum.

Possum rises slowly with a look of caution. With all that has been going on this afternoon, he must be thinking that another trick of some kind is on its way.

"As some of you know the championship game for the 1956 NBC tournament will be played this coming Thursday in Wichita. They expect a capacity house and have voted that Possum, here, be honored by throwing out the ceremonial first pitch," Mr. Davis nearly shouts.

The Bombers, without exception, jump up with cheers and applause.

Possum seems a bit flustered. He is likely already having worrisome thoughts about the details of making another trip up and down the turnpike.

Mr. Davis quickly jumps in. "Before you agree, Possum, I want you to know that the we have worked out a plan for getting you to Wichita for the ceremony and for your lodging at Hazel's that night. We also have been asked to invite Harold and Don, particularly, as well as any other member of the Bombers to attend the game."

Davis continues, "All you guys will need is your name tag and they will seat you in the players section for the championship game."

Possum has no choice. The response from the players is so overwhelming that he shakes his head and says, "Sounds good enough to me. I'll be glad to do it."

The evening ends with everyone except Mike and Steve sure they can get off work one more day. I know that Dad won't mind as long as I make the work up on other days and other hours.

We file out of Mr. Davis's house with arms slung around Steve and with many compliments for his fine "jeers" presentation. He enjoys the attention.

Chapter Thirty-Four

The First Pitch

With what will certainly be the final week for the Bombers to gather as a team, Monday starts off with a normal work schedule for all of us. Philip stops by the Logan Avenue building site at noon with an up-date on player plans for attending the championship game on Thursday.

Philip explains, "Mike got his promotion at the bank, so he has decided to stay in town on Thursday. Steve also has found a number of conflicts which will prevent him from attending. David has not yet got the day off. He says it is not promising. So, it looks like only six of us are going to make it so far, other than Harold and Don. I understand they will be riding with Mr. Davis and Possum to Wichita."

"You know, we were lucky to have had such a successful season with eleven guys working full time and playing baseball in nearly every spare minute," I say.

Philip volunteers to drive to Wichita leaving at the usual time of 5pm and invites me to join him. "I've no idea who else wants a ride. I imagine Peanuts will come along, and maybe Clyde."

We discuss the reasons for Harold and Don to be specifically invited along with Possum and we figure it must mean some kind of special recognition for them.

"I guess they have all-tournament awards, but I wonder if players from Alaska or California or Alabama will be coming all the way back to Wichita for awards, especially after their teams were eliminated some days ago."

"Well, at least Harold and Don will be there. This should be another fun time for us Bombers," Philip says.

Noon day, Tuesday, catches me by surprise. Dad and I sit down for our normal lunch break. After a moment of silence, Dad says, "Kenny, I waited until the baseball season was over to tell you that I have a lot of trouble breathing. So, I saw the doctor a few weeks ago. He said that I have the beginning signs of emphysema. He said it's going to get worse over the next few years and I need to think about slowing down on carpenter work.

I am startled with the news, especially with how concerned Dad seems with it. I know very little about the disease but have heard that some people die from it. "Are you feeling alright, now?" I ask, quietly.

"Pretty good right now, but other times it's really bad. The doctor says I need to quit smoking. I'm not sure how I will do that, though," Dad says softly.

"I tell you what. Let's make this house the best ever and plan to finish it up around Christmas time so you can sell it over the holidays," I say.

The First Pitch

Dad perks up with that and I know now that my concentration for the next few months will be on studies at E-State and doing my part on building this house.

The afternoon goes smoothly with Dad and me working well side-by-side.

Philip stops by again this Wednesday afternoon with specific details on the trip to Wichita tomorrow. "I guess we have a full car load. Looks like Peanuts, Clyde, Bob and Kenny will ride with us. We've decided not to wear our uniforms this time. We'll wear our name tags and sit with the rest of the crowd in the player's family section. Since the game doesn't start until 8, let's leave about five thirty."

I spend the evening hours visiting with Mom and Dad and reminiscing a little over the past baseball season. We agree it has been the experience of a lifetime. It is early to bed for all of us.

The next work day is uneventful. I rush home to change clothes and drive to the *Gazette* building.

What is our final trip down the turnpike to Wichita turns out to be a quiet one. It seems everyone is emotionally exhausted from all the baseball excitement and the normal end-of-work day fatigue. We rehash the reasons for Harold and Don to be specifically invited to the festivities at Lawrence Stadium, but agree that whatever honor it must be, it is well deserved. As for Possum, we have come to know him as one of the most sincere and respected people we have ever known.

"After only two games in the tournament, it's a wonder that Possum would be recognized above everyone else who may have managed for several more games. I understand that both teams tonight will have played ten games in the last fourteen days. Can you imagine?" Philip ponders.

We arrive at the stadium about seven thirty and are immediately escorted to the players-seating section. The ushers are incredibly courteous and surely make us feel welcome. We soon find out that the California Surfers, who beat us by only one run, made it all the way through the consolation bracket to finish in third place in a game played this afternoon.

The other team to beat us, also by one run, the Ft. Wayne Dairymen will play the Deming Washington Loggers for the tournament championship. How could we be in a better place right now? Excitement is all around us!

Within minutes, Bob motions for us to look near the home team dugout. He spotted Possum, Harold and Don standing next to several red-jacketed tournament ambassadors. We watch as a microphone is carried and set-up near the group. One of the ambassadors steps forward.

"Ladies and gentlemen, may I have your attention. Tonight, we are honored with a number of guests we would like to introduce. As many of you know, each year we recognize an All-Tournament team we consider best played their positions during the Tournament."

We watch as the outstanding infielders and pitchers are introduced. We notice a Surfer and a Dairyman are included.

The announcer continues, "Now for the outfielders, we have left-fielder, Homer Glasser from the Anchorage, Alaska Goldminers. He is not with us this evening." A scattering of applause.

The announcer raises his hand, "At center-field, we have Harold Turner of the Emporia Brown Bombers." The crowd erupts with strong applause and cheering.

"This fine player has just been signed by the St. Louis Cardinals and we all expect great things from him in the future," the announcer waves toward Harold.

The First Pitch

After the right-fielder award winner is next announced, we hear of an additional award. "Each year, the committee chooses a player who exemplifies what we all strive for; a respect for the game, for the opponent and for the fans who support us. This year, the Sportsmanship award goes to Don Graham, again of the Emporia Brown Bombers."

The six of us stand, yelling and cheering. The applause from the crowd is as loud as any heard yet this evening. Harold and Don stand together smiling and waving to the crowd.

After a few minutes, the announcer asks for the crowd to again be seated. "Now for the final recognition of the evening, I want to introduce to you a gentleman who has personified the ideals and goals of this tournament. He has taken a team of only eleven players from the countryside of his home town and formed them into one of the most outstanding town teams in America.

"His team, composed of seven blacks, three Mexicans and one white guy, won most of their regular season games and then traveled to Wichita for our NBC Tournament. They lost each of their two games by only one run. This statistic is even more remarkable in that one of the teams they played, the California Surfers, won third place this afternoon. And the other team, the Ft. Wayne Dairymen, will be playing for the championship in just a few minutes."

"Further," he continues, "our honoree is no stranger to Lawrence Stadium and the tournament. It was exactly twenty-one years ago, in 1935, that he played second base for a team facing Satchel Paige and the Bismarck Churchills. During that game, where Satchel struck out seventeen batters on his way to eventually striking out a total of sixty in four games, our man was badly injured and carried off the field to a local hospital. I understand that after one hundred twenty stitches and then

293

several weeks of recuperation, he played for a few more years on local town teams. His love for the game never diminished and finally, so many years later, he brought a fine group of young men to entertain us with excellent play and sportsmanship."

From our point of view in the stands, the crowd seems captured by the ceremony on the field.

The announcer continues, "We have selected this man for the honor of throwing out the first ball in this championship game. But, before that, we would like to ask William "Possum" Williams for a few words."

The crowd again applauds and cheers.

We look to each other with a bit of worry. However, it is short lived.

"Ladies and gentlemen, I cannot begin to thank all of you for following this amazing game of baseball and giving us such a fine welcome. The tournament has been a spectacular experience for the Brown Bombers. When we got together back in early June, we had no expectation of reaching Lawrence Stadium in late August. We started the summer with eleven players and ended the season with the same eleven players, most dressed in different uniforms," he smiles broadly.

Possum continues in a deep voice, unlike any we have heard all season. He seems a natural at the microphone. "Finally, I want to say thanks to the many sponsors we picked up over the season and especially to my players. As of this hour, our season ends. I will resume tomorrow morning my full-time job at my shoe shine stand in Fritz's barber shop and my eleven players will show up for work at their jobs. We will all likely go our separate ways, but the memory of this fine summer will never fade."

The crowd seems to recognize the uniqueness of the Brown Bombers and of Possum, erupting in loud support.

The First Pitch

"So, let's get this game underway. Where is my catcher?"

This brings laughter from many in the crowd as Possum strolls from the microphone to the mound, followed by the catcher of the home team Dairymen.

Rather than stride closer to home plate for the pitch as we have seen others do, Possum takes a firm stance on the rubber of the pitching mound and fires a fast ball directly into the catcher's glove. The crowd roars and Possum trots off the field.

We look at each other and I think I see tears in the eyes of my teammates. I cannot hide mine.

Epilogue

Today, some sixty years later, I still warmly recall memories from the summer of '56. Vivid images from that time include playing those many night games in very small towns under faint lights. Wins and losses have no sticking power, but by searching game summaries in the *Emporia Gazette,* I find triggers that stir clear visions.

Trips up and down the highways around Emporia offered more lasting memories than the games themselves. We were packed, six deep, in small 1940s automobiles, most often after a hard day's work and with no air conditioning.

Still, the deep passion for playing the game of baseball upstaged any idea of separate class or position in life. We were a group of young men who had found a singular outlet for daily frustrations and worry about our families, our jobs and our futures.

The summer of '56 may have been the last one for most of our team to play for the Brown Bombers. As far as I know, many of the players drifted either to playing baseball for other teams or to playing the very popular fast-pitch softball.

In that early fall, October 8, 1956, Don Larsen, the New York Yankee who pitched from the stretch, hurled the first no-hit game in World Series history, and better yet, the first perfect game. Somehow, I had found him early that summer as a model for my new pitching form.

I continued as a member of the E-State baseball team into the 1957-58 season with some success while continuing to pitch from the stretch. Late in the spring of that year, I was selected to pitch a game in front of several professional scouts looking at our very capable first-baseman. Word spread of their attendance and, naturally, the rest of the team, including myself, could not help but give our best effort.

With wind blowing strongly from my left to my right, I attempted to throw a curve-ball into the wind. It was more than my elbow could accommodate and it popped with a sound heard across the field. I struggled to finish the inning, but never again pitched with the same effectiveness. I picked up a knuckleball technique for the rest of my college baseball career, but my dreams of professional baseball ended on that day.

My homerun in Bushong turned out to be the only homerun of my career. I likely batted 50 more times in organized baseball, batting in the high .200s, but I never hit even one triple.

My first teaching job in the fall of 1959 required a distant move and consolidating my belongings became a priority. I sold my Mickey Mantle card for about twenty dollars but kept the Yogi Berra rookie card. In days when backyard trash fires were permitted, I tossed in old books, old clothes, other odds and ends and, finally, my "magic" broken, walnut bat. Perhaps an appropriate end for the hero it was.

The real and the imagined characters in this book continue to fan out before me on certain contemplative days.

Dad passed away at age 76 after suffering several years with emphysema. Mom died recently at age 98, after a long life of working and volunteering at her local hospital.

As for the Bombers, Harold Turner is a composite of many great center-fielders I played with and against. His long stride, deft hitting and carefree, kind personality did surely exist somewhere.

Don Graham, the aging, hard-working father clung to the game as many still do today. They just cannot let it go. I picture several friends just like him.

The Solis brothers are with me in so many ways, even today. Philip, whose stone-still catcher's glove set for me a target that I pitched to with the greatest confidence, shares occasional and enthusiastic telephone calls.

His brother, Jesse, called "Peanuts," excels in personality and in business skill. He serves on various community organizations and has received awards for those services. People in Kansas and Missouri follow a special community service recognition sponsored by the Kansas City Royals baseball club. For each game, a worthy volunteer is honored with a free pass and seating in the Buck O'Neil chair in Kauffman Stadium. Jesse was recently recognized with that honor.

Richard Solis passed away years after serving honorably in the Air Force and is still remembered as an excellent baseball umpire.

David Carter was a friend of mine in junior high school and disappeared until just before I began this book. Before I could interview him, though, he passed away. This is just one of my regrets, which we all have, when time catches up with us.

Mike Garcia's special personality reflects another one of my classmates who went on to serve in the movie industry in Hollywood, before passing away a few years ago.

Kenny Young and Bob Smith were real members of the Bombers but have been lost in my research.

Steve Jones is a composite of a young, troubled African-American with major family responsibilities and with limited possibilities for the future. When called to action, though, either with family emergencies or with job requirements, he rose to the occasion. He loved his "Jeers" collection and should have written a book on the subject.

Finally, Clyde might have inherited the farm he labored on for so many years. His boss may have had no children, so Clyde would be heir apparent. He then not only earned his high school diploma but went on to earn bachelor's and master's degrees in political science and, in my mind, he may have used his great empathy and understanding of the human condition to serve several terms as a Kansas state legislator.

Possum continued in real life occupying his shoe shine stand in Fritz's barber shop, following a few years later in Art's barber shop and, finally, in the Mit-Way Shine Parlor, all in Emporia.

I do not recall visiting any of the shops after that special season. As part of the research for this book, I recently found his obituary and was surprised by two discoveries. First, he was born in 1885, making him seventy years old during that 1956 season, which is a real surprise for such an energetic soul. Next, I found that he toured the country with a minstrel show in his youth, which might help explain his social ease in the company of any group of people and his ability to communicate with them.

I recently read a story relating to early Negro league baseball and found that both Brooklyn and Chicago had teams called the Brown Bombers. Reading further, their names were often abbreviated to the Brooklyn Bombers and the Chicago Bombers but, nevertheless, I was again proudly reminded of that summer experience in '56. It turns out, also, that I was not the first white boy to play for a Negro team. A former white big leaguer by the name of Eddie Klepp played for the Negro Cleveland Buckeyes in 1946. I was not a trailblazer after all.

Acknowledgments

I would like to acknowledge the following individuals who helped in the creation of this book: Don Pady, Lyle Baker, John Whittington, Jerry Brown, Diane Dufva Quantic, John Ellison, Al and 'G' Slappy, my sister, Bonnie Kuhns; my niece, Monica Scott; Jesse (Peanuts) Solis, Philip Solis, Jeff Dolezal, Tim Ohlmann, Will Bishop and Tom Ortiz.

My dear wife, Ruth, reminded me, even during my other writings, that my passion for those baseball times in the summer of '56 required that I write about them. Her reading and re-reading of the manuscript provided fresh ideas and helped shape and improve the narrative. A big thank you.

Special thanks to Kevin Jenks and the National Baseball Congress World Series in Wichita, Kansas. This book would not have been possible without your generosity and support. To Rosa Lee Waterman and the Emporia, Kansas public library, thank you for your deep research from those past times. To Mark Honer for very special encouragement. To Ken Harmon for your genius and motivation.

And a very special recognition to the Editor and staff of the *Emporia Gazette* for their professionalism, flexibility and guidance. Thank you for sharing so many critical moments of that memorable summer.

My friends at Mennonite Press, Judy Entz and Jim L.

Friesen, once again exhibited their creative guidance throughout this project and deserve my sincere gratitude.

Finally, my agent and cousin, Don Schrader, made a world of difference with his friendship and support.

About the Author

Ken Ohm is recently retired as professor emeritus after teaching for fifty years. He began his career as a high school physics teacher and as an astronomy professor at Kansas State University in Manhattan Kansas. He followed as a professor at Sheridan College  in Wyoming for twenty-six years before ending his career, after seventeen years, at Washburn University in Topeka Kansas.

His previous writings centered in his birth place in the Flint Hills of Kansas. As a lifetime baseball fan, he holds memories of his own baseball experiences far below the talent level of many of his fellow college and town team players. This writing reflects those times also in the shadow of his beloved Flint Hills.

He lives in Topeka, Kansas with his wife, Ruth and black cat, Lucy.